20-00

Communication for Development in the Third World

Communication for Development in the Third World

Theory and Practice

SRINIVAS R. MELKOTE

Sage Publications
New Delhi/Newbury Park/London

First published in 1991 by

Sage Publications India Pvt Ltd
M-32, Greater Kailash Market, I
New Delhi 110 048

Sage Publications Inc
2455 Teller Road
Newbury Park, California 91320

Sage Publications Ltd
6 Bonhill Street
London EC2A 4PU

Published by Tejeshwar Singh for Sage Publications India Pvt Ltd, photo-typeset by Jayigee Enterprises and printed by Chaman Offset Printers.

Library of Congress Cataloging-in-Publication Data

Melkote, Srinivas R., 1952–

    Communication for development in the Third World: theory and practice/ Srinivas R. Melkote.
      p.   cm.
    Includes bibliographical references and index.
    1. Communication in economic development—Developing Countries.
    2. Developing countries—Economic Policy. I. Title.
    HD76.M45 1991   338.9′009172′4—dc20   91-333

ISBN: 0-8039-9683-7(US-hbk) 81-7036-227-X(India-hbk)
       0-8039-9684-5(US-pbk) 81-7036-228-8(India-pbk)

Dedicated to the memory of Shri M.V. Rajagopal, my father and first guru, and Shri M.R. Krishna Iyengar, my maternal grandfather who encouraged me to excel in all that I did

Contents

Foreword

This volume chronicles the four-decade process through which intellectuals have gradually sharpened their insights into the development of Third World nations of Latin America, Africa, and Asia. Somewhat more than halfway through the 1950–1990 period, a dominant paradigm of development gave way to a more human view, stressing equality, widespread participation, and certain non-economic behaviors. This newer conception of development stems from the accumulated experience of development programs in Third World nations, which have been investigated extensively by social scientists. So the newer models of development are more informed by research; they also evolved out of the earlier model by critical analysis of what had gone before.

Professor Melkote's book is representative of this critical tradition, as he analyzes past theoretical perspectives and research approaches. The purpose is to find improved models and programs for development that may be more effective than those of the past, when the achievements of development programs have seldom lived up to expectations. Such a gloomy level of development progress over the past forty years understandably leads scholars like Professor Melkote, to be highly critical of previous models, and to seek improved understandings.

The present volume is organized in terms of historical eras, and is very comprehensive. While the central interest here is the role of communication in development, the wider context of communication (such as colonialism, religion, militarism, and technology) is also treated. The encyclopedic nature of the present book is indicated by the fact that, even though I am a specialist in this field, I learned a great deal from reading it. Despite the detailed breadth of this book, the reader does not get lost due to clear writing and to helpful chapter summaries.

Professor Melkote is one of the new wave of development communication scholars. He comes from a Third World nation, India (where his doctoral dissertation research was conducted), and he was trained by a scholar from a Third World nation. With such an academic pedigree, the author of this book may be better able to overcome the implicit Western biases in the theories of development created by older scholars in this field.

This book will be useful to scholars and students of communication for development, to officials in charge of development programs, and to others who wish to understand an important paradigm shift in a field of great importance to social science, and to the world.

Annenberg School for Communication　　　　**Everett M. Rogers**
University of Southern California

Preface

When I was an undergraduate student of communication in India, I was, like most others in my class, desperately dependent on my teacher for synopses of class lectures. The university library did not usually have the latest books, and even if it did, they were checked out by the faculty. I could not afford to buy my own copies since they were prohibitively expensive. Moreover, in subjects such as development communication, there was no *textbook* that put together all the relevant and important literature in the field. Since those days, it has been my objective to write a book that would, between two covers, define, describe, and analyze the field of development communication.

There are many people whose help I wish to acknowledge. Joe Ascroft, my academic advisor in graduate school and a dear friend, has been with me from the inception of this project. I profited from my discussions with him and am especially thankful for his input in the first chapter and the historical overview of development/development communication theories. Another person who has been very supportive is Ev Rogers, now at the University of Southern California. I am not sure I could have completed this project without their advice and support.

There are two institutions to which I am indebted. I owe a lot to the University of Iowa's School of Journalism and Mass Communication. I learned a great deal and honed my skills under the able guidance of Professors Joe Ascroft, Ken Starck, Al Talbott, and Don Smith. I also wish to acknowledge the School of Mass Communication at Bowling Green State University which provided me with a supportive environment during the period I wrote this book.

Finally, I wish to thank Doug Ferguson, my colleague at Bowling Green, for coming to my rescue whenever I got into problems with my word processor; and Deb Freyman and Sandhya Rao for helping me with the typing of the manuscript. Last, but certainly not the least, I am thankful to Malavika, my wife, Katya, my daughter, Mangutha, my mother-in-law, and Jaya, my mother for helping me retain my sanity during the past two years while I was writing this book.

Bowling Green, Ohio   **Srinivas R. Melkote**

Historical Overview of Third World Development/Underdevelopment*

I. Period of Great Development (3500 BC – 1700 AD)
Ancient World Civilizations

North Africa and West Asia: Mesopotamia *(3500 BC – 2000 BC); Egypt (3000 BC – 2100 BC)*

Indian Subcontinent: Indus Valley (2700 BC – 1700 BC)

China: Shang (1500 BC – 1000 BC); Han (350 BC – 200 AD); Ming (1368 AD – 1644 AD)

Sub-Saharan Africa: Axum (300 AD – 1100 AD); Ghana (700 AD – 1200 AD); Mali (1200 AD – 1400 AD); Songhai (1500 AD – 1700 AD); Zimbabwe (1200 AD – 1500 AD)

Central America: Mayan (500 AD – 1500 AD); Aztec (1325 AD – 1525 AD)

South America: Inca (1200 AD – 1525 AD)

II. Period of Colonization: Emergence of the Third World (16th – 20th century)
(*From a state of development to underdevelopment*)
Period of Pillage and Rise of European Commerce (16th – 17th century)

European Expansion to the Americas:
Iberian settler migration to South and Central America; Spanish Armada; English, French, North European settlers to North America

European Expansion to Africa:
Portuguese slave traders to Angola;
French and English commercial traders to West African Coast;
Dutch to Cape of Good Hope

European Expansion to Asia:
Portuguese to Malacca and coastal stations throughout East;
Foundations of British and Dutch East India Companies;

* Prepared with the help of Dr. Joseph R. Ascroft, University of Iowa, USA.

English acquire Indian coastal towns;
Dutch take Malacca, dominate Eastern trade;
Spanish conquer Pacific Islands, notably the Philippines
(1570)

Period of Dominance of Merchant Capital (18th century)

Main period of slave trade:
From Africa to Americas; Enforced labor through slavery and reduction to serfdom; Enrichment of metropolitan Europe, especially its rulers.

Protectionism:
Iberian Market closed to competing colonial produce; British textiles protected from Indian cloth imports (1700); raw agricultural produce, precious metals, spices became colonial export staples

Mercantilism:
Rise of merchant class; merchant marines, navy protection; colonies limited to trade only with motherland empires

Britain and France vie for Global Dominance:
British Industrial Revolution and the French Revolution
British expansion into India and the plunder of Bengal

Period of the Rise of Industrial Capital (19th Century)

Britain defeats Napoleon, gains worldwide naval supremacy
British opium wars against China
Chinese and Indian indentured labor to Africa and West Indies

French conquest of Algeria and expansion to West Africa
European revolutions of mid-1800s:
European settlers to White Dominions in Africa, Asia and Oceania

Period of New Imperialism: Late 19th century

Scramble for Africa (and rest of Asia) by European Powers (1880–1914)
Spanish-American War; US acquisition of the Philippines and other Pacific territories

III. Period of Decolonization (19th – 20th century)

(Emancipation of underdeveloped colonies)
Rise of European liberalism and decolonization in the Americas (early 19th century); Decolonization of Asia and most of Africa (1945 – 1970)

Historical Overview of Development Activities/Development Communication Theories since World War II*

I. **Genesis of Organized Development Assistance (ODA)**
   Birth of Multilateral Development Assistance (1945):
   International Monetary Fund (IMF), World Bank, the United Nations family of special agencies
   Emergence of bilateral development assistance (1949):
   Truman's Point Four Program

II. **Development of Emerging Third World: 1950s**
   Foster self-help by capital infusion and diffusion of modern innovations mostly from the West;
   Industrialization, Urbanization, and Westernization considered critical for development; Prescription of universal stages for industry-driven national growth (Walt Rostow); Emphasis on need for radical change in Third World social structure and individual attitudes and behavior;
   Subjugation of agriculture (large and small-scale) to priorities of industrialization

III. **First Decade of Development: 1960s**
   (Period of great optimism)
   Dominance of the Dominant Paradigm of Development
   Economic growth through industrialization and urbanization
   Capital-intensive technology
   Centralized economic planning
   Underdevelopment due to internal problems in a country:
   Biased social structure;
   Traditional attitudes and behavior that constrained development:
   (Example: the subculture of peasantry)

* Prepared with the help of Dr. Joseph R. Ascroft, University of Iowa, USA.

Dominance of the big mass media and powerful media effects

Belief in the Bullet theory of communication effects: powerful, direct, and uniform impact on people

Mass media considered as magic multipliers of development benefits

Mass media considered as agents and indices of modernization
Potential of mass media to give rise to Revolution of Rising Expectations

Setting of standards for minimum criteria of media availability for development:
10 newspapers, 5 radios, 2 televisions, and 2 cinema seats per 100 people

Importance attached to diffusion of modernizing (but mostly exogenous) innovations

IV. **Second Decade of Development: 1970s**
(Period of Pessimism)

Disappointment with rate and nature of development

Explication of the Development of Underdevelopment Hypothesis:
Focused on exploitation of the periphery (developing nations)
Underdevelopment of the Third World seen as a consequence of development of Europe

Weakness of the Dominant Paradigm: Neglect of social structural and political barriers to change: Too much emphasis on individual as locus of change and locus of blame

Problems with the use of mass media for development:
Potential to widen knowledge gaps between rich and poor;
Could lead to Revolution of Rising Frustrations;
Mass media not just an independent variable in development but dependent on other environmental factors

Weaknesses of the diffusion of innovations to help the poor due to:
Communication effects bias;
Pro-innovation bias;
Pro-source bias;
In-the-head variables bias;
Pro-persuasion bias;
Top-down flow bias of messages and decisions;
Authority-driven models rather than user-driven models;

Absence of a process orientation;
Widening of socio-economic benefits gap

V. **Alternative Conceptions of Development: 1970s**

Growth with Equity models: Reduce inequality and improve conditions of the poorest of poor

Emphasis on active participation of people at the grassroots

Encouragement of self-determination and self-reliance of local communities; freedom from external dependency

Opening of the Peoples Republic of China to the world and the lessons learnt from its successful development efforts

Importance given to small, indigenous technology

Emphasis on meeting basic needs of people: food, clean water, shelter, basic education, security of livelihood, transportation, participatory decision-making, and upholding of a person's self-respect

McNamara's (President, World Bank) New Directions Policy:

Integrated rural development—eliminate single factor determinism—all existing constraints to development need to be tackled simultaneously;

Distinguished between relative poverty and absolute poverty: relative poverty signifies that some countries/peoples are poorer than others while absolute poverty means a life degraded by denial of basic human necessities;

Failure of trickle-down concept—proposed reorientation of development policy to bring about equitable distribution of economic growth—switch from economic targets to meeting basic needs

Re-emergence of local culture in development activities: renewed interest in studying the positive role of local culture in social change

New roles for communication media in development:

Communication in self-development efforts, i.e. user initiated activity at the local level considered essential for successful development at the village level; communication should be a catalyst for change rather than the sole cause; dialogue between users and senders;

Highlighted the role of folk media in development activities;

Employed communication strategies to narrow knowledge gaps between the rich and poor, reduce pro-literacy bias through tailored messages and formative evaluations;

Attempted using communication media to conscientize the masses to the harsh realities in their environment

VI. **Third Development Decade: 1980s**
Greater focus on participatory decision-making
Knowledge-sharing on a co-equal basis between senders and receivers
Emphasis on <u>Right to Communicate</u>
Use of pluralistic, open-ended, and culture-sensitive models of development
Research into investigating gender gaps and ways to close them

Chapter 1

Introduction to the Study of Communication and Development in the Third World*

T here has indeed been a wealthy tradition of communication research geared toward Third World development needs, an area of concern which has now come to be known as *development communication*. This research flourished especially during the development decade of the sixties when it held much promise of assisting the development cause. The works of Daniel Lerner (1958), Wilbur Schramm (1964), Everett Rogers (1962, 1969), and many others like Fredrick Frey, Lucien Pye, and Lakshmana Rao, attest to this lively interest. However, it seems to have petered out, stymied perhaps by the corner into which it seems to have painted itself. In this introduction (and later in the other chapters), the intention is to show how development communication research has tended to create problems for itself, focusing too narrowly on peripheral issues, producing findings which have turned out to be misleading, confounding or culminating in dead-ends, seeming somehow to be *out of sync* with the felt needs of development practitioners.

The objective here is to undertake a brief historical reprise of Third World development initiatives since World War II in the context of which will be discussed the contributions of communication research and the resulting problems and biases. This section will set a tone for the material that follows in later chapters.

*This chapter is a revised version of Joseph Ascroft and Srinivas Melkote (1983), 'An Ethical Perspective on the Generation of Development Communication Research Useful to Policy Makers and Practitioners', Paper presented at the International Communication Association annual conference, Dallas, Texas, 1983.

COMMUNICATION FOR DEVELOPMENT:
A HISTORICAL REPRISE

It has been almost forty-five years since the end of World War II. This period witnessed the political emancipation of most of the Third World from colonization as well as the birth of the United Nations (UN) and its various executing agencies marking the formal beginning of development aid to Third World countries. In the early post-War years, the attention of the UN and its most influential member, the United States of America (USA), was consumed by relief and rehabilitation work in war-ravaged Europe. But starting in the fifties and on into the sixties, this attention turned increasingly to the Third World where two-thirds of the World's population resided. This population enjoyed, in 1955, only 15 percent of the World's income, being made up mainly of subsistence peasants (Van Soet, 1978).

What is the Third World?

It is quite common these days to read the label *Third World* used in books, journal articles and the mass media. What exactly is the *Third World?* At least in the Western countries, this label is used to describe developing nations of Asia, Africa, and Latin America. By default, the *First World* describes the industrialized countries of North America, Western Europe, Japan, Australia, New Zealand, South Africa, and Israel; while the *Second World* represents the nations of Eastern Europe and the Soviet Union. This characterization is considered ethnocentric by many outside the Western nations and is generally not adhered to by them when describing the world (Vogeler and De Souza, 1980).

There are many other ways of subdividing the world. Professor Joseph Ascroft has put together the following list of labels used in development and popular literature:

2 worlds	Political	East (Communist)–West (Capitalist)
2 worlds	Economic	Industrialized North, Agricultural South

3 worlds	Geo/Pol	West (I), East (II), South (III)
4 worlds	Soc/Eco	East, West, South (DCs), South (LDCs)
4 worlds	Economic	Industrialized North, NICs, DCs, LDCs
4 worlds	Pol/Eco	West (Free Market), East (Centrally Planned), South (Free Market), South (Centrally Planned)

*DC = Developing Countries
LDC = Less Developed Countries
NIC = Newly Industrialized Countries

Concern for the plight of these peasants moved US President Harry S. Truman to propose the 1949 Point Four Program, thus establishing a model which most of the developed world embraced. He observed that:

More than half of the people of the world are living in conditions approaching misery. Their food is inadequate. They are victims of disease. Their economic life is primitive and stagnant. Their poverty is a threat both to them and to more prosperous areas.
For the first time in history, humanity possesses the knowledge and skill to relieve the suffering of these people (Daniels, 1951: 10–11).

Relieving Third World suffering consisted of making available the Western cornucopia of advances in agriculture, commerce, industry, and health. The key to prosperity and peace, said Truman in his 1949 inaugural address, was 'greater production' through 'a wider and more vigorous application of modern scientific and technical knowledge' (Daniels, 1951: 11). The outcome of this proposal was called *development*.

Early Pro-Transfer of Innovations Period

Although the traditional practices of the peasants of developing countries had enabled them to survive for millennia, the prevailing wisdom of the times dismissed them without any evaluation. It was after all *known* that Western agriculture, medicines, tools, and techniques outstripped corresponding traditional practices manyfold. Therefore, it made unquestionable sense that the Third World peasantry discard unconditionally their *primitive* ways and embrace the technologies which had wrought such extraordinary progress in the *advanced* countries of the North. This orientation eventually came to be known as a *pro-innovation bias* (Rogers, 1976a), and has held fast to this day.

Initially, the pro-innovation transfer paradigm appeared alluringly simple and straightforward. It had been largely derived from the highly successful program under the Marshall Plan to resuscitate war-ravaged Europe. The essence of the Plan consisted of making resources of finance and material available for pre-existing European expertise to apply to reconstruction (Arkes, 1972). It was soon clear, however, that the post-colonial Third World problem was quite different. There was no adequate pre-existing base of expertise except within the erstwhile colonialists themselves. More significantly, people, masses of them, had to have their life ways changed radically, not merely helped to re-establish themselves. Development, therefore, involved not simply the transfer of technology but also the communication of ideas, knowledge, and skills to make possible the successful adoption of innovations.

Needed then was an expanded base of expertise to, *inter alia*, persuade and motivate the Third World peasantry to cast aside their traditional ways in favor of the new. To the pro-innovation bias, consequently, was added a *pro-persuasion* bias and, with it, the implicit acknowledgement that Third World peasants were not disposed to submit meekly to radical change. So, a burgeoning stream of Third World students flowed to the developed countries for training and education, reciprocated by a corresponding stream of *experts* representing multilateral (UNESCO, FAO), bilateral (USAID), and voluntary (Peace Corps, Catholic Relief Services) aid agencies gradually flooding the Third World.

Pro-Persuasion and Pro-Top-Down Biases

In the early days of development, before transistorization made possible the ubiquity of radio sets, the task of convincing people through persuasive communication to change their life ways, fell to the extension services. Extension had long been and continues to be regarded as the most logical, scientific, and systematic method for disseminating more productive and useful knowledge and skills to user receivers. Not only did extension operating methodology embrace the pro-innovation bias but also took it upon itself to decide what innovations were best for its clients, followed by campaigns to convince them of the wisdom of its choice. The original extension responsibility to collect, collate, and convey *all* relevant research-generated information to potential clients was no longer adequate. The information disseminating extension agent was now expected to evolve into a *change agent*: 'a professional person who attempts to influence adoption decisions in a direction that he feels is desirable' (Rogers, 1962: 283). And, so was set in motion a one-way flow of influence-oriented messages from change agencies at the top to the rural peasantry at the bottom, a process of communication which eventually earned itself the derisive sobriquet, *top-down communication*. This approach held that peasants were rational enough to see the value of adopting innovations selected for them but non-rational to be able to choose for themselves from among an array of alternatives put before them.

Figure 1.1: Pro-Persuasion Model of Development

Thus, the early pro-innovation transfer model became expanded as shown in Figure 1.1.

A thorny problem remained, however, serving to limit the effectiveness of the extension communication approach rather severely. The approach was almost totally reliant on agent-to-client face-to-face communication, augmented here and there by certain demonstration multiplier effects involving 'master farmers'. But the available pool of extension personnel, grossly outnumbered by the teeming masses of peasants spread over huge geographic areas difficult to get around in, was woefully unequal to the task. Besides, extension agents were first and foremost, subject-matter specialists (agriculture, health, and so on) to which was added a patina of communication skills which may have been useful in the interpersonal or the small group interaction situation. This certainly came no where near addressing the main problem which was one of mass communication.

So, extension tended to focus its attention mainly on the closest, most receptive, and thus, easiest to convince individuals who, as a class, as diffusion studies were to show later, had more education than the rest (Rogers, 1969). But the individuals so reached were very few. Needed was a great multiplier. The advent of transistorized radio in the late fifties, cheap, portable, and independent of electrification, accompanied by the publication of Daniel Lerner's premature pronouncement, 'The Passing of Traditional Society' in 1958, offered great promise of satisfying this need.

Pro-Mass Media and Pro-Literacy Biases

Lerner examined the correlations between the expansion of economic activity being equated with *development* and a set of *modernizing* variables, chief among which were urbanization, literacy, mass media use, and democratic participation. His findings suggested that the spread of literacy in an urban milieu and the emergence of a *mobile personality* highly *empathetic* to modernizing influences provided the means to create within Third World societies a *climate of acceptance* of change. Implicit in his formulations, and in those of Wilbur Schramm who followed him, was the belief that the interaction of literacy and mass media was the means by which the masses would eventually break free of their stupefying bonds of traditionalism, heralding, as it were, the *passing of traditional society*.

Thus were born two new biases: the *pro-mass media bias* and its concomitant, the *pro-literacy bias* to help multiply the effects of change-agency interpersonal communication.

Figure 1.2: Change-Agency Communication and Mass Media Model of Development

Under this model, the mass media would be responsible for creating widespread awareness of, and interest in, the innovations espoused by change agencies. Contained in their messages would be the persuasive components which, by some alchemy of the *bullet theory* of communication, would produce a *climate of acceptance*. Change agents would then furnish targeted segments of adopters with the details of information and the skills necessary to make adoption of the innovations feasible. Early adopters would then presumably constitute role models for others in their social system to emulate. By these *demonstration effects*, the innovations would *trickle down* to the rest of the community. Over time, therefore, the innovations would diffuse across whole social systems.

There were strong precedents for this expectation. Beginning with World War II, a new research tradition, the **Diffusion of Innovations**, was gaining momentum in the United States. Starting with the Ryan and Gross study of the diffusion of hybrid seed corn in 1943, much research data was gathered which tended to show that information about innovations was communicated by the mass media and extension agents to opinion leaders among relevant recipients, and from them to others in the social system (Rogers, 1962).

Even with the addition of the mass media and literacy, the expected diffusion of innovations in the Third World did not eventuate as it had done in the developed countries. When the rate with which an innovation diffused throughout a social system, from the earliest adopter to the last *laggard*, was cumulatively plotted over time, an S-shaped curve, peculiar to diffusion studies in the developed world, resulted. But when these studies were replicated in the Third World, the curves which resulted were considerably less than the total 'S', signifying adoption by very few people (Ascroft and Gleason, 1981). In the few instances where completed S-shaped curves were indeed struck, they occurred only in those Third World social systems which somehow had already developed a 'climate of acceptance' (Rogers, 1969).

How were these findings to be explained? Was there something wrong, something intrinsically unattractive about the innovations selected for diffusion? Were the channel linkages between source and receiver insufficient to the task of reaching all potential adopters adequately? Or was there something perversely recalcitrant about the Third World peasants? Of these questions, communication researchers of the sixties apparently chose to focus mainly on the last.

In-the-Head Psychological Constraints to Development

In the developed world, hard-headed non-adopters of innovations were labeled as *laggards* and described as *localite*, i.e. whose attention was 'fixed on the rear-view mirror' rather than 'on the road to change ahead' (Rogers, 1962: 171). Non-adopters in the Third World were regarded in the same vein. The problem was that whereas non-adopters in the developed nations constituted a small minority of holdouts, the Third World non-adopters were usually the vast majority. Curiously, this discrepancy alarmed nobody. The attitude seemed to be that most peasants were non-adopters, therefore laggard, and so recalcitrant. They were thus to blame for failing to adopt perfectly good innovations.

The research based on these suspicions 'confirmed' them. In 1969, Rogers, drawing upon the works of such development scholars as Lerner (1958), Hoselitz (1960), Hagen (1962), McClelland (1967), and Inkeles (1969), abstracted ten in-the-head socio-psychological factors which were held to constrain peasant adoption of innovations and synthesized them into what he termed the *subculture of peasantry* (Rogers, 1969). Thus, a new bias, the in-the-head psychological constraint bias, was now added to the rest, suggesting a major modification to the formerly fairly simple model of development.

The model implied that development of peasants would not ensue unless the psychological maladies afflicting them were first overcome. The burden that this orientation placed upon the powers of persuasion of change agents was onerous indeed. Changing peasants no longer consisted of simply convincing them of the superiority of Western innovations over their traditional ideas and practices: it now required the radical modification of a traditional mind set as a precondition of conviction.

Publication of the socio-psychological constraints had a chilling effect on development communication research. If the notion of a subculture of peasantry was true, then the prospect of producing change in such peasants was bleak indeed. To those concerned with designing strategies to bring about peasant development, the variables in question: familism, fatalism, and lack of deferred gratification, to mention a few, seemed essentially 'non-manipulable' (Roling, 1973).

External Socio-Economic Constraints on Development

By the seventies, US-trained Third World communication scholars began to assert themselves. In various ways, they began to take issue with the style and manner of US-dominated development communication research (Ascroft et al., 1973b; Beltran, 1976; Diaz-Bordenave, 1976; Rahim, 1976). Some were skeptical of the in-the-head variable bias which seemed to have led researchers into a *cul de sac*. They argued that the findings yielding the ten factors of the subculture of peasantry were an operationalizational artifact of the measurement instruments used. The factors seemed to be more in the eye of the beholders than in the reality of the peasants. This view led to an attempt to realign the focus between diffusion research and practice.

Field studies in Kenya seemed to support this hypothesis. There, researchers found at least six non-psychologically based factors which they termed 'bottlenecks', which together or in various combinations, appeared to be making it difficult, even impossible, for farmers to adopt recommended innovations (Ascroft et al., 1973a: Section I, page 6):

1. Lack of knowledge and skills about innovations to be adopted;
2. Lack of people involvement in the development planning process;
3. Lack of financial and material inputs necessary for adoption;
4. Inadequate market development for sale/purchase of produce;
5. Lack of infrastructure to facilitate distribution of information and material;
6. Lack of off-season employment opportunities in rural areas.

Of the six factors, the lack of knowledge and skills was arguably an in-the-head rather than an external variable. However, removal of this want depended upon receiving external inputs, not upon the individual changing long-held attitudes and beliefs.

The Kenya-based researchers showed that the removal of the above constraint plus the others resulted in an accelerated adoption of innovations (Ascroft et al., 1973b). To brand peasants as recalcitrant change-resisters without the prior removal of these bottlenecks constraining adoption, therefore, seemed tantamount to indicting them for a crime they had yet to have an opportunity to commit. Thus was created an alternative bias, the *external constraints on adoption bias*.

Similar conclusions about the prevalence of external constraints were being reached by development aid agencies. In 1973, Robert McNamara, then president of the World Bank, delivered his now famous 'New Directions in Development' speech in which he called for reassessment of existing development strategies (World Bank, 1973). His contention was that, taken as a whole, development strategies had so far failed to produce the desired advancement of Third World countries. Indeed the plight of their people seemed to have deteriorated during the sixties which, incidentally, had been proclaimed the *development decade* at an earlier time when optimism with existing strategies was running high.

A major shortcoming with existing strategies, McNamara felt, was the piecemeal approach to removing constraints. What was needed, he felt, was a multidisciplinary, broad-fronted *integrated rural development* approach which would seek, in one fell swoop, to remove all identifiable bottlenecks constraining adoption among peasants.

The findings about the external constraints on adoption, while perhaps not negating the possibility of internal psychological factors militating against adoption, at least provided a way out of the research *cul de sac*. For example, one of the major external constraints to development was the paucity of adequate, reliable, relevant, and timely information to overcome lack of knowledge and skills about recommended innovations among potential peasant adopters. If peasants were not receiving information at all, or if they were receiving it in a form which they were unable to translate into useful knowledge and skills, one would have expected researchers to subject the information sources and the messages they constructed to greater scrutiny; that is, to take up the questions mentioned earlier: namely, (*i*) were the mass and interpersonal messages somehow at fault—encoded, structured, and treated in ways not useful to consumers? (*ii*) were the channel linkages between sources and receivers too far to encompass all receivers?

Some students of development communication began to focus their attention on searching for factors which could presumably make development projects more relevant to the needs of the disadvantaged groups. They realized that many of the earlier projects had not given enough attention to the communication constraint. Their efforts, therefore, resulted in the conceptualization of communication as a dynamic support to development projects and activities and was termed as *development support communication* (DSC). The DSC specialist has the job of *bridging the communication gap* between the technical specialists with expertise in specific areas of knowledge—health matters, agriculture, etc.—and the users who are in need of such knowledge and its specific applications to improve their performance, increase their productivity, improve their health, etc. The DSC expert is expected to translate technical language and ideas into messages that would be comprehensible to users. It is in this context that this book will be relevant.

ORGANIZATION OF THE BOOK

This book aims to provide (*i*) a concise historical review of the field of development communication, and (*ii*) a comprehensive discussion of the theory and practice of development support communication. It will examine relevant models, points of view and arguments of important scholars in the field of communication and development, clarify concepts and critique them if necessary. As a teacher of development communication, I believe this effort fills an important void: it provides students with a book that synthesizes all pertinent material in development communication between two covers. There is a need for such a resource book which surveys work done in rural sociology, social psychology, social work, communication, and political economy, and presents it in an organized manner eliminating disciplinary jargon.

Though the perspectives of the role of communication in development as held in the fifties and sixties have changed since then, the need for development communication is as important today as it was thirty years ago. This book will trace the history of development support communication, critique the earlier paradigms and provide ideas and models for development communication in the eighties and nineties.

In Chapter 2, the reader is introduced to the dominant paradigm of development that was popular in the fifties and sixties. This chapter examines post-World War II development theories in sociology, social psychology, and economics; and discusses the role of culture in development as perceived in the sixties.

In Chapter 3, the focus of the discussion is on communication models and theories, especially as they related to modernization and diffusion of innovations in the fifties and sixties. The expected role of the mass media in national development efforts in the Third World during the post-World War II decades is discussed in detail in this chapter.

Chapters 4 and 5 critique the postulates of the dominant paradigm of development, modernization theories, and diffusion of innovations; question the relevance of the mass media in the development process as operationalized in the dominant paradigm, and critique their role.

The passing of the dominant paradigm in the early seventies, and the alternative perspectives of development that surfaced during this time is the focus of Chapter 6. It examines the ethical dimensions of the earlier theories of development, looks at the constructive role of local culture in development, examines indigenous channels of communication and their relevance as vehicles for development support, and sets the tone for the new role of communication in the eighties and nineties.

In the final chapter, the concerns of communication scholars in the eighties and nineties occupies center stage, namely: community and individual participation of beneficiaries in the development process. This chapter describes in detail the new paradigm of the eighties, sometimes termed as *Another Development*. The emerging new field of *development support communication*, its role and potential as a development support tool is also examined. This chapter discusses biases in communication in development projects and looks at ways in which they may be overcome using appropriate communication strategies.

Overview

This section deals with social and communication theories, techniques, and technologies suggested primarily by Western scholars, scientists, and administrators to guide the developing nations of Asia, Africa, and Latin America *develop* or *modernize* in the years following World War II.

Lest the reader feel that the chapters in this section are treated in a historical vacuum (as far as the Third World nations are concerned), a brief context is necessary to put the material in this section in a proper historical perspective.

A Brief History

A review of humankind's phylogenetic history will reveal that Europe, which was to dominate the rest of the world from the 16th to 19th centuries, did not lead the course in ancient times. It was the river valley civilizations of Mesopotamia (in West Asia), Egypt (in North Africa), Indus Valley (Indian subcontinent) and China which dominated during the period 3500 BC to 1500 BC in new technologies, architecture, arts and crafts, etc. The Roman civilization (500 BC) which followed the Greek age in Europe, paved the way for development of the European peoples who in recent history have come to dominate the world.

Throughout this long history of humankind, no nation or people have been the sole repository of knowledge. Instead, different cultures have generated new ideas, knowledge, etc. (Linton, 1936), which have accumulated over time and diffused from area to area and people to people. Some nations developed the ability to acquire and apply this knowledge faster than others and they used it to place themselves above others in wealth and power, to control the wealth and overall development of other nations in the world. Spurred by the rise of European merchant classes and the merchant marines, this ability emerged most decisively in Western Europe, circa 1500. The period from the 16th to early 20th century was one of expansionism and exploitation which saw the subjugation and reduction to serfdom of vast numbers of human beings across the southern two-thirds of the globe known as the Third World (Brookfield, 1975). The first period of European expansion ended in the early half of the 19th century, leading to the decolonization of the Americas and the suppression of slave trade (Goldthorpe, 1975). However, expansion continued unabated into interior parts of Africa and Asia. The voices of colonial dissatisfaction gathered in volume at the turn of the present century as some European colonial powers, such as the Dutch in the East Indies and the British in Africa, precipitated an era of *ethical concern*. This conceded some responsibility for the development and not just the exploitation of the subjugated people (Brookfield, 1975). The struggles for complete freedom from colonial rule were realized in the decades following World War II. First, the Asian colonies and then African colonies attained their independence by the 1960s.

Development Assistance: Both Money and Ideas

The years following World War II saw the birth of multilateral development assistance through the International Monetary Fund, the World Bank, and the United Nations family of specialized agencies, and the emergence of bilateral development assistance (i.e. President Truman's Point Four Program) to help the newly independent developing countries of Asia, Africa, and Latin America. While the Marshall Plan involved mainly capital investment to help Europe get back on its feet again, assistance to Third World countries comprised both monetary help as well as knowledge of scientific techniques and technologies in health, agriculture, mass media, etc. and human expertise to facilitate the acquisition of the new information. Thus was born Organized Development Assistance (ODA).

On the face of it, the task of modernizing the Third World seemed quite simple: determine appropriate innovations promising high payoffs and arrange to have them diffused to targeted beneficiaries. The reasons for the woeful state of affairs in the Third World countries were attributed to the inadequate industrial infrastructure, *backward* cultures of these nations, and certain characteristics of their citizens. That the long history of colonial exploitation and the oppressive social-structural conditions that it spawned may have anything to do with the backward state of these nations (and by extension, the modern state of the European countries) was not given a thought. Thus, Third World countries were considered to be in the same stage as the European nations in circa 1600, i.e. before the onset of the industrial age. Therefore, the *solution* to solving the problems of underdevelopment in Asia, Africa, and Latin America was simple and straightforward: by re-tracing the development path of the European countries (barring the colonization aspect), the Third World could be speeded through the different stages at a rate faster even than the advanced countries themselves experienced. It is this orientation which came to be known as the *Dominant Paradigm*.

The main purpose of talking about the dominant paradigm in this section, is to reveal a certain mind-set which was simple, linear, deterministic, and tinged with optimism. Wilbur Schramm, Daniel Lerner, Ithiel De Sola Pool, Lucien Pye, Walt Rostow, etc. believed that the process of development meant transition from traditionalism to modernization in a unidirectional way. Nations making the journey would have to pass through preordained stages such that those going ahead provided an emulative model for those following behind. The ultimate stage was to become like the Western countries.

Another reason to talk about the dominant paradigm is to show how this mind-set yielded an approach to communication for development which was, according to Ascroft and Masilela (1989), vertical in nature, authority-based, top-down, expert-driven, non-negotiable, well-intentioned, and thus hortatory in orientation.

Chapter 2

The Dominant Paradigm: Early Theories in Comparative International Development

> *Modernity exacts a high price on the level of meaning. Those who are unwilling to pay this price must be taken with utmost seriousness, and not be dismissed as 'backward' or 'irrational'*—Peter L. Berger (1976: xiii).

The transition of Europeon societies from a traditional and feudal structure toward more advanced social stages, has been an important concern of social theorists from the classical to the modern age. Considerable literature is available on the forces and set of relationships that propelled Europe from the largely agricultural-feudal order to the complex, highly differentiated, capitalist-industrial society. In fact, 'the issue of European transformation has given rise to what is, without doubt, the core of classic and of most modern sociological theory' (Portes, 1976: 56).

With the emergence of the Third World, theories and concepts which recapitulated the unique West European and North American transition from a traditional to a modern society, have generated in the last few decades a host of new models of development. An important concern among the 'developed' nations was how to develop the 'underdeveloped' societies just emancipated from centuries of colonial rule. The main trend in sociological theory was extrapolation of concepts generated from the West European and North American analysis to the study of national development in the Third World nations.

MODERNIZATION THEORIES

The dominant paradigm in the west *vis-á-vis* Third World development was based on an application of the evolutionary concept of Darwin to social change:

> Not only was change in one social sphere able to stimulate change in others, but social modernization was able to generate continuing change, and also to absorb the stress of change and adapt itself to changing demands. In other words, the process seemed relatively irreversible. Once the necessary conditions were established for take-off, a country took off, became modern, and stayed modern (Schramm, 1976: 46).

The notion of a *modern nation* was prescribed by Western scholars. As Fjes comments, 'it was generally assumed that a nation became truly modern and developed when it arrived at that point where it closely resembled Western industrial nations in terms of political and economic behavior and institutions, attitudes toward technology and innovation, and social and psychic mobility' (Fjes, 1976: 4).

Theories in Sociology of Development

In the 19th century, societies in Europe and North America were being transformed from rural, agriculture-based communities to take on a more industrial character. Social theorists during this time were concerned with the upheaval of the existing societies and the new social forms arising from industrialization, urbanization, and modernization.

These scholarly efforts resulted in various theories on social evolution. Portes (1976: 61) noted that Morgan, Comte, Spencer, Kidd, and Ward were the proponents of the evolutionary perspective in human societies. In their theories of development, the transformation of cultures was compared to the evolution of organisms as articulated in the biological sciences. In other words, these theorists saw very little difference in the phylogeny of biological species and human societies. The growth of cultures was inextricably tied, as in the growth of organisms, to a series of inevitable and irreversible stages. In these theories of social evolution, the development of societies followed a unilinear path and the major stages of growth were universal. However, it was quite transparent that these social theorists were preoccupied with the historical transformation of the Western countries. In their models, the highest stage of development or evolution was represented by advanced European nations of the 19th and early 20th centuries.

Charles Darwin's classic *On the Origin of Species* (1859) was the inspiration for the evolutionary view of social change. However, Darwin's thesis was applicable to the phylogeny of species. He argued that all organisms had evolved from simpler forms and that the general direction of biological evolution was unilinear, i.e., towards more complex forms. The early social theorists of the *evolutionist school* applied Darwin's ideas to the process of modernization of human societies. The more prominent of these theorists were Herbert Spencer and William Sumner. Spencer even applied Darwin's famous principle of *the survival of the fittest* to human cultures. He claimed that Western societies were superior to all other races and had excelled because they were better adapted to face the changing conditions in the process of modernization of societies. This school of thought, termed *Social Darwinism*, won acceptance even among intellectuals in the late 19th century (Berger, 1976; Ryan, 1976; Robertson, 1977).

The theories of social evolution influenced and gave rise to important concepts and hypotheses in the sociology of development. However, while the earlier theories were explanatory of the historical transformation of the West, the newer theories in the 20th century were used to compare the development of Third World nations with those in Europe and North America.

Tradition vs. Modernity

The earlier models were based on a dichotomous conception of tradition vs. modernity (Eisenstadt, 1976). These theories were essentially bipolar where the universal stages in the earlier theories of social evolution were reduced to ideal-typical end points. These ideal-typical extremes, however, were descriptive of the beginning and end points of the process of social transformation of the nations in Europe and North America. Portes (1976: 62) noted that 'theorists in this tradition were less concerned with encompassing the entire history of mankind than with apprehending that moment of

European transition from a feudal-agricultural to a capitalist-industrial order'. Several of these bipolar theories of modernization are given in Table 2.1.

TABLE 2.1
Bipolar Theories of Modernization

Maine (1907)	Status vs. Contract
Durkheim (1933)	Mechanic vs. Organic Solidarity
Toennies (1957)	*Gemeinschaft* vs. *Gesellschaft*
Lerner (1958)	Traditional vs. Modern Society
Cooley (1962)	Primary vs. Secondary Social Attachments
Redfield (1965)	Folk vs. Urban Societies

In all these theories, the earlier stage was the traditional society which was conceptualized as a small, mostly rural community where everybody knew each other, where interpersonal relations were close with strong group solidarity and kinship ties. The end stage, on the other hand, was a large, mostly urban society where interpersonal relations were impersonal, where there was hardly any group solidarity and close kinship ties. This society was conceptualized as a loose association of people and in which tradition and shared norms and values no longer had a dominant influence. Also, in these theories, as articulated cogently in Durkheim's analysis, the two ideal types differed on the basis of the social bond—mechanistic and organic. The transformation from the traditional to the modern society required greater functional specialization and structural differentiation.

Pattern Variables Scheme

The pattern variables scheme was a contribution of Parsons (1964a) to general social theory. However, this served as an extension of the classic bipolar theories and was used by the theorists of the functionalist perspective as a tool for diagnosing social change in different societies, particularly the contrast between the Western societies and those in the Third World (Portes, 1976: 62). Hoselitz (1960) used the pattern variables scheme as a model of the sociological aspects of economic growth.

In this scheme, traditional societies have certain common characteristics: ascribed roles which are functionally diffuse and oriented toward narrow particularistic goals. Modern societies, on the other hand, have roles assigned or acquired through achievement rather than birth, they are oriented toward broad, secular, and universal norms (Levy, 1966; Portes, 1976). When attempts were made to transform the pattern variables scheme as a theory of societal development, the consequence was a set of generalizations extrapolating concepts/notions from the European and North American historical experience to describe and prescribe modernization in Third World countries (Hoselitz, 1960).

Development as Social Differentiation

This notion of development was a direct extension of the social evolutionary theories of the 19th century. According to this theory of development, societies modernize through greater and greater differentiation in their institutions. In simpler societies, there is hardly any differentiation in social institutions. A single institution may perform several functions. For example, the family may not only serve the function of reproduction but also take care of socialization, education, and even economic production. However, human societies like organisms in biological theory pass through evolutionary stages to reach higher levels of complexity as exhibited through greater specialization of functions. A process of differentiation takes place where several institutions take over the functions that were hitherto undifferentiated and performed by one or a couple of institutions. The process of differentiation is accompanied by the concomitant process of integration. As Portes commented·

> the theory of society based on this notion is one in which pressures faced at a given point are eliminated through increasing specialization and differentiation, which, in turn, give rise to problems of integration, which are solved through emerging networks of interdependence. The whole process results in an ever-growing societal 'complexity' or 'systemness' (Portes, 1976: 63).

Again, this theory of social differentiation was employed for the comparative diagnosis of development in the developed and underdeveloped societies (Smelser, 1973).

Evolutionary Universals

This was another contribution of Parsons (1964b) to general social theory. He identified and described structural features of the systems in the West that helped them to survive in their environment in the process of societal development: bureaucratic organization, money, markets, democratic association, and a common legal system. These universals were prescribed as essential for modernization of the underdeveloped societies.

As Schramm noted, perhaps the best overall summary of this social approach was Karl Deutsch's (1961) concept of *social mobilization* defined as 'the process in which old social, economic, and psychological commitments are eroded and broken down and people become available for new patterns of socialization and behavior' (Schramm, 1976: 46). An index of this process included not only higher social differentiation and integration of roles and institutions but also the development of evolutionary universals described earlier.

In sum, the Western countries were treated as models of political, economic, social, and cultural modernization that the Third World nations would do well to emulate. The advanced Western nations had a wide range of systemic autonomy, i.e. their capacity to cope with a range of social, cultural, technological, and economic issues in the process of social change (Eisenstadt, 1976: 31). The Third World nations, on the other hand, lacking the higher differentiation of roles and institutions, the evolutionary universals, and other qualitative characteristics of industrial societies, were limited in their capacity to cope with problems or crises or even master their environment.

Unilinear Model of Development

Among the proponents of the unilinear model of development, Walt Rostow and Daniel Lerner deserve special mention. They stated explicitly that once key institutions and certain behavior patterns were established, development was more or less sustained. The changes were irreversible and the process of development moved in a common universal direction.

Rostow expounded his economic growth theory, in his *The Stages of Economic Growth: A Non-Communist Manifesto* (1960).

Essentially, he constructed a five-stage model of transition from a traditional economy to a modern industrial complex: the traditional society, preconditions for take-off, take-off, drive to maturity, and the age of high mass consumption. He believed that every society would pass through these five stages of economic growth leading finally to the last phase: the age of high mass consumption.

In Rostow's model (1960: 4–5), the traditional society was:

> hampered by limited production facilities; based on pre-Newtonian notions of science and technology, and constrained by rigid social structure and irrational psychological attitudes.

The preconditions for take-off were developed when insights of modern science were applied into new production functions in agriculture and industry. The idea spread that economic progress was possible and necessary for a better life, people were willing to save and take risks in pursuit of private profit, institutions such as banks appeared to mobilize savings, and there was development of infrastructure, notably in transportation and communications.

It was during the take-off stage that a nation developed from a traditional into a modern state:

> The take-off is the interval when the old blocks and resistances to steady growth are finally overcome. The forces making for economic progress, which yielded limited bursts and enclaves of modern activity, expand and come to dominate the society. Growth becomes its normal condition. Compound interest becomes built, as it were, into its habits and institutional structure (Rostow, 1960: 7).

During this period, the rate of investment and savings increased from 5 percent to 10 percent of the national income, new industries expanded yielding huge profits which were reinvested in new physical capital and in turn, the new factories stimulated the factors of capital and labor, and, finally, there were revolutionary improvements in the agricultural sector.

After the take-off, a steady rate of growth in the economy could be regularly sustained. Output was ahead of population increases, there was an improvement in technology giving rise to new and more efficient industries, and the economy found its place in profitable international trade. Finally, the society entered the stage of high mass consumption. Large numbers of people gained a command over consumption that went beyond basic necessities to include luxury goods and services. The United States, Japan, and countries of Western Europe constitute examples of nations that have reached the final stage of mass consumption.

Lerner saw the dynamic of social development as: a nucleus of mobile, change-accepting personalities, a growing mass media system to spread the ideas and attitudes of social mobility and change, then the interaction of urbanization, literacy, and industrialization, higher per capita income and political participation (Lerner, 1958).

Lerner believed that these institutional developments (which had already occurred in the Western nations) would lead to a take-off toward modernization. Lerner also suggested a psychological prerequisite among individuals called *empathy*. More will be said about this in the next section. Like other social theorists, Lerner saw a systemic interconnectedness between the various institutional developments. As Schramm noted: 'the essential point was that growth in one of these spheres stimulates growth in others, and all spheres of society moved forward together toward modernization' (1976: 45–46).

Theories on Individual Psychological Attributes

All the theories on modernization were not necessarily at the macro level. While institutional development in the Third World was considered necessary for modernization, it was not the character of society but the character of individuals that was important (Weiner, 1966). Weiner believed that attitudinal and value changes were prerequisites to creating a modern, socio-economic polity. However, the cause-effect relationship was hard to establish and there was no categorical answer to whether attitudes or institutions change first. Nevertheless, all scholars in this disciplinary area believed that neither modern science and technology nor modern institutions could be successfully grafted on a society whose people were basically traditional, uneducated, self-centered, or unscientific in their thinking and attitudes (Weiner, 1966).

Important scholars in this disciplinary field of development, which emphasized individual values and attitudes were: McClelland, Inkeles, Hagen, and Lerner. The intellectual source for this school of thought was Weber's thesis on the *Protestant Ethic* (1958) and the general trend in Amercian sociology on value-normative complexes.

However, Portes (1976) comments that while these scholars borrowed Weber's conceptualization, they did not necessarily use them within a proper historical-structural context. Weber's thesis on the *Protestant Ethic* was firmly anchored within the power relationships, structural constraints, and political-economic interests that obtained in Catholic Europe. Such was not the case with these writings regarding the value-normative complexes of individuals in Third World countries.

Let us review the main ideas of scholars in this area of development:

David McClelland (1966) was interested in identifying and measuring the variable that might be the impulse to modernization. There were several questions which interested him. Why did some nations 'take-off' into rapid economic growth while others stood still or declined? Why were the Greeks of 6th century BC very enterprising? Why did North America inhabited by the English develop faster than South America occupied by Spaniards at about the same time? In other words, McClelland was interested in what impulse produced economic growth and modernization. What was this impulse and where did it originate?

McClelland separated a *mental virus* that made people behave in a particularly energetic way (McClelland, 1966). This virus received the name *n-Ach* or need for achievement. It was identified in a sample of person's thoughts by examining whether the thoughts had to do with *doing something better* than it had been done before, doing things more efficiently and faster with less labor.

When the popular literature of a country was coded for the presence of n.Ach over long periods of time it was found that there was a direct relation between the virus and economic growth. For example, the literature of the Greeks in the 6th century BC had higher content of n.Ach than in later Greek literature. Similarly, English literature of the 16th century had more n.Ach content than Spanish literature of the same period.

Could it be that the n.Ach might be a part of the impulse to economic growth? McClelland found that this became more apparent when a nation's *infection level* with the virus was estimated by coding the imaginative stories the country used to teach its very young children (McClelland, 1966). It was found that this led to a spurt in economic activity a few years later. McClelland conducted an experiment in the city of Hyderabad in India where a group of businessmen were *injected* with the virus via a ten-day self-development course (McClelland, 1966). It was found later that these men took their work more seriously, became innovative, and there was overall a genuine desire to excel.

McClelland cautioned that n.Ach by itself was not enough. The other input which was equally important was social consciousness, i.e. working for the common good. Therefore, in summary, the impulse to modernization, according to McClelland, consisted in part of a personal variable—n.Ach—and in part of a social virtue—interest in the welfare of others (McClelland, 1966).

Everett Hagen (1962) attempted to empirically determine measures that influenced entrepreneurial activity. He introduced the concept of *withdrawal of status respect*, a complex psychoanalytic variable. Portes summarized this concept thus:

> Humiliations resulting from status withdrawal among parents have certain psychic consequences for their sons who, in turn, transmit them to their own children. After a complicated evolution of complexes and stages, the 'virus' finally matures and is ready to do its work in society (Portes, 1976: 70).

Thus, according to Hagen, certain creative individuals rejected traditional values, took on new roles and became innovative. He provided examples of Soviet Russia, Japan, and Germany where economic development was sustained by such creative individuals whose ancestors had suffered *withdrawal of status respect*. Clearly, according to Hagen, the impetus for socio-economic development was provided by a psychological characteristic present in certain groups of people.

Daniel Lerner (1958) based a substantial part of his elaborate theory of modernization on social-psychological variables. At the heart of his model was a nucleus of mobile, change-accepting individuals. These individuals could be distinguished by their high capacity for identification with new aspects of their environment. Lerner called this attribute *empathy*, which signified the capacity of a person to put himself/herself in another person's shoes. For example, a Turkish goatherd would exhibit empathy if he could imagine himself as the president of his country. Lerner believed that a high empathic capacity was the predominant personal style in Western countries which were also industrial, urban, literate, and participant. Lerner suggested the development of empathy as an indispensable skill for people moving out of traditional settings.

Alex Inkeles (1966) developed his conceptual model of individual modernity based on research in six developing countries. He argued that the transformation of individuals was both a means to an end and an end in itself of the development process. Inkeles used nine attitude items to construct standard scales of modernity which he later used to identify the character of the modern person: (*i*) readiness of new experiences and openness to innovation, (*ii*) disposition to form and hold opinions, (*iii*) democratic orientation, (*iv*) planning habits, (*v*) belief in human and personal efficacy, (*vi*) belief that the world is calculable, (*vii*) stress on personal and human dignity, (*viii*) faith in science and technology, and (*ix*) belief in distributive justice (Inkeles, 1969).

The psychological characteristics outlined above delineated Inkeles' concept of the spirit of modernity which he considered an essential prerequisite for economic growth.

Other scholars discussing the role of value-normative complexes in modernization prepared exhaustive lists of the social-psychological attributes of modernity. Some of these were: mobility, high participation in organizations and electoral process, interest articulation, interest aggregation, high ambitions for self and children, institutionalized political competition, secularism, appetite for national and international information, achievement motivation, desire for consumption of new goods and technology, preference for urban areas, new attitudes to wealth, work, savings and possibility of change, desire for geographical mobility, socio-economic and political discipline, and deferral of gratifications (Kahl, 1968; Horowitz, 1970; Schnaiberg, 1970; Portes, 1974).

Role of Culture in Modernization

In all the theories and models discussed so far, the implicit idea was that the Western cultures constituted ideal examples of what a modern society should be. The Third World nations could achieve the same results as the Western countries, but this meant dismantling all the non-Western traditional structures:

> The basic model that emerged out of all these researches assumed that the conditions for development of a viable, growth-sustaining, modern society were tantamount to continuous extension of modern components and to destruction of all traditional elements... the more thorough the disintegration of traditional elements, the more able a society would be to 'develop' continuously (Eisenstadt, 1976: 33).

Oriental values and religions were seen as a bulwark of traditionalism and a repository of ideas that were incompatible with modernity (Weber, 1964).

Buddhism

The founder of Buddhism was Gautama the Buddha, who lived around the 6th century BC. The story of his life is famed in legend and literature and in painting and sculpture.

The Buddha taught four noble truths: (i) there is suffering in this world; (ii) this suffering has a cause; (iii) the cause is desire, or thirst, as he called it; (iv) it is possible to put an end to suffering if desire is removed. To attain *nirvana* or freedom from birth and rebirth and, therefore, cessation of suffering, the Buddha said that one should know 'the right way'. This eight-fold path consists of the Right View, Right Resolution, Right Words, Right Action, Right Living, Right Effort, Right Thinking, and Right Concentration (*Social Studies*, 1969).

The Buddha proclaimed the uselessness of sacrifices and rejected the authority of the Vedas. He insisted upon simplicity of life. To him, social distinctions were of no consequence and he said that in order to lead a pure life, one need not be born into a high caste. Every person who wanted was thus admitted to the Buddhist order without any distinction. The Buddha taught in the language of the people which appealed to the common man.

The *sangha*, or the order of monks that the Buddha started, was a model of simplicity and perfect organization. The administration was democratic; disputes were referred to committees. The monks and the nuns travelled all year round preaching the doctrines, except during the four months in the rainy season when they stayed in the *viharas*, or monasteries, studying and meditating (*Social Studies*, 1969).

Ashoka, the Mauryan Emperor, helped spread Buddhism in India and abroad. He sent missionaries to Burma and Sri Lanka and also to some countries in West Asia. Later, missionaries such as Kumarajiva and Atisa Dipankara carried the Buddha's teachings to Central Asia and Tibet. From Central Asia, the religion spread to China, Korea, and Japan. Curiously, the religion practically died out in the land of its birth, India.

The most important Buddhist scriptures are the *Tripitakas*, or 'The Three Baskets'. These are the *Vinayapitaka* which deals with rules of discipline, the *Suttapitaka* which lays down the religious doctrines, and the *Abhiddammapitaka* which contains some philosophical principles. Another important work, the *Milinda-Panha*, explains the Buddhist doctrines in the form of a dialogue between King Milinda or Menander, the Greek king of northwestern India, and a Buddhist priest. All these works are in the Pali-Prakrit language, though several religious books of Buddhism were later written in Sanskrit (*Social Studies*, 1969).

Islam was criticized for its tradition-bound rigidity, Hinduism for its asceticism and Buddhism for its other-worldly emphasis. Following Max Weber's thesis, *Protestant Ethic and the Spirit of Capitalism*, several generations of sociologists sought to identify a set of cultural values in the Third World nations that inhibited modernization. In general, the Asian religions were seen as obstacles to progress (Bellah, 1965; Rose, 1970). Commenting on Weber's interpretation of Asian religions, Singer noted:

In his studies of India, China, and Asia generally, where he did not see anything resembling the development of European industrial capitalism, Weber reasoned that the religions of those countries must lack the counterparts of a *Protestant Ethic* that would provide the characterological foundation for the economic motivation required, as one among several factors, to spark and foster a development of industrial capitalism (Singer, 1972: 275–76).

For example, Weber identified the theological ideas of *samsara* (rebirth) and *karma* (fate) as the dogmatic foundation of Hinduism. When combined with caste ritualism, they made the rationalization of the economy, and progress and modernization impossible. The encouragement of asceticism was also perceived as a major problem. Shankara's philosophy of *advaita*, which called for renunciation of this world for an other-worldly asceticism, was considered as synonymous with Hindu theology. Shankara's concept of Hinduism was, therefore, criticized as life-negating and pessimistic by evangelizing Christians who sought to prove the superiority of Christianity over Hinduism (Srinivas, 1973).

Hinduism

Hinduism, as we now call it, is perhaps the oldest religion in the world. The peculiarity of Hinduism is that it had no founder. During its existence of thousands of years, it has come into contact with numerous beliefs, doctrines, and principles, some of which it has adopted. It has also undergone internal changes and shifts in emphasis. From very old times, the Hindu thinker has readily admitted other points of view and considered them worthy of attention. The Hindu believes in the existence of One Supreme Universal Spirit, but Hinduism allows the Hindu to worship Him in any form he likes. Many scholars thus think that Hinduism is henotheistic (*Social Studies*, 1969).

The Hindu believes in the doctrine of *karma*, which says that the present life of man is not an isolated existence but only a link in a series of existences. The soul within a body never dies. It is only the body that dies and is born again and again. Hinduism is a way of life and this way of life includes consideration of three ends. The first is *dharma*, or virtue, which is the spring of right action. The second is *artha*, which is acquisition of material things, guided in the path of *dharma*, or the righteous way. *Kama*, the third, is gratification of the physical senses, governed by a cultivated mind and rising above mere animal pleasure. These three, rightly pursued, lead to *moksha* or salvation, the coveted ideal of the cultivated mind (*Social Studies*, 1969).

According to Hinduism there are three ways to achieve salvation. The *karma marga* recommends the proper performance of rituals and sacrifices; the *gyana marga* is the path of knowledge; and the *bhakti marga* lays stress on personal devotion to a personal god—Vishnu, Krishna, or Rama.

Yet another characteristic of Hinduism to be mentioned here is *varna dharma*, popularly translated as the caste system, which was the very basis of Hindu society. It enjoins the individual to perform his duties faithfully, chiefly for the benefit of society. It emphasizes the social aspect of an individual's life. The rigidity that crept into the caste system is a later development and has been condemned by many social and religious reformers in India (*Social Studies*, 1969).

To sum up, the central principles of Hinduism have made it a living religion. It has never been a uniform, stationary, unalterable religion. It is in fact a tradition that kept growing. This feature of the religion has enabled it to adapt itself to changing circumstances and conditions of life as the religion of millions in India.

The scriptures of Hinduism are many in number. The most important of these are the four Vedas—the *Rigveda*, the *Samaveda*, the *Yajurveda* and the *Atharvaveda*—together with their *Brahmanas* and *Upanishads*. The Vedas have always been regarded as holy, though the original Vedic religion does not play a significant part in the life of a Hindu (*Social Studies*, 1969).

The *Brahmanas* prescribe the proper performance of rituals. The *Upanishads* lay stress on the acquisition of knowledge and record highly philosophical discussions on such fundamental problems as the nature of man and his soul and their relation with the universe and the ultimate reality of God. The *Bhagavad Gita* synthesizes three lines of thought on the way to achieve salvation through *karma marga*, *gyana marga*, and *bhakti marga*. It lays great stress on the *bhakti marga* and enjoins complete trust in God and the performance of one's duty without hope of reward, but does not reject the other two paths as unimportant or superfluous. The epics, the *Dharmashastras* and the *Puranas*, are the other important scriptures of the Hindus (*Social Studies*, 1969).

Weber's ideas were extended to provide a recipe for modernization of India. This called for the jettisoning of the caste system, the joint family, ritualism, and almost all other practices, institutions, and beliefs characteristic of Hinduism (Singer, 1972). In fact, Rose contends that it is these practices and institutions that have kept India economically backward. The joint family system, according to Rose, fosters dependency and submissiveness, whereas casteism hampers occupational mobility. Belief in superstitions and magic was rampant even among educated Indians. It was not uncommon for a top government official to consult astrologers about proper timing before any action. And, related to these irrational acts were others which were just as uneconomical. It was common in Asia to spend extravagant amounts of money over occasions such as marriage celebrations and religious festivals (Rose, 1970), all of which did not contribute to a rationalized economy.

Islam

Muhammad, the Prophet of Islam, was born in Mecca in Arabia in 570 AD. Mecca, the city of Muhammad's birth, was a commercial and religious center. The black rectangular stone set in a holy building called the *Kaaba*, was revered by the Arabs. It can still be seen in Mecca, the city to which Muslims make a pilgrimage.

Muhammad's visions completely convinced him that Allah was the only God and that he was a Prophet of God.

Islam teaches faith in the one all-powerful God, Allah, and in Muhammad, the Prophet of God. Islam speaks of life after death and of a last judgement when all men shall receive the reward for their earthly actions (*Social Studies*, 1969).

A Muslim has to regulate his life according to five principles: (*i*) he must proclaim the unity of God and the prophet-hood of Muhammad: *La-Ilaha illa Allah: Muhammad-ur-Rasul ullah* (There is no God but Allah and Muhammad is His Prophet); (*ii*) he must offer prayers five times every day and on Friday afternoons in the mosque; (*iii*) he must give alms to the poor as an offering to Allah and as a religious act; (*iv*) he must fast from dawn to dusk throughout Ramazan, the holy month of Islam; and (*v*) he should, if possible, go on a pilgrimage to Mecca, at least once in his lifetime (*Social Studies*, 1969).

Over and above these five principles, Islam lays down some observances and also forbids some practices. No Muslim should worship an idol. This is why no picture or sculpture of Muhammad exists. A Muslim must not eat pork, for the pig is unclean. He must not lend money on interest. He has to follow certain rules regarding marriage and divorce. The emphasis on a life of virtue and benevolence makes Islam one of the great humanitarian religions. The holy book of the Muslims, the *Quran*, emphasizes such virtues as 'to free the captive, or to feed, in a day of famine, the orphan who is of kin, or the poor man who lieth on the ground' (*Social Studies*, 1969).

Models for Economic Development

The dominant paradigm of development that ruled the social sciences prescribed a particular economic path to modernization: the neo-classical approach which had served as an important model for Western economists. Adam Smith in his *The Wealth of Nations* (1776) originally proposed this approach which was later supported and enriched by other Western economists—Ricardo, Schumpeter, Keynes, Albert Hirschman, Nurkse, and others.

The dominant paradigm was mainly concerned with economic growth as measured by the rate of growth of output (GNP). Thus, an important goal of economists was to accelerate and maintain high rates of growth. The theory of development in this orthodox economic approach was simple. There were two main factors that were important: (*i*) productive resources a society had, and (*ii*) economic institutions to utilize and guide the use of the resources (Weaver and Jameson, 1978: 9).

Productive Resources

The quantity of output of goods and services of a system was a function of several factor inputs: capital, labor, land, technology, and entrepreneurship. A brief discussion of the salient features of each input will be useful:

Labor. The emphasis was on increasing the quality and quantity of output by specialization and division of labor. The quality of labor could be enhanced and adapted to the needs of modern industry by improving its physical and mental capacities (Weaver and Jameson, 1978). Developing nations were persuaded to invest in the improvement of human resources mainly through upgrading of skills and attitude changes. These were to be brought about through institutional programs and other training sessions (Schultz, 1963).

Capital. Capital formation occupied a very important place. Individuals and entire societies were required to defer consumption and save capital so that it may be invested to build such physical capital as heavy industries, steel factories, mills, and dams (Weaver and Jameson, 1978). Development of heavy industry was significant since it was used to produce other goods and machinery. Thus, industrialisation, particularly the capital-intensive variety, was given utmost importance (Nurkse, 1953; Hirschman, 1958). In fact, industrialization was synonymous with development. One important way of generating sufficient capital for industrialization was through redistribution of income and resources to capitalists and entrepreneurs. The assumption was that these groups would reinvest the capital in productive ways to generate more capital. Weaver and Jameson summarize this approach very well:

> Theorists who take this starting point suggest that development will come about if profits can be increased, for that increases capitalists' income which will lead to increased savings, which will lead to increased investment in capital goods, which will lead to industrialization—which equals development (Weaver and Jameson, 1978: 12).

The approach of creating inequality initially by redistributing income and resources to capitalists with the hope of a *trickle-down* of benefits later to others in the population was a fond notion of several post-War economists: Arthur Lewis, Ragnar Nurkse, Harvey Leibenstein, to mention a few. It was articulated very well in the Harod-Domar and Mahalanobis planning model in India (Weaver and Jameson, 1978).

Land. Industrialization was dependent on efficient use of land. Many economists believed that industrial development had to be preceded by agricultural development (Johnston and Mellor, 1961;

Eicher and Witt, 1964; Schultz, 1964). At least, that is the way it had happened in the Western countries. Agriculture made several important contributions for an orderly and effective development of industry. It produced surplus food and labor that directly benefited the industrial sector. Also, the export of agricultural output provided resources for the import of physical capital such as machinery needed for local industry. Importantly, a developed agricultural sector provided an effective and efficient internal market for industrial output.

The key to greater productivity in the agricultural sector was to shift from human/animal labor-intensive techniques to a machine-intensive approach. Weaver and Jameson noted:

> This means more and more capital-intensive agriculture, and generally it means larger and larger farms with more and more output per worker. United States agriculture has carried this furthest: four percent of the labor force produces enough food for the whole population, plus a considerable amount for export. This is the pattern suggested for agriculture, and a similar pattern of capitalization is suggested for natural resource industries (Weaver and Jameson, 1978: 14).

Technology and Entrepreneurship. Technology was viewed as central to the growth of productive agricultural and industrial sectors (Schumpeter, 1934; Abramovitz, 1956; Denison, 1962; Veblen, 1966; Weaver and Jameson, 1978). Therefore, transfer of technical know-how from the developed Western nations was considered extremely crucial for development in the Third World nations.

Finally, the entrepreneur was the catalyst in the process of economic development. Like Lerner's grocer in Balgat, Turkey, the entrepreneur was a risk-taker. He/she wanted to discard the traditional way of doing things and imitate or supplant new techniques, especially those practiced in the West. Rogers (1962) and Schramm (1964) describe the entrepreneur as an innovator who 'destroys the old way and initiates a process which will replace the old way with an innovation which is organizationally more successful' (Weaver and Jameson, 1978: 15)

Economic Institutions

The second factor in the orthodox economic model was the strategies and institutions to guide the use of resources. The institutions in the capitalist model which had the best fit with the requirements and assumptions of the paradigm were (Weaver and Jameson, 1978):

1. Completely private ownership of all factors of production;
2. An interrelated market system for means of production (labor, land and capital) and for output;
3. A private capitalist firm for production of output (a private organization with no direct control from any other authority except itself, functioning rationally to produce the optimum profit in an orderly market);
4. Free trade at the international, national and local levels.

The development strategy that was emphasized was the principle of *laissez-faire*. In French, this would mean complete independence. Thus, in the orthodox paradigm, the capitalists and entrepreneurs were to be left alone by the government and other authorities. The role of government was to be confined to maintaining law and order and providing the right climate for the capitalist to engage in profitable production.

In sum, this was the economic model that had worked successfully in England and later in the United States and it was precisely the model that was prescribed for the development of Third World nations.

DOMINANT PARADIGM OF DEVELOPMENT

Implicit in the ideas discussed above was a certain philosophy of what development in the Third World should be, and how it should be brought about. Thus, a *dominant paradigm* guided intellectual thinking from the forties through the sixties and was influential in communication and development research and theory. Everett Rogers (1976b: 121) noted, 'this concept of development grew out of certain historical events, such as the Industrial Revolution in Europe and the United States, the colonial experience in Latin America, Africa, and Asia, the quantitative empiricism of North American social science, and capitalistic economic/political philosophy.' Rogers distilled the four essential elements in this conception of development (Rogers, 1976c: 49):

1. Economic growth through industrialisation and accompanying

urbanization was the key to development. It was approximately equal to passing through the Industrial Revolution. It was assumed that development performance could be quantified in economic terms: GNP, per capita income, etc.;

2. The choice of technology was to be capital-intensive, and labor-extensive[1] mainly imported from more developed nations;

3. In order to guide and speed up the process of development, planning should be centralized and controlled by economists and bankers;

4. Underdevelopment was mainly due to problems within the developing nations rather than in their external relationships with other countries.

A detailed analysis of these postulates is provided below.

Economic Growth

This was considered the key to development. Most problems plaguing the Third World nations were diagnosed as economic in nature. As Rogers noted (1976c), economists were clearly in charge of development plans. Five-year plans were launched in several countries to dovetail several development activities and help bring about orderly economic progress. Bilateral and multilateral (example, the World Bank) institutions were involved in these plans.

This approach was at the macro level. Problems were identified and solutions offered at the higher levels of the government. Information and other inputs were then channeled down to local communities. Participatory or autonomus development by local communities was considered slow, inefficient, and, more often than not, unlikely (Rogers, 1976c).

In the dominant paradigm, *industrialization* was considered the main route to impressive economic growth. At least, that was the path by which North America and West Europe had developed in the late 19th century. So, Third World countries were encouraged to invest in a program of industrialization such as hydroelectric projects, steel industries, and a diversity of manufacturing units.

The development performance was measured by *quantitative indicators* which included gross national product (GNP) rates, per

[1] This is defined as a strategy where little importance is paid to the use of human labor in development.

capita incomes, etc. These indicators were considered more straight-forward to measure (when compared with such concepts as freedom and justice) and objective. However, they could also have been chosen due to the quantitative and empirical bias of North American social sciences (Nordenstreng, 1968; Rogers, 1976c).

Capital-Intensive Technology

This constituted the core of the industrialization that was prescribed for developing countries. More often than not, the capital- and machine-intensive techniques substituted labor that was abundantly available in the Third World nations. The badly-needed capital for the new technology was provided by national governments and, often, supplemented by loans from bilateral and multilateral agencies and transnational corporations.

Internal Constraints to Development

In the dominant paradigm, underdevelopment was usually attri-buted to internal constraints within developing countries rather than external forces acting on these nations. Some of the causes of underdevelopment were (Rogers, 1976b: 127):

1. A biased social-structure which suffered from a top-heavy land tenure system and an inefficient and slow government machinery;
2. Traditional behavior and attitudes among the masses that acted as obstacles to modernization.

Everett Rogers (1969) did an impressive study on peasants in India, Nigeria, and Colombia. He chose to study peasants or sub-sistence farmers because they constituted a majority of the popula-tion in many Third World countries. And, for a country to moder-nize, it was necessary that the peasants were persuaded to change their traditional life ways. In order to better understand the peasants, Rogers delineated a *subculture of peasantry* that was characterized by ten elements:

1. Mutual distrust in interpersonal relations: In general,

peasants were suspicious, evasive and distrustful of others in the community and non-cooperative in interpersonal relations with peers;

2. Perceived limited good: Peasants believed that all good things in life are available in limited quantities. Thus, one could improve one's position only at somebody else's expense;

3. Dependence and hostility toward government authority: Peasants had an ambivalent attitude toward government officials. On the one hand, they depended upon them for solving many of their problems. However, there was a general distrust of government leaders;

4. Familism: The family played an important role in the life of the peasant. Peasants were prepared to subordinate their personal goals to those of the family;

5. Lack of innovativeness: Peasants were reluctant to adopt modernizing innovations, had a negative attitude toward change, and their behavior was not fully oriented toward rational economic considerations;

6. Fatalism: Peasants believed that their well-being was controlled by a supernatural fate. This had a dysfunctional consequence on directed social change;

7. Limited aspirations: Peasants exhibited low aspirations for advancement. Also, they had low levels of achievement motivation and a tendency toward inconspicuous consumption;

8. Lack of deferred gratifications: Peasants lacked the ability to postpone satisfaction of immediate needs in anticipation of better future rewards;

9. Limited view of the world: First, they were not time conscious. Second, they were localites.[2] They were oriented within their communities and had no orientation to the world beyond their narrow group. Consequently, they had very limited geographic mobility;

10. Low empathy: Peasants exhibited mental inertness. They could not imagine themselves in new situations or places.

Other prominent scholars, Daniel Lerner, David McClelland, and Everett Hagen among others, carried the *individual blame* bias in their theoretical writings on modernization. This view of traditional individuals, unperturbed by and unresponsive to calls for modernization, was the stereotypical view of *traditional individuals* in the dominant paradigm.

[2] Individuals who were oriented within their communities and not the outside world.

SUMMARY

With the emergence of the Third World, theories and concepts which recapitulated the development of West European and North American nations were used to generate models of development for the developing nations. In the modernization theories, the definition of a modern nation resembled Western industrialized nations in terms of political and economic behavior and institutions, attitudes toward technology, etc.

The earlier approaches in the sociology of development emphasized the theories of social evolution. These theories applied Darwin's ideas to the process of modernization of human societies. The theories of social evolution influenced and gave rise to important concepts in the sociology of development: for example, the various bipolar theories of modernization. In these theories, the universal stages in the earlier theories of social evolution were reduced to ideal-typical extremes: *Gemeinschaft* vs. *Gesellschaft*, traditional vs. modern societies, etc. The Third World nations were usually described as traditional while the industrialized nations of the West signified the modern counterpart. The advanced Western nations had a wide range of systemic autonomy, i.e. their capacity to cope with a range of social, cultural, technological, and economic issues in the process of social change (Eisenstadt, 1976: 31). The Third World nations, on the other hand, lacking the higher differentiation of roles and institutions, the evolutionary universals, and other qualitative characteristics of industrial societies, were limited in their capacity to cope with problems or crises or even master their environment.

At the micro level, theories on individual psychological attributes stressed that attitudinal and value changes among individuals were prerequisites to the creation of a modern society. Scholars such as David McClelland, Daniel Lerner, and Alex Inkeles described certain value-normative complexes which were responsible for the modernization of individuals in the West and which the Third World was lacking. These scholars posited that modernization of the Third World was dependent on changing the character of individuals living there to resemble more closely the attitudinal and value characteristics of people in West Europe and North America.

Another area of interest in the modernization theories was the role of culture in development. Using Max Weber's thesis in *The Protestant Ethic and the Spirit of Capitalism*, sociologists sought to identify a set of cultural values in Asian religions that inhibited modernization. The recommendation of these studies was to continuously extend the modern (i.e. Western) component and displace all traditional (i.e. Asian) elements in developing nations.

Finally, the economic model that was presented in modernization theories was the *neo-classical* approach which had served as an important model for Western economies. The dominant paradigm was mainly concerned with economic growth as measured by the GNP rates and encouragement of all factors and institutions that accelerated and maintained high growth rates such as capital-intensive industrialization, high technology, private ownership of factors of production, free trade and the principle of *laissez-faire*.

Chapter 3

Communication Approach of the Dominant Paradigm

> *It is perfectly reasonable that the peasant who each season courts hunger and all its consequences would hold a somewhat different opinion of risk-taking than the investor who is gambling 'off the top'.*
> —**James C. Scott (1976: 15).**

The *dominant paradigm* outlined in Chapter 2 prescribed a unique model of development for the developing nations—a model that was tested in the Western nations and found to be highly successful. This model of development underlined the importance of economic growth through industrialization, capital-intensive and machine-intensive technology, a top-down structure of authority with economists in charge, and a certain attitude and mind-set among individuals.

Teleconferencing and Development

A reliable telecommunications infrastructure can facilitate economic growth and promote national development aims. Telephone services to rural and remote areas can stimulate economic development and bring the rural resident closer to the mainstream of national life. There is also a growing feeling that access to communications facilities should be viewed as a social service to be provided by governments as they provide schools, and not merely looked at in terms of the bottom line of a balance sheet.

As these realizations grow, an increasing number of developing nations are investing in satellite-based telecommunications systems. Within the last decade, Indonesia, India, Brazil, Mexico, China, and a coalition of twenty-two Arab nations have launched their own satellites. Through INTELSAT, twenty-seven other developing countries have established domestic satellite-based communications systems. What was once regarded as the wave of the future is now a present-day reality. How can developing countries benefit from this 'telecommunications revolution?'

In 1980 the US Agency for International Development initiated the AID Rural Satellite Program to explore the potential of telecommunications to address basic development problems. Building on simple, interactive, and inexpensive telephone-based technologies, the program developed teleconferencing systems in Indonesia, the West Indies, and Peru as a means of extending scarce expert resources and expanding educational opportunities to remote and rural areas.

Unlike radio and television, the telephone offers two-way communication. Interaction is central to coordination, information exchange, and instructional and training efforts. With the addition of special equipment, the telephone can be transformed into a teleconferencing network linking many groups of people at one time for multisite, multiparticipant meetings, conferences, and seminars. It facilitates dialogue, questions and answers, and immediate response. Teleconferencing can thus provide an effective means of training, institutional outreach, and administration.

Not unlike an ordinary telephone call, teleconferencing allows for spontaneity, immediacy, and a certain 'intimacy'. The end equipment—simple microphones and speakers—is easily operated by the participants themselves, and the presenter is not separated from his audience by the time between taping and broadcast. Participants must come to predetermined conference locations; active participation and interaction, teleconferencing's key assets, necessitate that the audience remain small.

Two-way, telephone-based communications networks besides providing access to expert resources, quality training, new technologies and methodologies, also provide a means of communication with policy-makers, a chance to ask questions and discuss problems, and an opportunity to participate in the decision-making process.

Source: Karen Tietjen, 'Forging a New Development Tool: Teleconferencing', *Development Communication Report*, No. 57. 2, 1987.

The role of the mass media in development activities was very clearly implied in the dominant paradigm of development. For example, Wilbur Schramm (1964) reiterated that the modernization of industry or agricultural sectors in developing nations required the mobilization of human resources. Education and the mass media, then, were vested with crucial responsibility in the process of mobilization of human resources. He noted:

the task of the mass media of information and the 'new media' of education is to speed and ease the long, slow social transformation required for economic development, and, in particular, to speed and smooth the task of mobilizing human resources behind the national effort (Schramm, 1964: 27).

Some scholars went further to state that the major problem in developing countries was not a shortage of natural resources but underdevelopment of human resources. Thus, education and the mass media had the enormous task of building the human capital. Also, mass media channels were expected to prepare individuals for change by 'establishing a climate for modernization' (Rogers, 1976c).

This chapter is devoted to studying the various communication approaches of the dominant paradigm. The three areas which have contributed greatly to an understanding of the social-scientific foundations of communication and mass communication in general, and their role in development theory and practice in particular, have been: (*i*) Communication Effects Approach, (*ii*) Diffusion of Innovations Approach, and (*iii*) Mass Media and Modernization Approach.

COMMUNICATION EFFECTS APPROACH

The First World War can be considered to be a watershed in mass communication theory and research. The Libertarian theory of public communication which believed that individuals were by nature rational, proved to be increasingly unworkable with the advent of the War. In the West, people were bombarded with War-inspired propaganda and leaders began to get concerned over its apparent power of mobilizing people to fight and also maintain their morale in adverse conditions. Harold Lasswell came up with an innovative conceptualization of mass media effects during this period. His model of communication effects, which was strongly influenced by Freudian theory, was in direct contradiction to Libertarian philosophy (Davis and Baran, 1981). His verbal model suggested the following question: WHO says WHAT in which CHANNEL to WHOM and with what EFFECT? (Lasswell, 1948):

Figure 3.1: Graphic Presentation of Lasswell's Formula

While the Libertarian school emphasized the latent rationality in men and women, Lasswell in his model interpreted Freudian theory to mean that human behavior is essentially irrational. Based on this conceptualization, he developed a paradigm which has been called the '*hypodermic needle*' model (Berlo, 1960) of mass communication effects. This theory is also known by several other names: *bullet theory* (Schramm, 1971); and *stimulus-response theory* (DeFleur et al., 1975).

Concept of Mass Society

There were several theoretical concepts behind the concept of the *stimulus response* theory of mass media effects. Lowery and DeFleur (1988) noted that a starting point for understanding the development of the earliest theoretical models used to study mass communication effects was to review the term *mass society*: a description of modern Western societies in the early 19th century. These authors contended that there was indeed a close tie between the concept of Western countries as *mass societies* and the earlier theories on mass communication effects.

From the mid-18th century, certain trends occurred that transformed Western societies from feudal, agricultural, and pre-industrial communities to military-industrial complexes. These trends, identified broadly as *industrialization, urbanization,* and *modernization,* transformed the social relationships, norms, values, material culture, etc. quite drastically. For example, the Industrial Revolution changed the workplace, work ethics, and relationships, led to a factory system, migration into urban areas, the introduction of large-scale bureaucracy and so on. Urbanization led to a profound change in the social order, new institutions, norms, values and beliefs, while modernization led to further stratification of people through adoption of innovations and greater consumption of material goods (Lowery and DeFleur, 1988).

Thus, through these trends traditional loyalties, norms, and values eroded. There was widespread *anomie* among the inhabitants of the big cities, greater differentiation, distrust, and stratification. The strong interpersonal bonds between people and loyalties that characterized the pre-industrial communities were replaced by an impersonal and tedious life in the newly industrialized societies where everything was a contract. Sociologists, historians, and other scholars termed the new communities as *mass society*. This was, 'an image of a modern society as consisting of an aggregate of relatively *atomized* individuals acting according to their personal interests and little constrained by social ties and constraints' (McQuail and Windahl, 1981: 42). In this kind of society, the new mass media were perceived to have immense power because their impact would not be constrained by other competing social and psychological influences on individuals. In other words, people in *mass society* were more susceptible to the powerful influences of the mass media.

Thus, the earliest theoretical models on media effects conceptualized the impact of the mass media as **direct, powerful,** and **uniform** on individuals. The apparent success of propaganda during World War I and the Spanish-American War at the turn of the present century (which historians point out was a consequence of exaggerated reports from the newspapers owned by Pulitzer and Hearst) simply reinforced the view of powerful media effects. The *bullet theory* and the *hypodermic needle* theory were colorful terms used to describe the concept of powerful mass media. In the bullet theory, the mass media were the guns and the messages the bullets which were shot at passive and defenseless audiences. Similarly, in the hypodermic needle theory, the medicine was the media content injected into the veins of the passive audiences who offered no resistance to it.

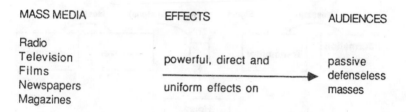

MASS MEDIA   EFFECTS   AUDIENCES

Radio
Television
Films
Newspapers
Magazines

powerful, direct and

uniform effects on

passive
defenseless
masses

Figure 3.2: Models Denoting Powerful Effects of Mass Media

The *stimulus-response* model also explained the same kind of effect. Every stimulus S (or message) was thought to produce a definite response R in the receiver O (McQuail and Windahl, 1981: 42).

With the addition of new media of mass communication, i.e. the film and the radio in the twenties, and the growth of advertising in the United States of America, the study of powerful and uniform effects gained additional momentum. During the period between the two World Wars, the mass media were viewed as powerful instruments which could be successfully used to manipulate people's opinions and attitudes, and thereby their behaviors, in a relatively short period of time. Katz (1963: 80) notes that, 'the model in the minds of the early researchers seems to have consisted of: (*i*) the all-powerful media, able to impress ideas on defenseless minds; and (*ii*) the atomized mass audience, connected to the mass media but not to each other'.

The predominance of interest in effects of media and effectiveness of channels led to other formulations. Communication became the object of scientific study. An influential model, the *telephone model*, was developed by Shannon and Weaver (1949). Diaz-Bordenave (1977) has noted that several concepts such as signal, code, message, channel, source, destination, encoding, and decoding were first described in the Shannon and Weaver model. While this model was developed in the area of information theory, it was used analogically by behavioral and communication scientists.

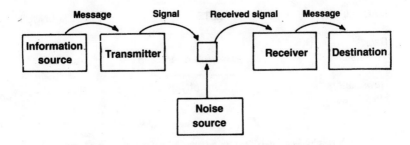

Figure 3.3: Shannon and Weaver's Model of Communication

SOURCE: Shannon and Weaver (1949:5). *The Mathematical Theory of Communication.* © University of Illinois Press. Copyright 1949 by the Board of Trustees of the University of Illinois Press. Reprinted by permission.

The other early models in communication developed by Schramm, Berlo, and others conceptualized communication as a linear and one-way process always flowing from the source of communication to a passive receiver.

The earlier models of Schramm and the SMCR model of Berlo conceptualized the communication flow as a simple, mechanistic process of message transmission (Diaz-Bordenave, 1977). In the post-World War II period, the SMCR model became popular with *communication for development* professionals.

All the models described in this section reinforced the *omnipotent source* and the *passive receiver* stereotype. McQuail and Windahl (1981: 43) explained this stereotype succinctly:

Active Source
Message/Signal
Passive Receiver

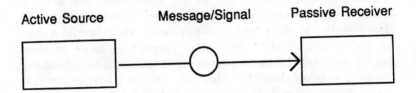

Figure 3.4 One-Way, Linear Model of Communication

> There is an assumption that contact from the media message will be related at some given level of probability to an effect. Thus, contact with the media tends to be equated with some degree of influence from the media, and those not reached are assumed to be unaffected.

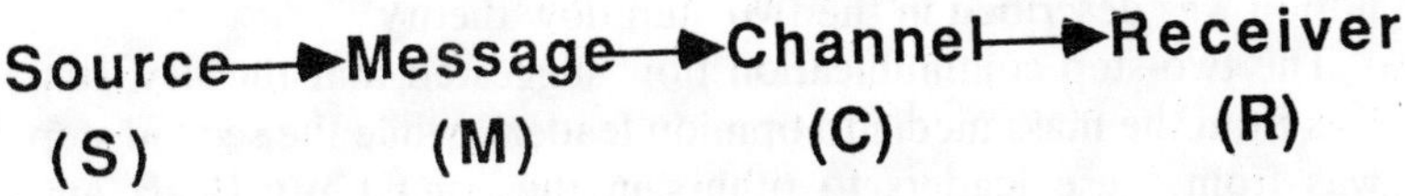

Source (S)
Message (M)
Channel (C)
Receiver (R)

Figure 3.5: Berlo's Formula for the Process of Communication

Theory of Minimal Effects of the Mass Media

The study of propaganda and the powerful effects of the mass media engaged some of the best minds in sociology, psychology, and political science. New areas of inquiry began to open up. Some of the newer questions asked were: What specific effects do the mass media have on individuals and the general community? What is the process by which these effects occur? (Severin and Tankard, 1979). Lazarsfeld, Berelson and Gaudet's work (1948) on political decision-making in the 1940 US presidential election campaigns is a major study which reconceptualized the process and effects of the mass media from one of dominant effects to one of a minimal impact. Also known as the *voter study*, this was an example of administrative research applied to critical questions.[1] The objective of this project was to measure the powerful nature of mass communication in society, people's exposure to mass media messages and the impact of the mass media in influencing people's political decisions. However, in this study, it was discovered that individuals were more influenced in their political decisions by members of their primary and peer groups than the combined mass media. The mass media seemed to have relatively little impact in influencing people's political decisions. Even exposure to the mass media was quite poor. Toward election day, the majority were somewhat exposed. But, on the whole, exposure was not high for the majority. The findings of this study, therefore, rejected the bullet theory of uniform and powerful effects of the mass media. However, there was one segment which was more exposed to the mass media than other individuals in the community. Researchers discovered that these influentials or opinion leaders then influenced others in the community. Thus, the effects of the mass media were seen as being indirect. This notion was described in the two-step flow theory.

The two-step communication flow suggested that the first step was from the mass media to opinion leaders, while the second step was from these leaders to others in the community (Katz and Lazarsfeld, 1955; Katz, 1957). The two-step flow theory was tested and confirmed in Decatur, Illinois in USA. Using the snowball sample, the researchers discovered that opinion leadership was not confined to the elite but was found at all levels of society (Katz and Lazarsfeld, 1955). The major finding of these voter studies was to suggest the weakness of the mass media in directly influencing personal decisions of individuals.

The work of some social scientists (Hovland et al., 1949, 1953; Klapper, 1960), further undermined the great power of the mass

---

[1] This important work lies in the areas of administrative and critical research. Administrative research dealt with structuring and operation of mass media industries to serve optimally the interest of the investors, media professionals, and the public. Critical research, on the other hand, examined broader questions involving human existence and the role of the mass media in a society. For more information, see Lazarsfeld (1941).

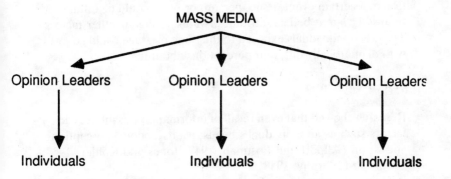

Figure 3.6: Two-Step Flow Model of Communication

media in bringing about direct and lasting effects on the audience. For example, Carl Hovland and colleagues did pioneering work in the area of communication and persuasion (Hovland et al., 1949). In his research on war propaganda films, Hovland was concerned with how and why individuals responded to persuasive messages. This research showed that the mass media were ineffective in improving attitudes of soldiers toward their allies and increasing motivation to fight. The findings showed that the social categories (for example, educational level) to which people belonged and individual differences were more predictive of certain effects than the mass media. People defended themselves against persuasive messages in three ways: *selective exposure, selective perception,* and *selective retention*:

Selective Exposure

Klapper (1960) suggested that people exposed themselves to messages selectively. There was a tendency for individuals to expose themselves relatively more to those items of communication that were consonant with their beliefs, ideas, values, etc.

Selective Perception

Regardless of exposure to communication, an individual's perception of a certain event, issue, person, or place could be influenced by his/her latent beliefs, attitudes, wants, needs or other factors. Thus, two individuals exposed to the same message could go away with diametrically different perceptions about it.

Selective Retention

Research showed that even recall of information was influenced by factors such as an individual's needs, wants, moods, perceptions, and so on (Allport and Postman, 1947; Jones and Kohler, 1958; Levine and Murphy, 1958).

Thus, what we learn from these selective processes is that the individual is not a defenseless target to persuasive communication. He/she is very active in receiving, processing, and interpreting information. The three selective processes outlined above could function as rings of defenses for the receiver with selective exposure constituting the outermost shield, followed by selective perception and selective retention (Severin and Tankard, 1979).

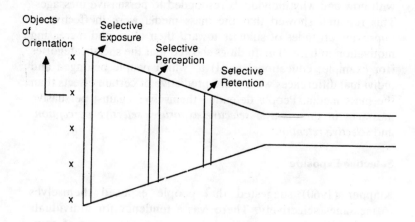

Figure 3.7: Rings of Defense of Receivers

In fact, Klapper (1960) suggested in his research that the mass media rather than being considered as causal agents of behavioral or attitudinal *change* in individuals, were more agents of *reinforcement*. The social categories to which people belonged, their individual characteristics, and social relationships had a far greater influence than the combined mass media (Lowery and DeFleur, 1988). All these research findings contradicted the earlier notion of the all-powerful mass media which could effectively convert anybody. On the other hand, people were not passive or defenseless against the onslaught of persuasive messages.

The theory of minimal mass media effects contributed positively to the refinement of both theoretical concepts and methodological tools in communication research.[2] The survey sampling designs of Lazarsfeld and colleagues at Columbia University, the experimental designs of Hovland and colleagues at Yale, the functionalistic and middle-range theories of Merton, Klapper, and others, have made significant contributions to our conceptualizations of communication effects. With greater refinement in theoretical concepts and methodological designs, the 'minimal effects' researchers were able to move away from the simplistic 'bullet theory' and 'hypodermic needle' concepts of mass media effects. They were able to discover and explain more adequately the role of interpersonal influences and other social-psychological variables of individuals.

While the research after World War II clearly showed the rather weak nature of the mass media in affecting important behavioral and attitudinal changes, this did not necessarily mean that they were discarded as agents of social change. For example, Davis and Baran (1981: 37) noted that even in the United States, Hovland's study (which indicated that the mass media were not very effective in changing people's attitudes and morale) was 'accepted for its *administrative* rather than *critical* research value. It was concerned with making communication more effective for immediate, short-term persuasion.' The findings of the minimal effects research aside, the mass media were increasingly used for persuasion and change. Particularly during the Cold War of the fifties, the mass

---

[2] For a detailed analysis and description of research pertaining to powerful and minimal effects of the mass media, see Lowery and DeFleur (1988).

media were used to play a useful role as propaganda tools for the United States in foreign countries. In the Third World countries, the orientations of communication as *transmission* of information and communication as *persuasion* were transferred to such diverse fields as agricultural extension, health education, and public relations (Diaz-Bordenave, 1977). The emphasis was on communication effects: creating awareness of new ideas and practices and generally bringing about attitudinal and behavioral changes in individuals.

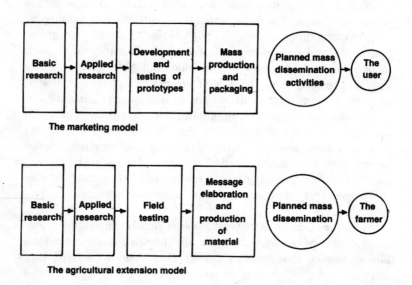

The marketing model

The agricultural extension model

Figure 3.8: Marketing and Agricultural Extension Models

SOURCE: Diaz-Bordenave (1977:13). Figures from *Communication and Rural Development.* © Unesco 1977. Reprinted with the permission of Unesco.

The marketing and agricultural extension models used in many Third World countries after World War II operationalized the effects orientation described earlier. The mass media of communication were widely perceived by administrators and policy-makers in Third World nations as important vehicles for bringing about speedy behavioral change among their peoples, particularly in favor of the modernizing objectives of the state. Diaz-Bordenave pointed out (1977 : 13–14):

> The pressures of economic development goals, the size and dispersion of target audiences in developing areas, the availability of modern communication technology, and an interest in selling expensive communication equipment all worked to make media an important element in rural development programs. Development personnel strived to use the latest gadgets in carrying out aggressive multimedia campaigns.

The preoccupation with effects suggests that the mechanistic stimulus-response model has not entirely vanished. It still constitutes an important theoretical model for a lot of the thinking about the nature and role of mass communication in society. It is almost as though the process of persuasion has become synonymous with the process of mass communication (McQuail and Windahl, 1981).

DIFFUSION OF INNOVATIONS RESEARCH

The diffusion of innovations theory has important theoretical links with communication effects research. As pointed out earlier, the emphasis was on communication effects: the ability of media messages and opinion leaders to create knowledge of new practices and ideas and persuade the target to adopt the exogenously introduced innovations.

History of Diffusion Studies

As recently as the turn of the present century, there was disagreement on the question of whether ideas were independently developed in different cultures, or whether an idea was invented in one culture and borrowed by or diffused into another. The dominant position initially was that of cultural evolutionists who put forth the hypothesis that there was natural, lawful, and individual development of each major culture (Frey, 1973). These ideas culminated in the 19th century into the *evolutionist school* of anthropology.

Around the year 1890, there was reaction in Europe and North America against the inconsistencies of the evolutionist theory (Heine-Geldern, 1968). Evidence indicated that in most cultures there was a predominance of borrowed or diffused elements over those that developed from within a particular culture (Linton, 1936; Kroeber, 1944; Herskovits, 1969). Three principal figures, Franz Boas in the United States, Gabriel Tarde in France, and Friedrich Ratzel in Germany, who were the proponents of the diffusionist theory, criticized the evolutionist school (Heine-Geldern, 1968).

Gabriel Tarde (1903), the French sociologist, was one of the first to propose the S-shaped curve of diffusion and also wrote about the important role of opinion leaders or change agents in the diffusion or 'imitation' process. However, it was the new awareness of the nature and role of mass communication effects (i.e. minimal effects of the mass media) in the forties that led to a renewed interest and need for theoretical and methodological reformulations in the field of communications. An important development was the reconciliation between mass communication and small group research. Katz (1963) noted that this effected a convergence of interest among mass communication researchers and rural sociologists who were studying the diffusion and acceptance of new farm practices. Mass communication researchers too gradually shifted their focus from a concern for interpersonal influence on individual decisions to a broader understanding of interpersonal networks of communication through which influence and innovations disseminated through society. A couple of the earliest studies in the United States that helped conceptualize the process of diffusion of innovations were the Ryan and Gross hybrid corn study in Iowa (1943) and the sociometric studies on physicians (Coleman et al., 1957).

The diffusion of innovations approach was rooted in the postulates and implicit assumptions of exogenous change theory. This approach, as Golding pointed out (1974: 43): -

suggests that static societies are brought to life by outside influences, technical aid, knowledge, resources and financial assistance and (in a slightly different form) by the diffusion of ideas.

The stranglehold of apathy, stoicism, fatalism, and simple idleness is held to have gripped the peasantry of the Third World until advanced countries produced both the tools and the know-how to coax them into action.

The notion of exogenously induced change permeated assumptions of fundamental concepts in diffusion research. The earliest definition of development was 'a type of social change in which new ideas are introduced into a social system in order to produce higher per capita incomes and levels of living through more modern production methods and improved social organization' (Rogers, 1969: 18). Modernization, or the 'development' of the individual, was seen as 'the process by which individuals change from a traditional way of life to a more complex, technologically advanced, and rapidly changing style of life' (Rogers, 1969: 48). The necessary route for this change from a traditional to a modern person was understood as the communication and acceptance of new ideas from sources external to the social system (Fjes, 1976).

Everett Rogers, whose work has been seminal in this area, identified the following main elements in any analysis of diffusion of an idea or innovation: (*i*) the *innovation* which is any idea considered as new by the recipient, and (*ii*) its *communication* through certain *channels*, (*iii*) among members of a *social system*, (*iv*) over *time* (Rogers with Shoemaker, 1971). Katz provided a similar definition of diffusion: 'the process of spread of a given new idea or practice, over time, via specifiable channels, through a social structure such as neighborhood, a factory, or a tribe' (Katz, 1963: 77).

The year 1960 may be considered a watershed in the export of diffusion studies from the West to the developing nations. This period saw a sharp increase in the number of diffusion studies in developing countries. Rogers noted that by the mid-seventies nearly half of all diffusion studies were being conducted in the Third World nations. The number of studies increased from a mere fifty-four in 1960 to over 800 by 1975 (Rogers, 1976a: 208). An apparent reason for this sharp rise may have been the technological determinism that reigned supreme during this period in the developing nations. Technology and the concomitant process of industrialization were thought to be the key to modernization. As Rogers aptly commented:

So, micro level investigations of the diffusion of technological innovations (e.g., in agriculture, health, family planning, etc.) among villagers were of direct relevance to development planners and other government officials in developing countries. These research results, and the general framework of diffusion, provided both a kind of theoretical approach and an evaluation procedure for development agencies (Rogers and Adhikarya, 1979: 70).

Model of Diffusion

Diffusion studies conceptualized, confirmed, and elaborated five stages in the adoption process of the individual decision-maker (Lionberger, 1960; Rogers, 1962; Frey, 1973). Adoption was defined as the process through which the individual arrived at the decision to adopt or reject the innovation from the time he/she first became aware of it. The five stages were: awareness, interest, evaluation, trial, and adoption.[3] At the awareness stage, the individual recipient was exposed to the innovation but lacked complete information on it. At the interest stage, the recipient sought more information on the innovation. Apparently, there was more interest regarding the innovation. At the evaluation stage, the individual mentally decided whether the innovation was compatible with present and future needs, and took the decision of trying it on a limited scale at the trial stage. At the adoption stage, the individual decided to continue full use of the innovation. The early diffusion studies also pointed out that at the awareness stage the mass media and cosmopolite information sources were reported as influential while at the evaluation and adoption stages, interpersonal and localite[4] sources of information seemed to be the dominant modes of influence (Rogers, 1962).

The starting point for the numerous studies of diffusion by rural sociologists was the collection of reports depicting the relative speed with which an innovation was adopted by members of a social system such as farmers living in small, well-defined communities (Frey, 1973). This data exhibited a consistent pattern across different communities for different kinds of innovations.

[3] In his later writings, Rogers introduced new terms to describe the stages in the innovation-decision process: knowledge, persuasion, decision, implementation, and confirmation (see Rogers 1983). However, the earlier terms described in the text have remained popular with extension professionals in developing countries.

[4] Localite communication channels are those from within the social system of the adopter (or rejector) such as close friends, neighbors, peers, and other significant members of the community. See Rogers (1962, 1983).

When the cumulative percentages of adoptions were graphically plotted against time, they formed the classic S-shaped curve. Thus the adoption rate of innovations had a rather slow start, then as the early adopters started to influence the rate, there was a fairly rapid rise slackening again at the top asymptotically forming the S-shape.

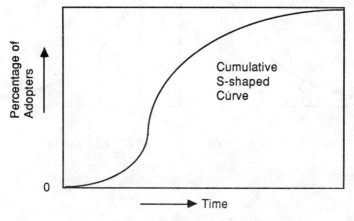

Figure 3.9: S-Shaped Curve of Diffusion

When the absolute number of adoptions were plotted for a distinct time period, a bell-shaped, approximately normal frequency curve was obtained as shown in Figure 3.10.

In this curve, the majority of adoptions was found to occur near the mean. The adopters were classified into five different categories on the basis of the two measures of the normal curve, the mean and the standard deviation. The categories were: innovators, early adopters, early majority, late majority, and laggards. The *innovators*, or the individuals who were the earliest in adopting innovations, constituted 2.5 per cent and lay at a distance of two units of standard deviation to the left of the mean. The next 13.5 percent of adopters lay between one and two standard deviations from the mean on the left and were called the *early adopters*. The *early majority* who comprised 34 percent of adopters lay between the mean and one standard deviation to the left. The next group of adopters were labeled *late majority* and they were located between the mean and one standard deviation to the right, while the last 16 percent of adopters were called *laggards* and placed at a distance of one standard deviation to the right of the mean (Rogers, 1969).

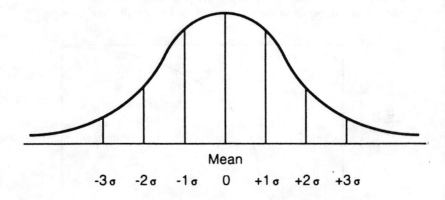

Figure 3.10: Standard Normal Diffusion Curve

The diffusion studies indicated a great difference among the adopter groups in terms of their personal characteristics, media behavior, and position in the social structure. The relatively early adopters were usually younger, they had a higher social status, they had a more favorable financial status, they engaged in more specialized operations, and were equipped with a superior mental ability than later adopters. In terms of communication behavior, earlier adopters used more impersonal and cosmopolite information sources and a greater number of other different sources of information. Also, the social relations of earlier adopters were more cosmopolite than for later categories, and the earlier adopters had more opinion leadership characteristics (Frey, 1973).

An important ingredient of the diffusion and adoption process was the innovation itself. The characteristics of an innovation, as perceived by the individuals in a social system, affected its rate of adoption. Five attributes were enumerated that would affect its rate of adoption: (*i*) relative advantage, or the degree to which an innovation was superior to the ideas it superseded; (*ii*) compatibility, or the degree to which an innovation was consistent with existing values and past experiences; (*iii*) complexity, or the degree to which an innovation was relatively difficult to understand and use; (*iv*) divisibility, or the degree to which an innovation could be tried on a limited basis; and (v) communicability, or the degree to which the results could be disseminated to others (Rogers, 1962).

Diffusion research pointed out interesting findings on the underlying power-influence structure in the peasant communities. Rogers discovered in a study of modern and traditional villages in Colombia that innovators were opinion leaders in the more modern villages, whereas in the traditional villages, where their distance from fellow villagers was great, they were accorded little opinion leadership (Rogers, 1969). Frey noted (1973: 396):

> In general, many diffusion studies suggest a picture of the underlying power-communication process that shows the innovator as an individual with comparatively strong communication links to more modern sectors outside his community. He may or may not have a conspicuously large opinion leadership domain himself, but in the more progressive community the innovators are either powerful themselves or at least linked to early adopters who are disproportionately influential in the community.

Diffusion of Innovations and Modernization

The diffusion of innovations research established the importance of communication in the modernization process at the local level. In the dominant paradigm, communication was visualized as the important link through which exogenous ideas entered the local communities. Diffusion of innovations then emphasized the nature and role of communication in facilitating further dissemination within the local communities:

> since invention within a closed system like a peasant village is a rare event, until there is communication of ideas from sources external to the village, little change can occur in peasant knowledge, attitudes, and behavior. Communication is, therefore, central to modernization in such circumstances (Rogers, 1969: 48).

Modernization was defined as the process by which 'individuals change from a traditional way of life to a more complex, technologically advanced, and rapidly changing style of life' (Rogers,

1969: 48). Thus, the diffusion of innovations paradigm by studying the communication of new ideas from external sources and their acceptance by peasants and others at the village level documented the impact of communication (interpersonal and mass media) on the change from a traditional to a modern way of life.

THE MASS MEDIA AND MODERNIZATION APPROACH

While rural sociologists were busy studying the modernizing role of communication in rural communities, political scientists, economists, and social psychologists in the fifties were laying out the functions of the mass media and measuring their influence in the modernization of developing countries. In the research and writing on modernization, communication was more than just an interplay between the source and receiver. It served as a social system fulfilling certain social functions (Hellman, 1980). Thus, the mass media came to serve as agents and indices of modernization in the Third World countries. Besides this macro-level analysis of the role of the mass media, researchers also focused on social-psychological characteristics of individuals which were considered necessary for a successful transition from a traditional to a modern society.

Daniel Lerner's *The Passing of the Traditional Society* (1958), illustrates the major ideas under the mass media and modernization approach. Modernization, according to Lerner, was essentially Westernization. However, since political leaders denounced the West for political reasons, the process of change suggested was called by a more neutral term: modernization. Lerner's model, in a nutshell, recapitulated the development of West Europe and North America from a feudal and traditional stage to modern, military-industrial societies. His social development model consisted of the following components: (*i*) a core of mobile individuals whose psychological orientation made it easier to accept rapid changes in their personal lives and the overall social system, (*ii*) an omnipotent mass media system that reinforced and accelerated societal and individual change by disseminating the new ideas and attitudes conducive to development, and (*iii*) the correlations between the important indices of urbanization, literacy, media exposure, and economic and political participation to establish a modern Western-type society.

According to Lerner, traditional society was non-participant. People were deployed by kinship into communities, isolated from one another and from the center, without an urban-rural division of labor. Thus, people developed few needs that required economic interdependence. Therefore, individuals' horizons were limited to their physical horizons and their decisions involved other known people in familiar situations. On the other hand, modern society was participant and functioned by consensus. Here, people went through formal schooling, read newspapers, were paid in cash for jobs they could legally change, used cash to consume goods in a free and open market, were free to vote in elections and express opinions on matters external to their personal lives. Lerner identified and explained a psychological pattern in individuals that was both required and reinforced by modern society: a mobile personality. This person was equipped with a high capacity for identification with new aspects of his/her environment and internalized the new demands made by the larger society. In other words, this person had a high degree of empathy. It was essentially the capacity to see oneself in the other's situation. Lerner stated that empathy fulfilled two important tasks. First, it enabled the person to operate efficiently in the modern society which was constantly changing. Second, it was an indispensable skill for individuals wanting to move out of their traditional settings which were characterized by a feudal system with regard to ownership of land, hierarchy based on kinship, a barter economy, etc. As Fjes (1976: 5–6) noted, 'empathy allows the individual to internalize the process of modernization by not only being able to cope with change, but expecting and demanding it... it is the psychic nexus of all the attitudes and behavior necessary in a modern society.'

The second element in Lerner's model was the mass media. They performed a special function: by exposing individuals to new people, ideas, attitudes, etc. they accelerated the process of modernization. Lerner posited that in the West, particularly in the United States, psychic mobility began with the expansion of physical travel. The expansion of physical or geographical mobility meant that more people commanded greater skill in imagining themselves as strange persons, living in strange situations and times than did people in any previous historical period. The development of the mass media accelerated this process even more. According to Lerner, the earlier increase of psychic experience through transportation was multiplied by the exposure to mediated experience through the mass media. Thus, the mass media were important agents of modernization. People in traditional societies could expand their empathy by exposure to the mass media which showed them new places, behavior, cultures, etc. In short, the mass media had the potential of blowing in the winds of modernization to isolated traditional communities and replacing the structure of life, values, and behavior there with ones seen in modern Western society.

In Lerner's model, the mass media were both an index and agent of modernization. The social change occurred in three phases. First and most crucial was urbanization. After about 10 percent urbanization was reached, the take-off occurred. In the second phase, literacy rates began to rise dramatically. With increasing rates of urbanization, literacy, and industrial development, in the third phase there was a great spurt in the growth of the modern mass media. Lerner said that the mass media systems flourished only in societies that were modern by other standards. Thus, the mass media functioned as important indices of modernization. In Lerner's model, there was a close reciprocal relationship between literacy and mass media exposure. The literate developed the media which in turn accelerated the spread of literacy. All these developments trigger a rise in political participation (such as voting) found in all advanced modern societies. While all these generalizations came out of the data collected in the Middle East, Lerner suggested that the historical sequence of these changes was natural as exemplified in the development of Western societies.

Like Lerner, Lakshmana Rao (1963) in his classic study suggested that communication was a prime mover in the development process. He selected two villages in India for his study: *Kothooru* or the village just about to modernize itself, and *Pathooru*, a village isolated and steeped in traditional customs and beliefs. Rao suggested that the laying of a new road to Kothooru from a nearby city started the process of modernization. Among other things, this road brought new people, ideas, and the mass media into the village while at the same time facilitating the villagers to visit the urban centers. All this new information opened up people's minds in Kothooru. They were not only ready for change but demanding and expecting it. The new ideas and innovations were first available to the elite and then trickled down to other sections in the village.

It was the quantity and quality of information that triggered change in Kothooru. The mass media brought in modern ideas and values from outside. Traditional ideas and modes of behavior as they existed in Pathooru were gradually dislodged. Education was given a great spur. Importantly, the new developments led to new jobs and higher productivity. As Schramm commented, 'More productivity leads to improved income, to widening consuming habits, to increased economic activity within the village (such as shops and restaurants), to new appetites for consumer goods, to a seeking after new opportunities, and so on in a chain of related development' (Schramm, 1964: 49).

While Lerner suggested the role of communication as the harbinger of new ideas from outside, Rao felt that new communication helped to smooth out the transition from a traditional to a modern community. If only attempts were made to open up a traditional society to modernizing influences, the new information available to the people at the top and its eventual and autonomous trickle down to others in the lower reaches of the hierarchy would increase empathy, open up new opportunities, and lead to a general breakdown of the traditional society.

Role of the Mass Media in Development: Optimism of the Fifties and the Sixties

The powerful role of the mass media in development was thus clearly implied in Lerner's and Rao's research and many other studies in the fifties and sixties. These studies complemented the postulates of the dominant paradigm of development. The mass media were the vehicles for transferring new ideas and models from the developed nations to the Third World and from urban areas to the rural countryside. Schramm echoed the dominant thinking during this historical period in his influential book, *Mass Media and National Development* (1964). He noted that in the Third World, '...villages are drowsing in their traditional patterns of life... the urge to develop economically and socially usually comes from seeing how the well-developed countries or the more fortunate people live' (Schramm, 1964: 41–42). The mass media thus functioned as a 'bridge to a wider world' (Schramm, 1964). Importantly, they were entrusted with the task of preparing individuals in developing nations for rapid social change by establishing a 'climate of modernization' (Rogers, 1976c). Lerner posited that the process of modernization began when something 'stimulates the peasant to want to be a freeholding farmer, the farmer's son to want to learn reading so he can work in the town, the farmer's wife to stop bearing children, the farmer's daughter to want to wear a dress and do her hair' (Lerner, 1963: 348). On a macro level, the modern mass media were very important for development. They were used in one-way and top-down communication by leaders to disseminate modern innovations to the public. Schramm recommended that 'the task of the mass media of information and the *new media* of education is to speed and ease the long, slow social transformation required for economic development, and, in particular, to speed and smooth the task of mobilizing human resources behind the national effort' (Schramm, 1964: 27).

Family Planning Messages via Music Videos

Who would have predicted that the most widely played song in Mexico in March 1986 would be a special record designed to encourage young teenagers to be sexually responsible?

The Population Communication Services project at The John Hopkins School of Hygiene and Public Health (JHU/PCS) put together two songs, *Cuando Estemos Juntos*, 'When We Are Together', by Juan Carlos Norona; and *Detente*, 'Wait', by Prisma on a 45 rpm record and music videos and targeted them at teenagers who compose about 30 percent of the total population of Latin America. The songs were sung by Tatiana, a young Mexican woman, and Johnny, a popular young singer from Puerto Rico.

Initial reception to the project was very encouraging. In Mexico, the most popular live television variety program—reaching nearly 150 million people every Sunday—requested to premiere the video. Monitoring by record companies and radio stations in Mexico indicated that the song was on top of the charts within a few weeks of its release.

This success story has some lessons for future development communication projects: choose the most appropriate medium

which has a big audience, enlist professionals experienced in
the chosen medium, and develop a high-quality product that
will attract commercial sponsors and thus help defray expenses
and insure income generation.
Source: Patrick Coleman, 'Music Carries a Message to Youths',
Development Communication Report, No. 53, Spring 1986.

The mass media were thought to have a powerful, uniform, and
direct influence on individuals. Thus, the bullet theory model of
mass media effects seemed to hold in the Third World countries in
the fifties and sixties, even though this model was discarded in
North America in the forties. The strength of the mass media lay
in their one-way, top-down and simultaneous and wide dissemination. And, since the elites in every nation were required to
modernize others in the population, the control of the prestigious
mass media by them served their economic and political interests.
Moreover, influential research at this time, such as Lerner's (1958)
Middle East study and Lakshmana Rao's Indian study (1963),
generated high expectations from the mass media. They were considered as *magic multipliers* of development benefits in Third
World nations. Administrators, researchers, and field workers
sincerely believed in the great power of the mass media as harbingers of modernizing influences. This period in development
history was characterized by a spirit of optimism. There were other
contributory factors:

Certainly, the media were expanding during the 1950s and
1960s. Literacy was becoming more widespread in most
developing nations, leading to greater print media exposure.
Transistor radios were penetrating every village. A predominantly one-way flow of communication from government development agencies to the people was implied by the
dominant paradigm. And, the mass media seemed ideally
suited to this role (Rogers, 1976b: 134).

This period was also characterized by a spate of research activity
to demonstrate the correlation between exposure to the mass
media and modernity. Surveys conducted by Frey (1966) in
Turkey, Rogers (1965, 1969) in Colombia, and Inkeles and Smith

(1974) in six developing nations, and Paul Neurath's field experiments in India (1962) on the effectiveness of radio forums, provided impressive evidence for the impact of the mass media on modernization. Rogers (1969) too in his survey of peasants in Colombia, India, Kenya, and Brazil was able to show the role of the mass media as an intervening variable between functional literacy and various measures of modernization such as empathy, agricultural innovativeness, political knowledge, and educational aspirations for children.

Therefore, the connection between the availability of mass media and national development was crucial. Both Lerner (1958) and Schramm (1964) showed a high correlation between the indices of modernity and availability of mass media: more developed the nation, higher was the availability of mass media outlets. The converse was also true. As Schramm notes, 'the less-developed countries have less-developed mass communication systems also, and less development in the services that support the growth of mass communication' (Schramm, 1964: 112). In an attempt to reduce the gap between nations labeled as mass media *haves and have-nots*, Unesco suggested a minimum standard for mass media availability in the Third World. This *Unesco minima* recommended that every nation should aim to provide for every 100 of its inhabitants ten copies of daily newspapers, five radio receivers, two television receivers, and two cinema seats (Schramm, 1964). Researchers had demonstrated a strong and statistically significant positive correlation between the development of the mass media and important indices in the economic, social, and political spheres. Thus, the establishment of the critical minimum of mass media outlets was strongly encouraged if the developing nations were to achieve overall national development.

Ecological Awareness through Television in India

A population of nearly 800 million takes a heavy toll on India's natural resources. But India is taking steps to protect her natural and cultural heritage while providing for the needs of her people by educating her citizens about the country's environmental problems and possible solutions—using video.

Many of India's schools (at least in urban areas) now have access to television and video players. So, in collaboration with the US Fish and Wildlife Service (FWS), the Indian government has begun to develop environmental television programs for the country's school systems. The Children's Environmental Education Television Project (CEETV), a collaborative effort of the Center for Environment Education (CEE) in Ahmedabad, India, and the State University of New York, College of Environmental Science and Forestry (ESF) in Syracuse, USA, combines advances in educational technology with up-to-date environmental information to promote knowledge and awareness about the environment among India's youth. CEETV will produce a series of educational videos focusing on various aspects of India's environment as part of larger environment education modules. The modules will also include teachers' guides, workbooks, and other classroom materials targeted to reach Indian school children 10–14 years old. The project is administered by CEE.

The project settled on a magazine format for the videos. Each program consists of individual segments tied together by a major theme. Programs can feature segments of real people in actual settings, puppets or animated sequences. The segments do not follow a rigid structure and are connected by storylines and major themes. Common opening and closing credits, theme music and characters used throughout the series provide additional continuity. Thus, the magazine format remains cohesive while allowing for creativity of individual program producers.

The first video produced and directed by Indian film maker Sai Paranjpye tells the story of Somu, a young village lad and his cow Drakhi. When drought strikes his village, Somu is forced to take the cow to a public cattle camp. During the journey, Somu learns about drought, its effects on the environment, and how he can help his village prepare for the next one.

A major goal of the project is to create a sense of individual capability and motivation among the students. Modules are designed to foster discussion and participation. Students are encouraged to believe that they can improve their environment and are provided with skills and knowledge to do so. Teachers are also encouraged to develop creative activities to complement programs.

Source: Kreg Ettenger, 'Television for the Environment in India', *Development Communication Report*, No. 65, 2, 1989, pp. 7–9.

Therefore, information was considered as the missing link in the development chain. The quality of information available and its wide dissemination was a key factor in the speed and smoothness of development (Schramm, 1964). Adequate mass media outlets and information would act as a spur to education, commerce, and a chain of other related development activities.

SUMMARY

This chapter was devoted to studying the various communication approaches of the dominant paradigm of development. The chapter covers the period spanning the forties until the sixties—the age of big media, powerful effects orientation, and top-down persuasion models. It examined the following three areas which have made rich contributions to our understanding of the role of communication in development theory and practice: (*i*) Communication effects approach; (*ii*) Diffusion of innovations approach; and (*iii*) Mass media and modernization approach.

Communication Effects Approach: The earliest models of mass media effects conceptualized the impact of the mass media as direct, powerful, and uniform on individuals living in modern, industrial societies termed as *mass societies* by sociologists. The *bullet* and *hypodermic needle* theories were colorful terms used to describe the concept of powerful mass media effects. The early models developed by Lasswell, Shannon and Weaver, Berlo, Schramm, etc. conceptualized communication as a linear and one-way process flowing from a powerful source to a passive receiver. However, there was a shift in opinion among scholars after World War II. New research showed the rather weak nature of the mass media in affecting important behavioral and attitudinal changes among receivers. Communication scholars suggested that the mass media rather than being sole agents of attitudinal and behavioral change were more agents of reinforcement.

The shift in emphasis regarding the role of the mass media from one of dominant and powerful influence to that of minimal effects did not make any significant difference to formulations advocating the use of the mass media for development in Third World countries.

Here, the orientations of communication as *transmission* of information and communication as *persuasion* were transferred to fields such as agricultural extension, health, education, and public relations. The mass media were perceived by administrators and policy-makers in the Third World as important means of bringing about quick behavioral change among their people, particularly in favor of the *modernizing* objectives of the state. The powerful effects idea still constitutes an important theoretical model for a lot of the premises regarding the nature and role of the mass media in developing nations.

Diffusion of Innovations theory has important theoretical links with effects research. The emphasis is again on communication effects, i.e. the ability of media messages and opinion leaders to create knowledge of new practices and ideas among the target audience and to persuade them to adopt the exogenously conceived and introduced innovations. It was firmly believed that the necessary route to the *development* of an individual from a traditional to a modern person was the acceptance of new ideas from sources external to the social system.

Everett Rogers, whose work has been seminal in this area, identified the following elements in the diffusion of an idea or an innovation: the *innovation* which is any idea considered as new by the recipient, and its *communication* through certain *channels* among members of a *social system* over *time*. Adoption was defined as the process through which the individual arrived at the decision to adopt or reject an innovation from the time of first awareness. The five stages were: awareness, interest, evaluation, trial, and adoption. The diffusion studies indicated differences among adopter groups in terms of their personal characteristics, media behavior, and position in society. The early adopters were usually younger, had higher social and financial status, and were equipped with superior mental ability than later adopters.

The diffusion of innovations research established the importance of communication in the modernization process at the local level. In the dominant paradigm communication was visualized as the important link through which exogenous ideas entered the local communities. Diffusion of innovations then emphasized the nature and role of communication in facilitating further dissemination within the local communities.

In the *Mass media and modernization approach* the mass media served as agents and indices of modernization in the developing nations. At the micro level, research in this tradition focused on social-psychological characteristics of individuals which were considered necessary for a successful transition from a traditional to a modern society.

Daniel Lerner's *The Passing of the Traditional Society* illustrates the major ideas under the mass media and modernization approach. He posited that people in traditional societies could expand their empathy by exposure to the mass media which showed them new places, behavior, cultures, etc. In short, the mass media had the potential of blowing the winds of modernization into isolated traditional communities and replacing the structure of life, values, and behavior there with ones seen in modern Western society.

In this approach, the mass media were considered as the ideal vehicles for transferring new ideas and models from the developed nations to the Third World and from urban areas to the rural countryside. The mass media were entrusted with the task of preparing individuals in developing nations for rapid social change by establishing a *climate of modernization*. They were thought to have powerful, uniform, and direct effects on individuals in the Third World even though this premise was discarded in North America in the forties.

Research in this tradition generated high expectations from the mass media. They were considered as *magic multipliers* of development benefits in Third World nations. Administrators, researchers and field workers sincerely believed in the great power of the mass media as harbingers of modernizing influences. Also, the connection between the availability of mass media and national development was considered crucial. Both Lerner and Schramm showed a high correlation between the indices of modernity and availability of mass media: more developed the nation, higher was the availability of mass media outlets. The converse was also true.

Information, therefore, was considered to be the missing link in the development chain. The quality of information available and its wide dissemination was a key factor in the speed and smoothness of development (Schramm, 1964). Adequate mass media outlets and information would act as a spur to education, commerce, and chain of other related development activities.

Overview

The early seventies may be considered a watershed in the literature on communication for development. Scholars, researchers, and administrators became increasingly restive with the notion of *development* and its progress in the preceding two decades. Ironically, the plight of the very poor in the developing nations had not improved significantly since the sixties. In fact, the situation seemed to have deteriorated (Illich, 1969; Seers, 1977a; Weaver and Jameson 1978; Wang and Dissanayake, 1984a; Smythe, 1985). The process of development had *developed* a minority of nations in the world, and a small number of individuals and groups in the remaining nations. However, it had *underdeveloped* a majority of individuals and groups, especially in the Third World nations. Poverty, unemployment, and income inequality seemed to be on the rise in the Third World.

The initial critique of the dominant paradigm came from development scholars in Latin America—Frank, Diaz-Bordenave, Cardoso, Beltran, among others. While their special focus was on Latin America, it would be possible to generalize their findings to Asia and Africa as well. They showed how in the preceding decades economic policies, international aid, trade, etc. focused on the exploitation of the periphery (i.e. Third World nations) by the center (i.e. industrial countries); they emphasized structural imbalance between the periphery and the center which was responsible for the *development of underdevelopment* of the Third World (Frank, 1969). These scholars of the Dependency School explained to the academic community how and why the *trickle down* of economic and social benefits of development was not being felt in the periphery.

On another front, scholars such as Milton Singer and M.N. Srinivas were attacking the fairly well-established views of Max Weber and other like-minded sociologists regarding the debilitating role of Eastern cultures in development. They were able to show that the dominant view regarding Eastern religions was anti-historical, oversimplified, and highly exaggerated.

The decade of the seventies, therefore, was a period of ferment in the field of development in general, and development communication in particular. There were more scholars interested in the field of development communication and they were more likely to be from Asia, Africa, and Latin America (Rogers, 1987). When these scholars also became important contributors to this field, the stereotypes and cultural assumptions of the preceding two decades that guided thinking and research in this field, were shattered.

Chapter 4

Denigration of the Dominant Paradigm: Critical Analysis of Early Approaches to Third World Development

> *The conviction, or assumption, that the term 'modern' designates something desirable, stands or falls, I submit with the belief that progress in human affairs can be relied upon as inevitable*—**Wilfred Smith (1965: 2).**

The old paradigm of development started to break down in the late sixties and early seventies. The development of Third World nations simply did not fit the assumptions implicit in the paradigm. At the very least, the paradigm worked better as a description of what had happened in West Europe and North America than as a predictor of change in developing countries (Eisenstadt, 1976). The criticisms of the sociology of development models were directed at several fronts.

SOCIOLOGY OF DEVELOPMENT MODELS REVISITED

Abstractness

The propositions based on the theories of social evolution were excessively abstract. While they served as a comprehensive tool for an understanding of social change in general, they had limited utility when applied to concrete problems of development in Third World countries (Portes, 1976).

To make the diagnosis, for example, that social transformations occur in the passage from underdevelopment (backwardness, undifferentiation, ruralism, etc.) toward modernization (industrialization, social complexity, urbanization, etc.) is to beg the entire question. Such descriptions are not the end point of scientific inquiry into the problem but the beginning. The question is why such transformations occur in some societies and not others, why they take place at different rates and in different forms, under which conditions such processes are paralyzed or even reversed, and under which they successfully overcome structural obstacles (Portes, 1976: 64).

The bipolar theories presented ideal-typical extremes of the process of change without providing insight into the determinants and constraints of developmental processes (Portes, 1976). Other theorists pointed out that actual developmental changes that took place in developing countries went against the empirical relationships proposed in the old paradigm (Eisenstadt, 1976: 36):

> Several countries in Central and Eastern Europe, Latin America, and Asia seemed to have reached at certain levels a negative correlation between such socio-demographic indices as literacy, spread of mass media, formal education, or urbanization on the one hand and the institutional ability to sustain growth or to develop libertarian or 'rational' institutions on the other.

In other situations, the empirical facts were different from the relationships proposed in the paradigm, yet they led to the same conclusions. For example, India had very low urbanization and relatively little industrialization but still it was able to evolve a stable, viable, modern political system (Eisenstadt, 1976).

Ahistorical

The Rostowian thesis on economic growth was also found wanting. Some writers pointed out that Rostow had taken the prerequisites of economic growth from the historical experience of Western democracies as they had happened in the past and applied them as preconditions for growth in non-Western nations in the future. Also, the model distorted history:

Rostow has compressed epochs of economic struggle in the history of nations into a neatly drawn five-stage model of transition that does not extend more than two centuries at the most.... Rostow's historical evidence is based on the limited experience of a few countries that constituted a highly homogenous sample (excluding Japan) (Abraham, 1980: 47).

Other criticisms of the Rostow model were directed at its unilinear evolutionary nature. He had proposed that every society would pass through the first four stages of his model in order to reach the golden age of mass consumption. However, the history-specific setting of the newly-independent developing countries from colonial rule made it extremely difficult, if not impossible, for them to recreate the developmental path of the Western nations. As Abraham notes (1980: 47):

it is, however, highly unlikely that the developing societies of today with their history of colonial exploitation, current population explosion and a wide variety of geographical and cultural differences will be able to go through the process of growth which developed countries treaded.

Incorrect Indicators

In the old paradigm, wrong dimensions were identified as indicative of development (Portes, 1976). For example, Parsons (1964b) identified several 'evolutionary universals' such as money, markets, and bureaucracy as strategic for development. However, for a majority of Third World countries, these 'evolutionary universals' were nothing new:

Minimal familiarity with Third World nations would indicate that, by these standards, most of them are already 'developed.' Such features as money and markets, extensive bureaucratic regulation, and formal legal systems have been long known and present in underdeveloped countries. It is perhaps for this reason that when the abstract discussion of 'universals' reaches for concrete examples, it selects primitive tribal societies as poles of contrast to modern Western nations. Such comparisons are, of course, entirely irrelevant to the problem of national development. Third World nations, regardless of stereotypes dear to theorists, are not in the tribal stage (Portes, 1976: 67).

Another evolutionary universal suggested by Parsons was the democratic form of government. However, many countries in Africa and Latin America that followed the path of West European nations and set up a democratic form of government achieved mixed results. 'Democratic politics in these societies did not greatly increase the adaptive capacity of their social systems' (Portes, 1976: 68). Instead, they perpetuated and even legitimized the inequality that existed due to internal contradictions and external subjugation of their economies into a dependent status (Zeitlin, 1968).

Development of Underdevelopment

Serious criticisms were leveled against the old paradigmatic models by several neo-Marxist theorists such as Andre Gunder Frank, Denis Goulet, Dos Santos, Paul Baran, and Samir Amin. Underdevelopment, according to these writers, was not a process distinctly different from development. In fact, they constituted two facets of the same process. The 'development of under-development' in Third World nations was and is related to the economic development of West Europe and North America (Frank, 1969). Frank (1969: 9) argued that:

underdevelopment is not due to the survival of archaic insti-tutions and the existence of capital shortage in regions that have remained isolated from the stream of world history. On the contrary, underdevelopment was and still is generated by the very same historical process which also generated econ-omic development: the development of capitalism itself.

Marxist writers maintained that the underdevelopment of Third World nations could be regarded as the consequence of the deve-lopment of Europe and North America which satellized the former and exploited them in order to help their own economic growth.

In the old paradigm, Third World societies were conceived as autonomous with respect to changes which were thought to be due to internal forces. Portes (1976: 67) points out that:

it fails completely, however, to provide a framework for understanding the insertion of individual countries in an evolving international system. Distinctions between core and peripheral economic regions are foreign to the theory. Nor does it grasp the possibility that 'autonomous competitors' in the developmental race may be integral parts of transnational units in which weaker states are kept in place by a context of overwhelming political and economic forces.

Ancient World Civilizations: Mesopotamian Civilization

The Mesopotamian Civilization is one of the oldest recorded civilizations. *Mesopotamia*, which means *the land between two rivers*, was irrigated by the Tigris and Euphrates rivers in modern-day Iraq. By 3000 BC, this civilization had reached a high level of achievement. The cities of Erech, Eridu, Lagash, and Ur which were developed as centers for control of irrigation, became important centers of commerce and industry. Ur, a city-state, was divided into three areas: sacred area, walled city on the mound, and the outer town. The temple of god called *ziggurat* was built of bricks in the sacred area and was more than 20 meters tall and in three storeys. The sacred area also served as an administrative center with storehouses and offices. The walled city and outer town were residential areas. The houses were built along a uniform pattern and had a central courtyard with rooms around it (*Social Studies*, 1969).

The king was regarded as god's representative. The priests, king's officers, and scribes constituted the upper class. The middle class was comprised of merchants, landowners, craftsmen, and shopkeepers. The slaves, mostly prisoners of war, were at the bottom of the social scale. As life became complicated laws had to be made to regulate people's activities. Hammurabi, the greatest ruler of Babylonia, gave his people a system of laws which covered every aspect of life. The Mesopotamians believed in a number of gods though each city had one special god. Rent from the land was collected and all government regulations were carried on in his name.

Agriculture was the main occupation of the people. Before metals were used, the sickles were made of baked clay which were hardened so that they did not break easily. To ensure permanent supply of water, the people diverted flood waters through canals to big reservoirs. They used cattle to draw the plough.

A great many metal objects such as exquisitely designed jewelry, harps, and helmets have been discovered in the royal cemetery at Ur. This shows that by 2500 BC the metal workers had developed high technical skills in their craft. Also, there is some evidence of a guild system among the metal workers. The potter's wheel was perhaps first used in Mesopotamia and they were probably also the first to make glassware. For transportation on land, Mesopotamians had wheeled carts while rafts were used to carry goods on water (*Social Studies*, 1969).

The Sumerians were the first people to evolve a system of writing. The *cuneiform* script that they developed was written with a stylus on smooth clay tablets which were then baked. Each tablet was like a page of a book. Some of the tablets discovered include business documents such as deeds of sale and contracts.

The people in Mesopotamia counted by sixties. While their sexagesimal system of counting is no longer in use, we still use it a basis of division of time into minutes and seconds and of circles into 360 degrees. In geometry, they had discovered the Pythagoras theorem. This proved to be a great help in building and computing distances. In astronomy, the Mesopotamians divided the whole day into twenty-four hours, a system followed today. They divided the sky into twelve parts and assigned each a name. This has come down to us as the twelve signs of the zodiac. The Mesopotamian calendar was lunar-based and thus was prone to some error. The lunar year is about eleven days shorter than the solar year. In spite of this error the Mesopotamian calendar was a great achievement for its time) (Social Studies, 1969).

The old paradigm denied history to developing nations. The assumption was that during an earlier period, the Third World nations resembled earlier stages of the history of West European nations. Marxist scholars contend that this was not true. Underdevelopment in the Third World does not signify an earlier stage of European development history but instead 'is in large part the historical product of the past and continuing economic and other relations between the satellite underdeveloped and the now developed metropolitian countries' (Frank, 1969: 4).

Frank posited several hypotheses in the theory of imperalism which he then supported using empirical and historical observations (1969: 9–13):

1. In contrast to the development of the world metropolis which is no one's satellite, the development of the national and other subordinate metropolises is limited by their satellite status.
2. The satellites experience their greatest economic development and especially their most classically capitalist industrial development if and when their ties to their metropolis are weakest, and
3. The regions which are the most underdeveloped and feudal-seeming today are the ones which had the closest ties to the metropolis in the past.

When Third World nations are viewed as part of a larger world system, the evolutionary universals too could be indicative of exploitation leading to underdevelopment rather than as adaptive mechanisms leading to greater development. As Portes (1976: 67) points out:

Since colonial times, extensive legal and bureaucratic regulation of dependent territories has been employed by metropolitan centers as a means of ensuring their hegemony. The historical dialectics by which 'modern' structural features serve to perpetuate weak and stagnant societies are not understood by proponents of the evolutionary perspective.

Ancient World Civilizations: Egyptian Civilization

Historians divide the history of Egypt into three periods: the Old Kingdom, the Middle Kingdom, and the New Kingdom. The Old Kingdom is also called the Age of the Pyramids. The civilization of Egypt with its advances in art, religion, and sciences was developed during this period (3000–2000 BC) and during the Middle Kingdom (2000–1750 BC). But in the 18th century BC, Egypt was overrun by invaders called the Hyksos, who came from the east.

The Egyptian king was called the pharaoh. He had absolute power. The land belonged to him; his word was law. He was also looked upon as a god and his statues were put up in temples. Next to the pharaoh came priests, officials, artists, and craftsmen. Below them were the farmers who lived beyond the cities, and then came the slaves, who were really prisoners of war and owned by the king (*Social Studies*, 1969).

Agriculture was the most important occupation of the people. The rivers fertilized the land every year, and the people worked together to build canals to make it possible to grow crops all year round. They appear to have used oxen to draw the plough as early as 3000 BC and sickles with flint flakes mounted on stout sticks. The chief crops were wheat, barley, and millet. They also grew dates, figs, apples, peaches, and mulberries.

The Egyptians started using metals on a large scale gradually. Perhaps, this skill came to them from the Hyksos. During the period of the Middle Kingdom, the potter's wheel came into use. The Egyptians made beautiful stone vases which they exported. Like the Mesopotamians, they also developed the art of making glass and produced glassware of graceful shapes. Their carpenters made beautiful furniture, inlaid with ivory and precious stones, which was well preserved in the royal tombs (*Social Studies*, 1969).

The pyramids were the most remarkable Egyptian buildings in the early period. Still in existence as achievements of those years are thirty large pyramids and a number of small ones. Most imposing of all is the Great Pyramid of Gizeh near Cairo. It was built by Pharaoh Cheops (Khufu) of the Old Kingdom in about 2650 BC. It is said that 100,000 men worked for twenty years to complete this structure which is made of huge blocks of stone. These blocks were cut into shape and rolled up a slope and fitted together skillfully and carefully. This required an amazing degree of engineering skill. The pyramids undoubtedly deserve their place among the seven wonders of the ancient world (*Social Studies*, 1969).

A second peculiar specimen of Egyptian architecture is the sphinx. The sphinx is a mythological animal with the body of a lion and the head of a man. Each sphinx was carved out of a single solid stone. Egyptian temples are also remarkable. The temple at Karnak, lavishly adorned with statues and sculptures, has a hall of 130 impressive columns and an avenue of sphinxes leading from the temple to the river. Another famous temple is the great temple of Abu Simbel, cut out of sandstone cliffs.

The Egyptian script is known as hieroglyphic, which means sacred writing'. It consisted of twenty-four signs, each of which stood for a single consonant. Vowels were not written. Later, the Egyptians started using symbols for ideas and the total number of signs rose to about 500. The writers, who were an important section of society, wrote with reed pens on the leaves of a plant called papyrus from which we get the word paper (*Social Studies*, 1969).

The Egyptians made significant advance in many fields of knowledge. They developed a decimal system of numeration. Numbers from one to nine were represented by one sign repeated to give a desired number. They could calculate the area of a triangle or a rectangle. The measurement of land, the amazing achievements in the art of building, and the calendar are evidence of their mathematical skills. The crowning achievement of the Egyptians was the solar calendar. Egyptians concluded that the year had 365 days. The year was then divided into twelve months, each of thirty days. The extra five days were set apart for the celebration of religious festivals.

The Egyptians' practice of preserving the bodies of their dead by embalming was a stimulus to science. It added to the knowledge of the structure of the human body, and to skill in surgery (*Social Studies*, 1969).

The sociology of development models invoked a very limited time perspective of twenty-five to 100 years at most. If the time frame for an analysis of Third World development were to go back in history, it would be seen that countries such as India, China, Egypt and Peru, were centers of sophisticated civilizations. Paul Harrison (1979:33) puts it across very succinctly:

All three continents of what is now the Third World were home of sophisticated civilizations. Many of their cities were centers of fabulous wealth far in advance of anything their first European visitors knew back home. Mathematics, astronomy, medicine were all highly developed among the Arabs, the Indians, and the Chinese. It is wrong to call these civilizations backward. In an intellectual, moral and spiritual sense, several of them were far in advance of Europe. Europe was able to bring them all to their knees for one reason only: because she was more developed in purely material respects. She had achieved breakthroughs in the technology of war and of sea travel which were the basis of her military conquests. And she had developed industrial capitalism, along with its peculiar contempt for and exploitation of human beings and of nature.

The critical stimulus to investment which spurred economic growth in West Europe was provided, to a great extent, by the surplus appropriated from the slave-plantation colonies (Williams, 1964). It was the unlimited overseas market captured by British commerce through empire and superior naval power that fueled the Industrial Revolution in England (Hobsbawm, 1968). Also, *laissez-faire* was not in vogue at the time England was striving to be an industrial power. For instance, in the year 1700, British textile manufacturers had to be protected from the imports of textiles from India, at the time one of the biggest exporters of textiles. 'Deindustrialization of India thus flowed from British industrialization' (Brookfield, 1975: 4).

Ancient World Civilizations: Indus Valley Civilization

The Indus Valley Civilization seems to have flourished about 2500 BC and extended over a larger area than any of the other contemporary civilizations. This has led some historians to think that it was created by a people who had come from outside and who already had some experience in an urban culture (*Social Studies*, 1969).

The cities of Harappa and Mohenjodaro were well planned and thickly populated. Their roads were straight and wide and cut each other at right angles. The main road in Mohenjodaro was about 10 meters wide and 800 meters long. The houses were situated along the roads and made of burnt bricks; some had more than one storey. Every house was furnished with a well and a bathroom. The drainage system found in Mohenjo-daro was magnificent, and the house drains emptied all waste water into the street drains.

In Mohenjodaro was found a great tank, now called the Great Bath. A flight of steps led to the water and all round the tank were small rooms. In Harappa has been found what is now known as the Citadel. It stood on raised ground and contained structures that seem to have been public buildings. Almost all the cities had huge granaries, perhaps to store grain from the countryside.

Most of the people, however, were farmers who lived beyond the walls of the cities. They grew wheat, barley, and peas, and perhaps rice in some places. Cotton was also culti-vated and probably cotton fabric was common. Some scholars suppose that the Indus people exported cotton cloth to Mes-opotamia. Fish seems to have been part of their diet. Domesti-cated animals included humped and humpless cattle, goats and buffaloes, and possibly elephants (*Social Studies*, 1969).

Harappa pottery was all wheel-made, a sign of an advanced culture. Plain pottery was produced for common use and some of the finest specimens have been discovered. These reveal the high artistic achievements of the Harappa potters. The variety of shapes and sizes is amazing. Large jars with narrow necks, drinking cups with handles, and black on red decoration are the most distinguishing features of Harappan pottery. The designs are intricate.

A large variety of clay toys have been dug up in the various sites of the Indus civilization. Countless carts with wheels and animals yoked to them, models of birds with long stick-like legs, figures with movable arms, clay bulls with nodding heads have been discovered—these reveal that the children of Harappa knew the joy of playthings (*Social Studies*, 1969).

The people used metals for their implements and utensils. They also used earthen pots of various shapes and sizes that they turned out on the potter's wheel. The bronze figure of a dancing girl found at Mohenjodaro is a wonderful example of their workmanship. Archaeologists have discovered thousands of seals decorated with beautiful impressions of animals such as the bull, rhinoceros, tiger, and elephant.

Beads similar to those in Mohenjodaro, a golden monkey on a pin, and seals have been uncovered in Mesopotamia. In one city, a large number of seals of the Harappa type have been found. These findings point to direct trade between the Indus Valley and Mesopotamia. To avoid the difficulties of overland routes, trade was carried on by sea, Telmun or modern Bahrein being the great center of exchange between the Indus Valley and Mesopotamia. We infer that the Harappa traders took pottery, grains, cotton goods, spices, stone beads, pearls and eye-paint and brought back metal wares (*Social Studies,* 1969).

A large number of seals depict the humped bull which may have been considered sacred. The impression of a god-like being on a seal is now believed to be an early form of the Hindu God Shiva. Small figures of men have been found, as well as figures of a goddess. Scholars thus believe that both kings and the mother goddess were worshipped. The Great Bath in Mohenjodaro might have been a place of religious bathing.

The seals unearthed are the most distinctive products of the Harappa culture. Some of them are square tablets of clay, with boss on one side and engraving on the other. After they were cut, they were glazed over. Animals such as the bull, rhinoceros, tiger, elephant, and crocodile have been engraved very vividly and beautifully. Some of the seals have inscriptions, but the script has not yet been deciphered. The extraordinary skill in moulding the animal figures with such minute details is very impressive (*Social Studies,* 1969).

By 1500 BC, the Indus civilization came to an end. How, or why, is not known. The destruction seems to have come rather suddenly and perhaps it was caused by a flood. Many historians and archaeologists, however, think that the invading Aryans destroyed it (*Social Studies.* 1969).

The underdevelopment of countries in Asia, Africa, and Latin America, therefore, was not by choice. Due to their colonized status they were forced to be either deindustrialized or kept in a state of underdevelopment—providing raw materials for the factories in Europe and being captive markets for their finished goods. For example, on the eve of colonialism (circa 1500), China, India, the Middle East, and Europe were at the same level of development—they were all agricultural communities and well-versed in the technology of that time: plough culture. However, by the year 1945, much of Asia, Africa, and the Middle East was still predominantly agricultural using the same primitive technology of circa 1500, whereas European nations such as England, France, and The Netherlands, were military-industrial giants. 'It is possible that industrial civilization might have emerged spontaneously in China or India. But it is futile to speculate; Europe evolved first as an industrial force, and that fact alone changed the entire situation, crippling what industry existed in Asia and giving Europe an advantage that would last at least two hundred years' (Harrison, 1979: 38).

Ancient World Civilizations: Chinese Civilization

The earliest Chinese civilization of which archaeologists tell us is the Shang civilization. The Shang rulers are believed to have been in power from 1765 to 1122 BC. According to archaeological evidence, by the 14th century BC the Shang people had developed a high level of culture, comparable with centers of the other river valley civilizations. They seem to have been skilled in the use of metals and to have known the art of writing. They must have been good craftsmen as well, for their graves have yielded objects of exquisite quality (Social Studies, 1969).

One of the primary duties of the Shang king was to protect his people from invasions and to preserve the benefits of urban life and prosperity. Below the king in Chinese society came a number of noblemen. Apparently the king distributed lands among the nobles, who in return helped him in wars and conquests. Some scholars regard this arrangement as a kind of feudal system. The next social class of importance was perhaps merchants and craftsmen. The bulk of the population was composed of farmers, and at the lowest end stood the slaves, who were, as in other cultures of the time, prisoners of war. The Shang kings spent considerable time in wars and conquests. The soldiers wore bronze helmets and perhaps a metal body armor. Bronze daggers, axes, bows, and metal-tipped arrows have been discovered. The army fought mainly from horse-drawn chariots.

As in the other three river valley cultures, the prosperity of the Shang people depended on agriculture. Millet was the main cereal cultivated. Wheat was introduced later. The Shang people also came to cultivate rice on a large scale. The Chinese worked out an elaborate system of irrigation which reduced the distress caused by floods. Thus, a surplus of foodgrains was available, and this helped the progress of their civilization.By the time of the Shang rule, the Chinese had domesticated cattle, sheep, fowl, pigs, and dogs. The war chariots, as has been said, were drawn by horses. Perhaps elephants were also used in war (*Social Studies*, 1969).

The Chinese wore linen clothing. There is evidence that the Shang people also used silk. Breeding of silkworms was begun, and silk production became an important industry of the Chinese. The Chinense made very fine pottery which they learned to glaze. Soon they also learned to make dishes of porcelain, and we still call porcelain dishes chinaware, or simply china.

The use of metals was known to the Shang people even before they settled down in the Hwang-Ho valley. The specimens found tell us that the Chinese metal worker was a master of his craft. He often worked patterns on vases, which shows that he was an artist as well. Some of the bronze articles of the Shang period are superior to many produced later.

Timber was found in plenty in China and was used extensively in buildings. Palace walls were of polished wood. Much of the woodwork has naturally perished, but the few carvings on wood that have survived are proof that the Chinese were excellent carpenters. Some of the woodwork was also inlaid with ivory (*Social Studies*, 1969).

Ancestor worship was the most popular practice of the ancient Chinese. They believed that death transformed a mortal into a spirit and that the spirit possessed great powers.

The Chinese script started as a pictographic script but it was independently developed as an ideographic script in which a sign represents an idea. It is remarkable that the Chinese script has changed very little since the earliest times. Writers wrote on silk or bamboo slips with a brush.

> The Chinese calendar was a combination of solar and lunar calculations. The months were lunar and consisted of twenty-nine or thirty days, but the length of the year was correctly calculated as 365 $^1/_4$ days. The difference between the solar and lunar calculations was resolved every nineteen years. It appears that the Chinese scholars could correctly foretell lunar eclipses (*Social Studies*, 1969).

Thus, the sociology of development theories by relating the backwardness of the Third World nations and their peoples to internal constraints such as native cultures, religions, individual characteristics of psyche, were adding insult to grave injury.

CRITIQUE OF THE CULTURAL MODEL

Chapter 2 delineated the popular notion among sociologists and anthropologists regarding the normative structure of communities in Asia, Africa, and Latin America. The blame for the relative economic backwardness in the Third World was ascribed to traditional values and institutions and the dominant religions. German sociologist Max Weber and a host of sociologists who followed him, regarded Buddhism, Islam, Hinduism, and Confucianism as fostering values and beliefs that were incompatible with modern science, technology, and the ideology of progress (Singer, 1966).

In recent years, Weber's ideas, particularly in regard to Asian religions, have been criticized. Leading anthropologists feel that Weber downgraded the importance of the political and economic factors in change, his ideas were oversimplified and sometimes even anti-historical (Singer, 1972; Srinivas, 1973). For instance, Srinivas wondered why Weber chose the theological ideas of *samsara* (rebirth) and *karma* (fate) and not any other ideas as the dogmatic foundation of Hinduism. He even questioned the existence of a dogmatic foundation in Hinduism (1973: 279–80):

Hinduism is so fundamentally different from Judaism, Christianity and Islam, the three Mediterranean religions, that ideas and biases carried over from them may stand in the way of understanding it. Hinduism is an acephalous religion. It has nothing corresponding to the religious hierarchy of Christianity or even Islam. It does not state that it is the only true religion and all others are false. There is no formal provision of conversion. It is not congregational. Crucial ideas such as *samsara* and the sanctity of the *Vedas* have been rejected by one or another sect which has managed to remain within the Hindu fold.

Again, Weber projected a view of Asian religions in general, and Hinduism in particular, which made them incapable of change. Critics charge that this view was patently anti-historical. Hinduism, the oldest continuous religion in the world, has been changing and adapting since 5000 BC. The ideas in the earliest holy text—the early *Vedas*—changed in the later texts, the later *Vedas* and the *Upanishads*. The dominant ethic of Hinduism changed since the days of the Indo-Aryans who ate meat and drank liquor to vegetarianism and abstinence from liquor among a great many Hindus today (Srinivas, 1973). Also, during its long history, there have been several religious revivals. Importantly, it survived the enormous challenge posed by Buddhism (which had almost eclipsed Hinduism) to come back as the dominant religion of the region. Moreover, the fact that it survived almost seven hundred years of Islamic and then Christian rule in India, speaks volumes for its adaptability and resilience.

There were other conceptual problems with Weber's thesis. He and other Western indologists regarded Shankara's *advaita* philosophy as synonymous with Hindu theology. *Advaita*, which propagated asceticism and other-worldliness, is not the only school of philosophy or even the most important in Hindu theology. However, indologists who regarded *advaita* as the dominant idea in Hinduism, criticized it for its other-world emphasis and asceticism. This neglected the diversity of religious ideas in Hindu theology. A substantial portion of Hindu texts, literature, and folklore deal with duties and action in this world. For example, in the *Bhagavad Gita*, the holy book of the Hindus, a central concern is the problem of action. Srinivas (1973: 282) has noted:

> It must be mentioned that there is in the *Gita* an undoubted emphasis on performing the duties of one's caste and status. Duty conscientiously performed, without attachment to the fruits of the action, leads to salvation.... Duty properly

performed, makes the entire life an offering to God. It is interesting that during the last 70 years or more, Indian leaders and intellectuals, including Tilak, Gandhi, and Aurobindo, turned to the *Gita* to justify their involvement in political and social action. It is difficult to understand why Weber failed to see that the *Gita* was a major scriptural source for a 'work ethic' and for political and social activism....

Also, attainment of salvation or eternal life in the other world was just one goal in Hindu texts. The other three goals stressed a person's obligations in the present world. They are: *dharma* (morality), *artha* (pursuit of wealth), and *kama* (sex within marriage). Singer and Srinivas, who have conducted several studies in India, note that there is compartmentalization in that society. The office and factory symbolize the modern life whereas the home is a place for traditions. Indians are able to move quite easily between these two worlds. As one informant aptly put it, 'when I put on my shirt and go to the factory, I take off my caste. When I come home and take off my shirt, I put on my caste.' Thus, the advantages Hindus have is that they move from the traditional role to the modern without schizophrenia (Singer, 1966). These observations indicate the coexistence of traditional and modern life styles and cast doubts on the widespread belief among certain Western sociologists that traditional beliefs and practices are always obstacles to modernization.

Research conducted by anthropologists provides evidence that other religions such as Islam and Buddhism do not necessarily foster piety, resignation, or fatalism among the people. For example, while the giving of *dana* (alms) in Buddhism and going on pilgrimages in Islam might seem on the surface to be economically irrational, they actually motivate very rational behavior. In order to fulfill these traditional obligations, individuals will need to work hard and save (Goldthorpe, 1975). Also, traditional forms, arrangements, and institutions are not an antithesis of development. Singer and Srinivas expose the fallaciousness of such arguments by showing how caste, joint family, etc. could contribute to profitable entrepreneurial behavior and rational bureaucracy:

The joint family, for instance, provides a pool of trusted personnel for commercial and industrial activity in India today, just as in the rural setting it enables large farms to be managed at a particular technological and organizational level. Since

the running of big farms, commercial undertakings, and
industries needs political backing and bureaucratic clearance,
one or more members of the joint family are allowed to
specialize in the cultivation of politicians, bureaucrats, and
influence-peddlers (Srinivas, 1973: 283).

All the ensuing discussions bring us back to re-question the
utility of traditional institutions and arrangements *vis-á-vis* progress and change. The dominant paradigm of development took
a very negative view of tradition. It had to be destroyed if the
Third World nations and peoples wanted to modernize. This
notion does not have too many supporters in recent times. The
importance of tradition in the process of development has been
recognized. Eisenstadt points out that, 'the mere destruction of
traditional settings—the family, the community, or even the
political order—led to disorganization, delinquency, and chaos
rather than to a viable modern order' (Eisenstadt, 1976: 35).
Finally, the cultural model in the old paradigm was riddled
with contradictions. First, there was excessive emphasis on
religion as an inhibiting factor in Third World countries. This
may not be true. Goldthorpe (1975: 236) points out examples of
Chinese, Muslims, and Asian Indian groups, who were associated with entrepreneurial zeal and innovative energy when they
migrated to other lands:

> For example, it is possible to explain the economic backward-
> ness of China before the Communist triumph of 1964 in terms
> of passivity, the Confucian ideal of the cultivated man of the
> world, lavish expenditure on funerals and weddings, non-
> rational magical beliefs, and the like....Yet, when Chinese
> migrated to Indonesia, Malaya, Singapore, Thailand, or
> even Hong Kong they suddenly became energetic innovators
> whose industry and enterprise stimulated the economy of the
> region into new life; and it does not seem to have been the
> case that the religious beliefs and ritual customs of the over-
> seas Chinese were in any important respect different from
> those of the homeland.

Another assumption that seems to have been uncritically accepted was the notion that a Western person was always rational.
Several researchers indicate the contrary. Traditional attributes
such as particularism, favoritism, belief in astrologers, and lavish

A Reductionist Approach to Rationality

The dominant view in the West is that knowledge is out there in the world. Reality is something undeterminate—a gray blob. The mind copies the knowledge from nature, categorizes it and makes sense of it. This knowledge then makes the undeterminate world more determinate, ordered, rational, etc. This approach to rationality is reductionist.

Any body of knowledge or school of thought cannot and will not incorporate everything out there in the world. Something is invariably left out. Therefore, when one adopts a pluralistic view, one would assume that there may be different systems of knowledge to describe the world. Thus, schools of knowledge outside the Western 'rational' empirical view can also be rational. Until now, most of the scholarly writing in the West, particularly in political science, sociology, economics, etc. implied that the Western logical positivism was the 'best' and 'most rational' method of explaining reality.

For example, in the interpretation of the history of the East, mainly China and India, by Western scholars, there was the explicit notion that orientals were irrational in their practices, observed 'strange' customs and unnecessary rituals. This was reinterpretation of Hindu reality by the Western scholar through his/her 'superior' logical positivist models. These scholars were reinterpreting knowledge of ancient Hindus not only to the world but to the Hindus themselves. This new knowledge was not in terms of what the rituals and practices meant to the Hindu at that particular point in history when they were practiced and in their socio-cultural milieu, but in a period and setting far removed from their actual origin. This kind of interpretation practiced in the 19th century made subjective statements about the orientals on their cultural practices much before the system of ideological analysis was well developed.

It is ethnocentric to assume that the Western or any other method of inquiry and analysis is superior to others. From an epistemological viewpoint, the scholars in the West do not know enough about other systems of knowledge to dismiss them as irrational, bizarre, or disorderly. Most such value judgements are merely ideological rather than scientific.

expenditure on social/religious occasions are widely prevalent in the advanced countries whereas modern attributes such as universalism, secularism, and strict criteria for merit may be found in developing nations. For example, Abraham (1980: 76) noted that:

1. Several practices in the United States make the political system there very particularistic: influence of family tradition on voting; preferring individual candidates over political parties and letting elected officers such as the president or mayors return political favors by rewarding friends with administrative assignments;
2. There is a preponderance of local news and local newspapers in American small towns making the value orientations of the average person very local-oriented. However, in the developing nations the average 'traditional' person is universally-oriented since his/her regional newspaper is more national and international than local;
3. Serious contradictions prevail in terms of attributes fostered by traditional cultures vis-a-vis the value orientations instilled by modern societies. For example, even the most orthodox Hindu person exhibits religious tolerance and the belief that all religions ultimately lead to the same destination, thus exemplifying universalism of the highest order. However, many 'progressive' individuals in Western nations exhibit particularism as reflected in their attempts at proselytization and conversion to their 'true' religion;
4. Universities in many Third World countries, particularly in Asia and Africa, have a universalistic system of examinations where the students' papers are graded by examiners from other schools or universities.

In addition to the above observations, several more could be posited to highlight the inconsistencies and contradictions in the cultural model proposed by the old paradigm. For example, the observation that top government officials in the Third World countries consult astrologers and look at the position of the stars in the constellation before planning important projects is not something unique to developing countries. In the summer of 1988, the mass media all over the world reported how President Ronald Reagen of the United States consulted an astrologer in San Francisco to plan his duties and even marked his personal calendar with pens of different colors to signify good, bad, and neutral days. Again, individuals in traditional cultures were faulted for spending huge amounts of money and other resources on social and religious ceremonies. This behavior is quite common in the West too. In the United States, ostentatious Christmas celebrations and parties are not uncommon. Individuals shop months ahead of Christmas so that they may buy gifts for all relatives and friends. Several people run into debt simply to fulfill their gift-buying obligations.

All these observations were intended to demonstrate that labels such as 'traditional' and 'modern' may be misplaced, and in many situations, the line dividing the two could be very thin indeed.

VALUE-ENACTMENT MODEL REVISITED

Chapter 2 outlined the theories of McClelland, Inkeles, Lerner, and Hagen on the relationship between the personality structure of individuals and the modernization of their societies. These theorists conceptualized the attributes of the 'modern' person which comprised an ideal mix of certain belief systems, patterns of behavior, and attitudinal structure. All these made modernization and economic growth in their societies almost automatic.

This perspective of development has been quite controversial. The critique of this mode of analysis is presented under two headings (Portes, 1976).

Social-Political Vacuum

The value-enactment theories did not address or take into consideration the influence of structural constraints on individual action. Theorists of this perspective resolutely avoided looking into the effects of political and economic interests at the national and international levels on individual independence, action, and opportunities (Frank, 1969). For example, the structural obstacles faced by black Africans in South Africa, the lower castes in South Asia and the racial minorities in the United States override and nullify whatever achievement motivation, aspirations, or empathy they may have had. Portes (1976: 72) points out that:

> an active set of individuals, motivated by whatever psychological mechanism one may wish to posit, must still cope with existing economic and political arrangements. One way of doing so is to attempt to transform them, in which case 'entrepreneurs' must organize themselves and enter the political arena in conflict with entrenched interest groups. The transformation of 'modernity' or 'n-achievement' into potential rebellion and ideologically committed elites is a possibility seldom contemplated in these theories.

Thus, McClelland's *n-Ach* may not be an independent variable but rather a dependent variable—dependent on the sanctions, norms, political and economic interest groups that prevail in a society. As Abraham notes, 'achievement motivation itself is a highly institutionalized function of a system of stratification that distributes motivation differently and unevenly over different social strata' (Abraham, 1980: 86).

Some critics argue that the existence of highly motivated achievers may be irrelevant or even harmful to a nation attempting to bring about socio-economic development. Thus, these critics argue that what is important for a developing nation is not just a mass of individuals with high levels of aspirations, empathy, or achievement motivation, but articulating clearly the goals toward which the energies and creativity of such individuals are channeled. In fact, Portes (1976) points out several dysfunctions arising from the role of such individuals:

1. Highly motivated individuals could be quite effective in maintaining or supporting the existing unequal structural relationships in their societies;
2. They could be effective as managers of companies owned by multinational corporations. Thus, as Marxist scholars would contend, their energies could be used to perpetuate the unequal international economic structure;
3. Highly motivated individuals could emigrate to the United States, Australia, Canada, or other advanced nations (as has been the case with engineers and medical doctors) leading to a 'brain drain'

Conspicuous Consumption

Lerner and Inkeles outlined in their theories several characteristics of a 'modern' person. Overall, such a person was to tailor his/her behavior, values, life style to be consistent with that of a Western person. Empathy was, after all, the ability to lift oneself out of the traditional environs and be placed in a Western urban-industrial society. However, this could very well lead not to a *revolution of rising expectations* among the people in the Third World nations but to a *revolution of rising frustrations* (Lerner, 1958). The reason for this is because a developing nation cannot support the consumption patterns of individuals in advanced countries. In fact, excessive consumption could be dysfunctional to a poor country with scarce and limited resources which could be better utilized for long-term development. Portes (1976) cautions that the emphasis on consumption could also constrain the flexibility of governments in choosing between different development strategies. The temptation could be to succumb to immediate consumption which would produce mass political support, whereas curbing of immediate consumption for long-term development objectives could result in mass protests and concomitant political problems.

The Case of the Irrational Peasants

In the literature on mass media and modernization, the major blame for the relative backwardness of developing nations was attributed to the traditional behavior and attitudes of the masses. The value-normative complexes of scholars such as McClelland, Hagen, Inkeles, and Rogers painted a rather grim picture of the anti-change attitudes and values of individuals in the Third World. As a group, the subsistence farmers or peasants were more often the subjects of study by social scientists. Everett Rogers described a *subculture of peasantry* which was characterized by ten functionally related variables. The *subculture of peasantry* was a comprehensive account of what was known about peasants until then. It indicated that their ideas and behavior were irrational and that they constituted a formidable obstacle to modernization and change in Third World countries (Rogers, 1969). In all this, the investigation was at a very micro level. Consequently, the peasant was the locus of blame for the sluggish pace of progress and change in developing nations. A macro analysis looking at the entire society, its history, tribulations, social structure, power relationships, etc. may have placed the blame elsewhere. For example, social-psychological variables such as mutual distrust in interpersonal relations, perceived limited good, dependence on and hostility toward government authority, familism, lack of innovativeness and limited aspirations of peasants, while seeming irrational at the individual level, would seem perfectly logical when one considered the long history of oppression and exploitation that peasants have suffered under the elites in their societies. An equally convincing argument may be made that these socio-psychological variables were probably the consequences rather than the causes of underdevelopment. Thus, while the objective was to understand better the life styles of the peasants, the findings of the earlier studies actually distorted the image of peasants.

The development of peasant agriculture so that it can make a positive contribution to ventures designed to improve agricultural production depends crucially on how one views the nature of the peasantry and its enterprises. The earlier theories in the dominant paradigm held the stereotypical view that the peasantry, as a class, constituted the traditional sector which was necessarily in conflict with modernization and change. Therefore, innovations had to flow from outside into these *traditional* enclaves and somehow *modernize* them. This conceptualization on the nature of peasants and their enterprises seemed overly abstract and unreal (Schultz, 1964; Gusfield 1971). Thus, there is a need to understand better the nature of the peasantry and its household resource allocation. Why are the peasants averse to risk? What is their attitude toward work? Are they traditionalists unwilling to change? Let us attempt to examine some of these stereotypes.

Classical Economics Approach

Much of the work on peasant economic orientation and behavior has been done by Western researchers trained in the discipline of classical and neo-classical economics. The underlying assumptions of this approach were not only that Western-type economic and industrial development was the best choice for societies all over the world, but also that the economic theories and analytical tools had universal application. Consequently, these economic anthropologists set out to study peasant cultures very different from Western societies using the tools, concepts, and abstractions with which they used to work. Some notable examples of this can be seen in the works of Raymond Firth (1964, 1965) where he attempted to use the concepts of neo-classical economics to explain the behavior of 'primitive' and peasant peoples. Analyzing peasant society in Polynesia, Firth (1965) explained that they lack a money economy, markets, prices, and other concomitant Western economic factors. He labeled them as primitive for lacking all these factors and then went ahead and analyzed their economic behavior as though they were Western-type entrepreneurs functioning in a cash economy. Daniel Thorner (1968: 507) summarized how this approach equated the peasant household with a capitalistic enterprise:

> When the 'farm business' method is applied to analysis of peasant agriculture, the peasant's land and livestock, equipment, and other goods are equated with those of a small firm. The peasant's behavior is then treated in terms of the theory of the firm as developed for business enterprises. It is taken for granted that the peasant's aim is to rationalize his operations so as to obtain the maximum profit.

In the above approach, the expenses of the peasant family on such things as equipment and wages were deducted from the gross income to obtain the net profit. When the expenses exceeded the total income, the farm was said to be operating at a loss. This approach, then, failed to explain some obvious realities in the developing nations. For example, as Thorner (1968) posited, how was one to explain how peasants in many developing nations survived in spite of engaging in 'uneconomic farming' decade after decade? Many of these observed anomalies, however, were explained earlier by a group of economists working with Russian peasants. This came to be labeled the *Production and Consumption* school of thought.

Production and Consumption Approach

The classical economics approach to peasant agriculture was challenged by a group of Russian scholars: Kablukov, Kosinskii,

Chelintsev, Makarov, Studenskii, and Chayanov. They based their arguments on the data they had collected and analyzed from Russian peasants in the decades following 1880. They argued that the economic orientation of the peasant enterprise could not be treated as if it were a business firm. The primary motive of the peasant family was to eat, make the required payments—such as to the landlord and the state—and somehow survive. It was not possible to impute money value to the labor performed by the peasant family. The sheer pressure exerted on the family made the members behave in a way which could be considered 'irrational' according to capitalistic business standards. If the consumption needs of the family demanded extra labor, the members would expend that labor even if the additional product that was obtained was very small. Since labor was in abundance, the peasant family would rent or buy extra land regardless of its price. Chayanov argued that since hired hands were not employed, the concepts of classic and neo-classical economics could not be applied to peasant farm families (Thorner, 1966).

One of the notable contributions of Chayanov to a clearer understanding of the peasant household economy was the labor-consumer balance. As he put it, 'We can state positively that the degree of self-exploitation of labor is established by some relationship between the measures of demand satisfaction and the measure of the burden of labor' (Chayanov, 1966: 81). According to this, the production and consumption decisions in the household economy were interrelated. Each household worked to the point where the household's subjective evaluation of the marginal disutility of work equaled its estimate of the marginal utility of the output gained. This statement is represented graphically in Figure 4.1.

In the figure, **AB** indicates the degree of drudgery of work, **CD** represents marginal utility of output (rubles). The curve **CD** cuts **AB** at the point **X** which corresponds to a sum of 67 rubles received per year. At this output level, the subjective evaluation of output obtained equals the subjective evaluation of the drudgery involved in the agricultural work. From this point onwards, as the curves indicate, each succeeding ruble will be evaluated lower than the drudgery of winning it.

Chayanov drew similar curves and showed how, for different families, the balance between demand satisfaction and irksomeness of work was influenced by the size of the family and the ratio

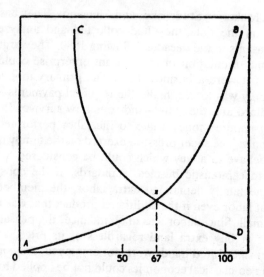

Figure 4.1: Chayanov's Curves of Utility/Disutility of Output and Drudgery of Labor.

SOURCE: Chayanov (1966:82). 'Measure of Self-Exploitation of the Peasant Family Labour Force'. *In* D. Thorner et al. (eds.), *The Theory of Peasant Economy.* Copyright American Economic Association. Reprinted by permission.

of working members to non-working members. Thus, Chayanov and his colleagues proved that the peasant exhibited a totally different rationality when it came to questions such as adoption of innovations, subsistence farming, and risk-aversion. Kerblay (1971: 159) noted that though Chayanov's thesis worked better for thinly populated countries, it was, nevertheless, still relevant to peasant populations in other Third World nations:

> The problem raised over forty years ago by the leader of the Russian organizational school, and the basic approach focusing analysis of peasant economies on the dynamics and structures of family farms, are just as pertinent today for developing countries where peasant economies still predominate.

Subsistence Ethic of Peasants

Several scholars such as Migdal (1974), Scott (1976), Popkin

(1979), and Hyden (1980) have been increasingly concerned with peasants. Their models are consistent with the findings of Chayanov, who did not explicitly discuss some of the issues they raised, but did imply them in his studies. These scholars agreed on the precarious existence of peasants in the Third World today: living dangerously close to the subsistence level. Scott posited: 'If the Great Depression left an indelible mark on the fears, values, and habits of a whole generation of Americans, can we imagine the impact of periodic food crises on the fears, values and habits of rice farmers in monsoon Asia?' (Scott, 1976: 2). He argued that the fear of food shortages in peasant societies had given rise to a *subsistence ethic*. This ethic was the consequence of living so close to the margin and could be compared to the ethic of peasants in 19th century France, Russia, and Italy. Scott placed the subsistence ethic at the center of the analysis of peasant politics. The peasant family's major objective was to produce enough rice to feed the family, buy necessities, and pay land rents and taxes. Living dangerously close to the margin, where one bad crop meant starvation, the peasants had perfected ways of keeping alive. For example, the local tradition of seed varieties, planting methods, and timing were designed after centuries of trial and error to produce the minimum subsistence even under very difficult circumstances (Scott, 1976). Scott (1976: 3) pointed out that several social arrangements served the same end:

> Patterns of reciprocity, forced generosity, communal land, and work-sharing helped to even out the inevitable troughs in a family's resources which might otherwise have thrown them below subsistence.

Safety-First Principle

Scott (1976) asserted that it was the *safety-first* principle that anchored many of the social, moral, and technical arrangements of the peasant agrarian order. Given the imminent possibility of facing hunger, starvation or malnutrition every year, it was reasonable to assume that the peasant would have a different perspective *vis-á-vis* adoption of risky innovations. In other words, the 'peasant household has little scope for the profit maximization calculus of traditional neo-classical economics' (Scott, 1976: 4).

Thus, the objective was to stabilize returns and minimize risks even if this meant reduced returns for labor expended:

> In decision-making parlance his behavior is risk-averse; he minimizes the subjective probability of the maximum loss. If treating the peasant as a would-be Schumpeterian entrepreneur misses his key existential dilemma, so do the normal power-maximizing assumptions fail to do justice to his political behavior. To begin instead with the need for a reliable subsistence as the primordial goal of the peasant cultivator and then to examine his relationships to his neighbors, to elites, and to the state in terms of whether they aid or hinder in meeting that need, is to recast many issues (Scott, 1976: 4–5)

Through his subsistence ethic and safety-first principle, the peasant was desperately trying to earn a *minimum income*. It is usual in advanced nations for the state to guarantee a minimal standard of living through social security, unemployment compensation, medical care, and so on. The Third World peasant did not have this safety net and it seemed irrational for him to engage in innovative, achievement-oriented, and profit-maximizing behavior.

CRITIQUE OF THE ECONOMIC MODEL

The neo-classical economic model in the dominant paradigm that suggested a 'trickle-down' approach to development benefits, started losing credibility in the seventies. Dudley Seers (1977b: 3) documents some of the reasons for this:

1. The social problems of developed nations were spreading concern about the environmental costs of economic growth;
2. Despite substantial transfers of capital and technology from the developed nations to the Third World, the gap between per capita incomes between the two blocs was growing;
3. Third World nations with impressive rates of growth did not achieve either the political status or social equity expected of them;

4. Income inequality was rising all over the Third World countries;
5. Unemployment rates were refusing to go down in spite of impressive growth rates;
6. Power was being concentrated among an elite coterie who benefited from the growth, who then used that power to preserve the inequality in their societies.

In the dominant paradigm, economic growth was synonymous with development. Per capita incomes and GNP rates constituted reliable criteria to measure progress. However, there were other economic indicators that were equally important but given a short

---

The Misleading Nature of GNP Measure

Published figures of GNP per head if taken too literally can be misleading, maybe even inaccurate. GNP measures exaggerate the real differences of living standards between the rich and poor countries, making the poor countries look worse than they really are.

First, since they are average figures, they do not reveal the differential income levels between the rich and poor people within a country. Second, because of the vagaries of exchange rates between national currencies, they are usually misleading. Official rates of exchange are not accurate indicators of the 'purchasing power parity' of currencies. Importantly, the official rates of exchange put a low value on currencies of poor countries. Third, GNP statistics in poor countries undervalue goods and services which are locally produced and consumed and which, very often, do not go through the marketing process. Fourth, in industrial economies, many goods and services which are bought and sold may not be 'life enhancing' but instead be a cost rather than a benefit. For example, driving long distances to work and the cost of gasoline, wear and tear on automobiles, etc. are more a hassle than a form of desired consumption. Another example is the fast-food packaging and retail distribution system. A fruit is no more tasty or nutritious when eaten straight off the vendor's cart than

> when packaged and sold in supermarkets in plastic bags. Yet the cost of packaging, retailing, transportation, etc. in developed countries are calculated in national income accounts (Goldthorpe, 1975: 82).
>
> Thus, ordinary estimates of GNP per head, in money terms, converted to United States dollars mask and exaggerate the true difference in living standards between rich and poor countries. It may be more accurate to multiply the average incomes of the poorest countries by three to arrive at a truer comparison (Goldthorpe, 1975: 84).

shrift in the 'trickle-down' approach. Seers (1977a: 3) put it very well:

> the questions to ask about a country's development are therefore: what has been happening to poverty? What has been happening to unemployment? What has been happening to inequality? If all three of these have declined from high levels, then beyond doubt this has been a period of development for the country concerned.

Unfortunately, progress in eradicating unemployment, poverty, and income inequality has been dismal. Weaver and Jameson (1978) note that in each of these areas, the poor benefited very little, and their plight has deteriorated over the last thirty years. Let us examine each in detail:

Unemployment

During the development decade of the sixties, unemployment rates actually went up rather than down. And, this was the period during which the economies of developed nations were doing very well. Available data indicate that the rate of increase of unemployment was concomitant with high rates of growth (Weaver and Jameson, 1978).

Inequality

Income inequality increased all over the Third World. Weaver and Jameson (1978) document the trend in several Third World countries such as Kenya, Brazil, Ecuador, and Turkey. In these countries, the share of national income was concentrated in the hands of a very small minority. For example, in Brazil in the sixties, the top 5 percent cornered as much as 46 percent of the national income.

While the trickle-down model encouraged some initial inequality as necessary to generate savings and incentives, the rate of inequality that actually emerged was dysfunctional to economic growth. Seers (1977a: 4) questioned the need to generate inequality for a later-day trickle-down effect:

> I find the argument that the need for savings justifies inequality unconvincing in the Third World today. Savings propensities are after all very low precisely in countries with highly unequal distributions; the industrial countries with less concentration of income have, by contrast, much higher savings propensities.

Weaver and Jameson (1978: 36–37) constructed the Lorenz curve which could be used to compute Gini coefficient—a measure of income distribution. Figure 4.2 is the graph they obtained.

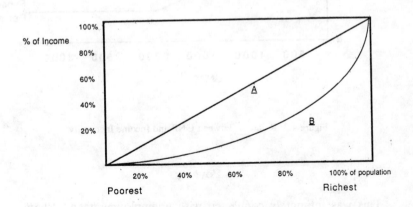

Figure 4.2: Lorenz Curve

In this figure, the vertical axis denotes income distribution and the horizontal axis the spread of the population. Perfect equality of income distribution is denoted by the diagonal line. For example, 40 percent of the population will get 40 percent of income. However, actual data obtained would show points falling on a curved line or the Lorenz curve. The narrower the distance between the curved line and the horizontal axis, the greater the income inequality. Gini coefficent was computed by the ratio **A/(A+B)**. Thus, if there was extreme inequality (i.e. area **A** covered the whole area of the graph), the Gini coefficient would be unity. If there was perfect equality (area **A** was zero), Gini coefficient would be zero.

According to the theoretical assumption of the trickle-down model, the measure of inequality would reduce as the economies grew. However, Weaver and Jameson (1978: 37) using data from Chenery et al. (1974) showed (Figure 4.3) that such was not the case. Income inequality once established did not decline.

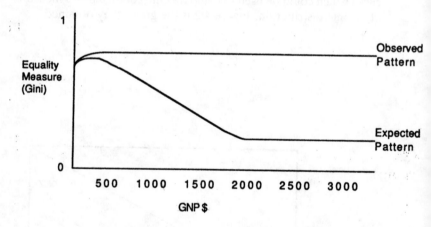

Figure 4.3: Relation Between GNP and Income Inequality

Poverty

This was intimately connected with unemployment and income inequality. Any negative growth in these two areas would have a detrimental effect on poverty rates. For the purpose of this discussion, poverty is defined as the inability of people to meet basic necessities such as minimal food, clothing, footwear, and shelter. Research studies found that as economic expansion proceeded the income of the bottom 40 percent of people in developing countries fell not only relatively (which was to be expected during the initial period) but in absolute terms as well (Adelman and Morris, 1973). In other words, the bottom half of the population in several countries such as Pakistan, India, Brazil, and Mexico had less income (in absolute dollars) at the end of the seventies than they had in the early sixties (Adelman and Morris, 1973).

In a nutshell, the economic planning using models in the old paradigm brought about mixed results. Many developing nations showed very impressive increases in their GNP rates until the sixties. Some even doubled and tripled the rates. For example, in Brazil the GNP rates showed a 7 percent increase every year from the mid-sixties, whereas in Korea, since 1974, GNP was growing at 10 percent per year. However, unemployment, poverty, and income inequality were increasing as well. The poor, therefore, benefited very little from the economic growth in their countries. As Weaver and Jameson (1978: 39) conclude:

> this model led to increasing inequality and also led to increasing poverty...what planning seems to have brought is an enhancement in the good life of a small elite class, while increasing the good life for the poor very little or perhaps even removing them further from the attainment of the good life.

Why did the trickle-down model not work to alleviate the poverty of the very needy and poor in developing nations, who incidentally, constituted a fairly large proportion of the population? Several explanations are offered by researchers:

1. In the old paradigmatic model, the emphasis was on economic growth and not equitable distribution of the fruits of development. Thus, high GNP rates constituted development regardless of who they may have benefited. Therefore, those who controlled economic and political power benefited from the growth;

2. Those who derived greatest benefit from the economic expansion were slow to tackle problems of poverty. Instead, as Seers noted, 'they will inevitably try to find ways of main-

taining privilege, resorting (as dozens of historical examples show) to political violence than give it up' (Seers, 1977a: 5). The basic problem here lay in the conception of trickle-down strategy. In the Third World, it was very difficult to 'grow now and trickle down later.' The unequal structures and the concomitant economic and political power of those who controlled the rules of the game prevented redistribution of benefits. Moreover, the new profits and income were converted into goods such as expensive college education, luxury houses, and imported cars which could not be redistributed (Weaver and Jameson, 1978);

3. Also, the profits and high incomes derived from economic growth were not adequately reinvested in the development process. Either they went into projects with low priority for development or they were sent abroad. And, it fueled conspicuous consumption on goods and services with a high foreign exchange content. This proved dysfunctional to a country suffering from foreign exchange difficulties (Seers, 1977a: 4);

4. A substantial part of domestic funds and foreign aid and investment was directed at capital-intensive projects. Quite often, foreign aid was earmarked for such projects. This made capital cheap relative to labor. However, in reality, developing countries were labor-rich and capital-poor (Weaver and Jameson, 1978).

DECLINE OF THE DOMINANT PARADIGM

Chapter 2 has already outlined the main ideas in the dominant paradigm of development. This section will take a critical look at the postulates of the dominant paradigm of development. This will provide a good base for a later discussion on the many shortcomings of several theories and ideas in development communication.

Quantification of Development

In the dominant paradigm, development was quantified, usually in terms of economic indicators—the gross national product (GNP), per capita income, etc. This approach did not consider the question of equality of the benefits of development. The emphasis was on absolute growth and not its equitable distribution:

> The 'growth-first-and-let-equality-come-later' mentality often was justified by the trickle-down theory that leading sectors, once advanced, would then spread their advantage to the lagging sectors (Rogers, 1976b: 125).

Little attention was paid in this approach to the fundamental contradictions of societies in the developing nations where economic and political power were concentrated in the hands of a small elite and where large sectors of the population had no significant share in the political and economic resources. Further, the perspective of economic growth through industrialization obscured the fact that there was monopolized control of technology of development, i.e. the know-how, production, and distribution of modern technologies was vested in the industrialized nations rather than in the Third World, and the location of such centers was in the metropolitan decision-making centers (Institute of Social Studies, 1980).

The paradigm assumed that the standard of living would be improved in the Third World nations if innovations of new technology were communicated down through the social structure but leaving the structure of dependence in these societies (where a small elite controlled a disproportionate amount of political and economic power) intact (Institute of Social Studies, 1980). Thus, most of the efforts of such 'development' brought further stagnation, a greater concentration of income and power in a few hands, high unemployment rates, and an ever-widening gap between the rich and the disadvantaged sectors (Rogers, 1976b).

Capital-Intensive Technology

In the dominant paradigm, a big push was given to capital-intensive and labor-extensive technology which was mainly imported from more developed nations. Here, the term 'capital-intensive' meant an approach which relied heavily on infusion of capital, whereas the 'labor-extensive' strategy was one which placed little importance on human labor factor in development. These definitions tend to be confusing because capital is required in labor-intensive strategies as well. Labor-intensive approaches too cannot function without adequate capital. So, what was implied as a capital-intensive strategy in the dominant paradigm was, in fact, a machine-intensive approach. This approach can be viewed as a predominantly urban-based strategy depending crucially on large-scale industries using machines and huge capital but with little labor input. A low priority was accorded to industries employing labor-intensive strategies.

Machines that were to be used in the machine-intensive approach were not locally produced in the developing nations. They had to be purchased from the industrialized nations, paying in scarce foreign exchange funds. Thus, instead of using the abundant mass of cheap labor already existing in Third World countries, precious capital was used to buy machines. Very soon, nations employing the machine-intensive approach ran into problems as suggested by high underemployment and unemployment rates and other maladjustments, leading to a deterioration in the quality of life (Oshima, 1976a).

There was another undesirable facet to this problem. The huge capital required for the technology had to be provided by international agencies, multinational firms, and such other institutions usually controlled by the industrialized nations. This made the developing countries indebted to the richer nations, giving rise to economic colonialism.

The labor-intensive strategy, on the other hand, would have let the capital remain in the Third World nations and also provided employment to the great mass of labor in these nations. As Oshima (1976a: 22) noted:

a shift to a more labor intensive strategy becomes inevitable if the economy is to create sufficient jobs for new workers coming into the labor market and is to continue to grow. Capital-intensive technology cannot raise levels of productivity and income of the low income groups as it is far too sophisticated and expensive for these groups.

However, a labor-intensive strategy is not without problems. This strategy has to contend with a large number of small and traditional units of production, such as workshops, farms, and stores, and administration of these myriad units demands effective management techniques. In fact, Hirschman (1958) argued that a predominantly capital-intensive strategy was due to the extreme difficulties of dealing with a great mass of small peasants and other producers, and the limited expertise and knowledge available on effective management techniques. In these circumstances, it was far easier to deal with a small number of big industrial units located in a few big centers.

Internal Causes of Underdevelopment

The dominant paradigm focused its attention on development constraints within a nation-state. Invariably, the reasons for underdevelopment were thought to be the social-psychological make-up of individuals or the 'traditional' nature of peasants in the Third World. They seemed to lack achievement motivation, were fatalistic, unresponsive to technological innovations, were unempathetic, and they suffered from a host of other factors epitomized by the *subculture of peasantry* (Rogers, 1969).

Little attention was paid in the Western models of development to external constraints to national development. As Fjes (1976: 23) noted:

Viewing development solely in terms of individual nation states, obscures what may today be fundamentally a more important development dynamic, that of the relationships between the underdeveloped and developed nations. The contemporary web of trade and financial relationships, military alliances and political blocs, a vast international network dominated by the countries of the industrialized West, is rarely given any degree of attention in mainstream development literature.

The nation-state as the unit of analysis in the dominant paradigm of development, was, therefore, questionable. It projected the erroneous view that a developing nation could work out its own destiny outside the context of international political, economic, and cultural ties (Fjes, 1976). Rogers pointed out that technical assistance programs guided by the postulates of the dominant paradigm were slow to realize the importance of outside constraints

on a nation's progress: 'international terms of trade, the economic imperialism of international corporations, and the vulner-
ability and dependence of the recipients of technical assistance
programs' (Rogers, 1976b: 127). In other words, it was a classic
example of blaming the victim, i.e. the developing nations for all
their problems.

Centralized Planning

The dominant paradigm underlined that central planning of
development, usually by economists and bankers, was a legitimate
and reasonable means by which the country could seek its development goals' (Rogers, 1976b). Most nations in Africa, Asia, and
Latin America responded during the fifties and sixties by setting
up national development and planning commissions comprised of
prominent economists and bankers. The assumption by these
economists was that local communities could be developed eventually by such central development strategies. Autonomous self-
development of local units was thought to be very unlikely. However, development did not go very well with nations that closely
followed the paradigm. Oshima (1976b) noted that as the economic
development strategy, which was at the heart and core of planning, was wrong, it was inevitable that development planning
was not as successful as desired.

Examples of successful development in the People's Republic of
China and to a limited extent in Tanzania showed that 'people
cannot *be* developed, they can only develop themselves. And this
realization was demonstrated not only in communist and socialist
nations, but also in such capitalistic settings as Korea and Taiwan'
(Rogers, 1976b: 131).

The approach of centralized planning by a few economists and
bankers was a top-down form of development which allowed very
little participation of people who were the target of all this planning. This approach, therefore, could not reflect the new concern
for self-reliance in development, and popular participation in
decentralized development planning and execution as it did not
accommodate a two-way, participatory, and bottom-up flow of
communication.

One of the important alternatives suggested to the top-down

approach has been the bottom-up orientation to development communication (Rogers, 1976c; Schramm, 1977). However, this approach left crucial questions unanswered. Who among the people is to be selected for participating in this bottom-up communication? Is it to be the development chiefs, politicians or the common man in the village? How are these people to be selected and by whom? Finally, how could the scholars who had condemned the mass of peasants as traditional and lacking in motivation, aspirations, innovativeness, empathy, and a plethora of other factors constituting the *subculture of peasantry*, also suggest that these very peasants be in the vanguard of such bottom-up approaches to communication? Such apparent contradictions and the lack of viable strategies for bringing about successful grass-roots participation may be some of the reasons why top-down approaches still prevail in much of development communication.

SUMMARY

The development process in the Third World countries did not fit the assumptions implicit in the dominant paradigm of development. The dominant paradigm worked better as a description of social change in West Europe and North America than as a predictor of change in developing countries.

The criticism of the sociology of development models was directed at: (*i*) the abstractness of the social theories. They served as comprehensive tools for an understanding of social change in general but had limited utility when applied to concrete problems of development in Third World countries; (*ii*) the ahistorical nature of the propositions. Critics argued that many of the models, such as Rostow's Growth Theory, distorted history of the developing countries; and (*iii*) incorrect nature of development indicators such as the development of money, markets, and bureaucracies that constituted the 'evolutionary universals' of Parsons.

Also, serious criticisms were leveled against the old paradigmatic models by several neo-Marxist scholars. To them, underdevelopment was not a process distinctly different from development. In fact, they constituted two facets of the same process. The *development of underdevelopment* in Third World nations was and is related to the economic development of West Europe and North America.

The cultural model of development also came in for serious criticism. The dominant paradigm of development took a very negative view of tradition. It had to be destroyed if the Third World nations and peoples wanted to modernize. This notion does not have too many supporters in recent times. The importance of tradition in the process of development has been recognized. In the cultural model of the dominant paradigm, the blame for relative economic backwardness in the Third World was ascribed to traditional values and institutions and the dominant religions. Max Weber and a host of sociologists who followed him regarded Buddhism, Islam, Hinduism, and Confucianism as fostering values and beliefs that were incompatible with modern science, technology, and the ideology of progress. However, in recent years, leading anthropologists feel that Weber downgraded the importance of the political and economic factors in change, that his ideas were oversimplified and sometimes even anti-historical.

Another assumption that was uncritically accepted was the notion that a Western person was always rational. Many researchers indicate the contrary. Traditional attributes such as particularism, favoritism, belief in astrologers, and lavish expenditure on social/religious occasions are widely prevalent in the advanced countries whereas modern attributes such as universalism, secularism, and strict criteria for merit may be found in developing nations. Thus, labels such as *traditional* and *modern* may be misplaced, and in many situations, the line dividing the two may be very thin.

The value-enactment models of McClelland, Hagen, Inkeles and Smith, and Lerner, were criticized for neglecting to account for the influence of structural constraints on individual action and enterprise. Theorists of this perspective resolutely avoided looking into the effects of political and economic interests at the national and international levels on individual independence, action, and opportunities. Some critics argue that the existence of highly motivated achievers may be irrelevant or even harmful to a nation attempting to bring about socio-economic development. Thus, these critics argue that what is important for a developing nation is not just a mass of individuals with high levels of aspirations, empathy, or achievement motivation, but articulating clearly the goals toward which the energies and creativity of such individuals are channeled.

The neo-classical economic model that suggested a *trickle-down* approach to development benefits started losing credibility in the seventies. In this economic model, economic growth was synonymous with development and not an equitable distribution of the fruits of development. Per capita income and GNP rates constituted reliable criteria to measure progress. However, other economic indicators that were equally important were given a short shrift in the *trickle-down* approach. For example, unemployment rates, poverty, and income inequality were increasing all over the developing nations. The poor, therefore, benefited very little from economic growth in their countries.

The dominant paradigm itself was found wanting in several respects. It was criticized for (*i*) defining development only in terms of certain quantifiable characteristics such as GNP, and per capita income; (*ii*) for encouraging capital-intensive techniques in capital-poor developing nations and neglecting labor-intensive strategies; (*iii*) focusing only on constraints to development that existed within a developing nation and largely ignoring constraints that were imposed from outside; and (*iv*) supporting a top-down approach to planning and development. This approach did not reflect the new concern for self-reliance and popular participation in development activities.

Chapter 5

Critique of the Dominant Paradigm's Communication Approach

Mass media have proved in many, many countries to be a necessary but not a sufficient condition for development.
–Wilbur Schramm (1977: 4).

T he general note of optimism that reigned in the fifties and sixties regarding the role and potential of the mass media in the development·process in the Third World, turned sour in the seventies. Administrators and researchers alike realized that the development process was not as straightforward and clear-cut as it was earlier conceptualized. There were too many extraneous variables that impacted on the process. The mass media, far from being the independent variable in the change process, were themselves affected by the extraneous factors.

The following comments from Beltran (1976: 19) conveyed the new concerns of scholars from the Third World:

1. Overall change of social structure is the fundamental prerequisite for the attainment of genuinely human and democratic development;
2. Communication, as it exists in the region, not only is by nature impotent to cause national development by itself, but it often works against development—again, in favor of the ruling minorities;
3. Communication itself is so subdued to the influence of the prevailing organizational arrangements of society that it can hardly be expected to act independently as a main contributor to profound and widespread social transformation.

By the seventies it became increasingly clear in Asia and in Latin America that social-structural constraints diminished and even eliminated the influences of the media in overcoming development problems (Rogers, 1976b: 137).

THE MASS MEDIA AND MODERNIZATION APPROACH: A CRITIQUE

In his classic study, *The Passing of the Traditional Society* (1958), Daniel Lerner showed that there was a strong correlation between the indices of the mass media and socio-economic and political development of a nation. In other words, he showed that the mass media were both an index and agent of modernization in societies. However, Lerner implied causality among the variables based on the strength of the correlations (Fjes, 1976). Correlational measures are necessary but not sufficient indicators of causality. In fact, attempts by several researchers to prove causality among the various indices of development and media availability have not proved successful (Shaw, 1966; Schramm and Ruggels, 1967).

Golding (1974) pointed out an ethnocentric bias in Lerner's assertions. The Western model of democracy was considered as the dependent variable of political development in his model. Thus, there was a clear imposition of a Western liberal model on Third World countries. Any failure to attain the Western form of political arrangement was used to categorize the Third World nations as underdeveloped (Douglass, 1971; Fjes, 1976).

A factor that was largely ignored in the modernization approach was the unequal power relationships in Third World countries. Consequently, many dependent variables of modernity such as leadership, cosmopoliteness, and reference groups lacked face validity. Beltran, reviewing the research of Cuellar and Gutierrez, noted that the socio-structural situation in a society provided a totally different meaning to several variables. Thus,

the concept of 'leadership' hides 'elite' or 'oligarchy,' that 'cosmopoliteness' disguises the connection of interests between rural and urban power-holders, and that the term 'reference group' may serve to dilute the reality of 'internal domination' which victimizes the peasantry (Beltran, 1976: 21).

Lerner, Schramm, and Lakshmana Rao indicated a dual society in Third World nations: a traditional sector existing alongside a modern entity. The traditional sector not only preceded the modern sector in temporal sequence but was also backward because of its traditionalism and antichange attributes. They visualized the day when the modern sector would, through the process of diffusion, dominate and get rid of the traditional set-up. The mass media were seen as important vehicles for speeding up this process of disintegration of the traditional sector. However, a lack of interest in studying the social-structural constraints obfuscated the reality in developing nations. Fjes (1976: 25) cautioned that:

> often times it is not in the modern sector's interest... to modernize the so-called traditional sector. Rather than being isolated from the modern sector, the so-called traditional sector often exists in a relationship of oppressive dependency, its human and material resources being exploited for the benefit of the modern sector. Rather than the traditional and modern sectors existing as two distinct systems, each more or less separate from the other, the modern and traditional systems exist within one system of economic, political and social relationships, with the modern sector dominating the traditional.

Thus, quite often, the perpetuation of the traditional set-up served the interests of the modern sector.

Recently, serious ethical problems have been identified in the way Lerner's study was conceptualized and executed (Samarajiwa, 1987). Lerner's classic study was not originally intended as a survey on the relationship between empathy and development. Instead, as Samarajiwa (1987: 10) points out, 'the objective of the project was audience research in the broader sense of identifying target audiences, as well as in the narrow sense of obtaining *nuts and bolts* information about how *Voice of America* (VOA) broadcasts were received and how the VOA was evaluated in relation to competing broadcasters.' This scholar also points out that Lerner's study was funded by the United States Department of State at the height of the Cold War. Thus, there was more than academic interest in the role of the mass media *vis-á-vis* social change. One clandestine objective was to identify vulnerable audience segments within the Middle East populations and then to target VOA propaganda messages at these groups (Samarajiwa, 1987).

Social-Structural and Political Constraints to Change

An important conceptual problem in theories of modernization was the level at which change was sought to be introduced. The unit of analysis was predominantly centered within the individual (Fair, 1989).

Individual as Locus of Change

The underlying theme in this approach was that the benefits of modernization would accrue by changing the traditional attitudes, values, and aspirations of the individual peasants in developing nations. Exposure to new ideas and practices, usually through the mass media, could help remove traditional attitudes which posed impediments to progress (Lerner, 1958; Shore 1980). This psychological bias in research, Rogers stated, could be traced to the fact that several early scholars in communication had psychological backgrounds and so it was obvious that their views of communication and change neglected the influence of social-structural variables that affect communication (Rogers, 1976a). Much of the early research, therefore, placed an exaggerated emphasis on the individual as the locus of control for change to the neglect of the group and also the relations between sources and receivers. This resulted in the individual constituting the unit of response and the unit of analysis, and consequently, the unit of change (Coleman, 1958; Rogers, 1976a).

There were other reasons for the individual orientation besides the psychological bias. The research design employed, to a great extent, favored the individual approach. The use of the survey design forced researchers to concentrate on a random sample of individuals, rather than a group, as the unit of analysis. Most often the respondents chosen were the heads of households and this obfuscated some very real social realities. It biased the data to the views of one individual in a family and ignored the views of all the other members. The use of sample survey for collection of data also resulted in further obscuring the dynamic, on-going interactions between people as it ripped the individual from his social-structural context (Beltran, 1976). The structure and function of peasant society became hazy or completely disappeared in this methodological/conceptual approach:

> Using random sampling of individuals, the survey is a socio-
> logical meat grinder, tearing the individual from his social

context and guaranteeing that nobody in the study interacts with anyone else in it. It is a little like a biologist putting his experimental animals through a hamburger machine and looking at every hundredth cell through a microscope; anatomy and physiology get lost; structure and function disappear and one is left with cell biology (Barton, 1968: 1).

The survey was clearly an inadequate research tool. It did not record the relational and transactional aspects between individuals in a society. It is only recently that the level of analysis has moved from the monad to the dyad or network of individuals largely through the network analysis and general systems approach (Beltran, 1976; Rogers, 1976a).

The individual approach to change also has its roots in the individual bias of American empirical research. A great majority of quantitative studies in the United States have employed the individual as the unit of response and analysis. This bias has been carried into the Third World without first making sure if individuals were the right unit of response in developing nations. In much of the Third World, individual decisions are not common and are overruled by the decisions of the reference group. So, the overuse of the individual as the locus of change may have masked the fact that the unit of response and analysis could have been the group—such as the immediate family, clan, tribe, caste, or some other subgrouping of individuals.

Ironically, the individual-centered approach ran contrary to the dominant theoretical position:

> One of the significant achievements of American communications research is that it has shown, contrary to the expectations of mass society theorists, that within a highly developed industrial society the individual is not an isolated, atomized entity, but an ongoing, active member of one or a number of the myriad of social subgroups that exist.... However, in turning their attention upon the peoples of the underdeveloped world, communication researchers tend to ignore this insight and view underdeveloped populations as being homogenous, atomized, and lacking any significant group ties (Fjes, 1976: 12).

Individual-Blame

A consequence of the psychological, methodological, and

individual bias in communication research was that it held the individual responsible for all the attendant problems. Little or no attention was given to investigating the anomalies of the system. 'Person-blame rather than system-blame permeates most definitions of social problems; seldom are the definers able to change the system, so they accept it. Such acceptance encourages a focus on psychological variables in communication research' (Rogers, 1976a: 213). A high degree of person-blame is also present in studies pertaining to communication and development. Beltran succinctly summarizes this dominant thinking in much of the earlier diffusion research: 'If peasants do not adopt the technology of modernization, it is their fault, not that of those communicating the modern technology to them. It is the peasantry itself which is to be blamed for its ill fate, not the society which enslaves and exploits it' (Beltran, 1976: 25). Much of the earlier communication research with its exaggerated emphasis on the individual-blame causal hypothesis to social problems, obfuscated the social-structural, political, and institutional constraints acting in concert against the individual's efforts to change. Thus, the use of the individual as the unit of response and analysis has led to the use of the individual as the unit of change and consequently, the unit of blame.

Social-Structural Barriers to Change

More recently, communication research has given increasing attention to the role of larger social-structural and economic factors in a particular society rather than individual factors in development. It was observed that these structural constraints have produced an unequal distribution of important resources such as wealth, land, skills, and information among the people in Third World countries (Narula and Pearce, 1986). These inequalities have had a deleterious effect on the nature of innovation diffusion and who among the recipients reaps the advantages and disadvantages of such change (Rogers, 1976a). It has been found that the socio-economic structure has invariably favored adoption of innovations by individuals with higher socio-economic status, i.e., those who own more land, have higher economic and educational status, and ample mass communication activities, thus resulting in greater inequality (Beltran, 1976; Rogers and Adhikarya, 1979). In short, in developing nations, the mass media communicated innovations down the social structure leaving the structure of dependence intact.

The influence of social-structural variables as mediating factors in communication and change has led to a reconceptualization of the role of communication in national development. What is apparent 'from the results of research in rural development over the past two decades, is the need to consider communication not as a simple independent variable but as both a dependent and independent variable in a complex set of relationships with social, economic and political structures and processes' (Shore, 1980: 21). Also, the influence of the social structure on the individual adopter points to the fact that the main barriers to development, at least in Latin America, are not psychological or primarily informative, as assumed, but mainly structural, and that a restructuring of society is a prerequisite for the achievement of humane development (Eapen, 1973; Diaz-Bordenave, 1976; Beltran, 1976; Rogers and Adhikarya, 1979; McAnany, 1980b).

Political Constraints to Change

Research has shown that in the Third World, quite often the people who are supposed to be the prime beneficiaries of development are not reached at all, or only a smaller segment of the groups is actually exposed to the message (Lenglet, 1980). Access of subsistence peasants to media resources is a crucial constraint in many developing countries:

> Those farmers with higher education, higher reading ability, greater exposure to other media, and higher standards of living (half of whom were already well-informed and had less need for the information) attended programs (media shows) more frequently than those with less education, less reading ability, limited exposure to other media, and a lower standard of living (Shingi and Mody, 1976: 94).

These findings confirm that the highest attendence is usually among those who have access to other sources of information. The rural poor in developing nations have very limited access to the media. In most of these countries there is an unequal distribution of mass media characterized by urban concentration and rural starvation of media materials. And, recent research indicates that there is an important imbalance within rural areas itself where the elite have better access and exposure to media sources (Beltran, 1974; Eapen, 1975; Shore, 1980; Khan, 1987).

The quality and content of mass media messages too leave much to be desired. The modern media in most Third World nations are controlled by the urbanites and other elite sources and the quality and content of messages are not well-suited for rural audiences (Beltran, 1974; Eapen, 1975). Further, very little time and space are accorded to developmental information in the mass media. Shore (1980) quoted studies on the content of newspapers, radio, and television which suggest that information relevant to development is given less preference than trivial and non-development oriented subjects. Thus, it is seen that the poor, disadvantaged sections in rural areas of the Third World live in a state of 'under-communication'.

Attempts at improving the lot of the rural poor, however, face political constraints. Though the rural poor need all the help they can get, local governments do not have the political will to ameliorate their present condition. McAnany (1980a) pointed out that though communication projects for the rural people promise to save money, most often the costs are based upon comparison with delivering information to urban audiences or the highly motivated elite in rural areas and not the most disadvantaged rural masses. He concluded, 'the approach to a "solution" to the problems of the rural poor is a political one, rooted in the history of the country and the structures that continue to support the status quo' (McAnany, 1980a: 11).

McAnany's comment deserves attention particularly when reviewing the recent history of many developing nations in Asia and Africa. These nations gained independence from European colonial powers only in the preceding twenty-five to forty years, and the political structures that exist today have been largely developed after their independence. The histories of these nations have been distorted by the colonial powers and restoration to an independent status has only created new problems (Eapen, 1973). National geographic boundaries were drawn arbitrarily by the colonial powers before political independence, leading to frequent factional fights and boundary disputes between neighboring countries. Furthermore, the governments and political structures left behind in many of the new nations did not usually fit into the traditional mold, giving rise to complex problems. Thus, the

political structures in many of these nations have become square
pegs in round holes.

Ideological Constraints

Why was there a benign neglect of social-structural and political
constraints to development in the mass media and modernization
theories in the fifties and sixties? Latin American scholars contended that this neglect was neither conspiratorial nor accidental.
Instead, in developing nations, the field of scientific thought in
general, and communication research in particular, was influenced
by *alien premises, objects and methods* (Beltran, 1976). The definitions of concepts, the role and functions of the mass media, indeed
the field itself were incompatible or irrelevant to the needs and
problems of the Third World.

Latin American scholars such as Beltran and Diaz-Bordenave
noted that much of the initial work in the discipline of communication was done principally in the United States of America, and
mostly by psychologists, political scientists, and sociologists. The
study of communication was strongly influenced by the disciplinary
perspectives of these other social sciences. In the infant stage,
communication models stressed political persuasion and propaganda. The problems were uniquely American: the nation was at
war during the First and Second World Wars; the mass media were
used to gain internal support and cohesion, and for propaganda
against the enemy. However, after the War, the knowledge gained
in media effects was applied to other important objectives in
peace-time America. It was used to improve commercial advertising techniques, radio ratings, and in election campaigns.

In the fifties and sixties, the communication models were exported
to the Third World nations. Here is when the mismatch occurred.
Quite clearly, the scientific knowledge, research, models, etc. that
were exported were best suited to the socio-economic, political,
cultural, and structural arrangement in the United States. And,
the United States was no Third World. Beltran (1976: 23) noted:

> What kind of society hosted these remarkable scientific ex-
> periments and advancements? Was it an unhappy one

burdened by poverty, afflicted by social conflict, and shaken by instability? Not at all. It was basically a prosperous, content, peaceful and stable society.... It was also a society where individuality was predominant over collectivism, competition was more determinant than cooperation, and economic efficiency and technological wisdom were more important than cultural growth, social justice, and spiritual enhancement.

Obviously, the knowledge generated by such a society would strive to achieve the conformity of individuals to the prevailing norms and behaviors. In other words, it would be a science striving to maintain the status quo. The discipline of communication had similar objectives. If the need was to help individuals adjust to the dominant social ethic, 'communication scientists had to find those personality traits which would render them amenable to persuasion. Accordingly, they had to invent media and message strategies able to produce in them the desired behaviors' (Beltran, 1976: 23).

Thus, the emphasis was on curbing individual aberrance. An early, influential communication model of Lasswell, was obsessed with persuasion of the receiver to the objectives of the source. The social context, however, was irrelevant. The functionalistic paradigm of Merton and other American sociologists further supported the need to help individuals be persuaded to conform to the existing arrangements in the society. The locus of change then was not the society but the aberrant individual.

The scenario in Latin America and the newly independent nations in Asia and Africa was quite different from that of the United States or West Europe. These nations were afflicted by poverty, gross inequality among their citizens, a rigid social structure, political instability, and other negative consequences of their earlier colonized status. The models of adjustment and conformity and persuasion of individuals toward a status quo were clearly incompatible with and irrelevant to the problems these nations were facing. The locus of attention was to be the entire society. Beltran (1976: 26) outlined several questions that the mass media had to address in the Third World nations:

Who owns the media today and to which interest groups are they responsive? Are there ethical limits to persuasion proficiency? Must feedback forever remain no more than a tool for securing the intended response? Does the state exert any control over North American communication interests overseas? How far should advertising be allowed to keep exacerbating consuming behavior in a time of serious economic crisis?

Diaz-Bordenave (1976: 54) posited other concerns:

How autonomous or independent is the country from external forces which affect its economy and its political decisions? How is the rural structure organized and what influence does it exert over individual decision-making? Who controls the economic institutions, particularly the market, credit, and input supply organizations?

These questions, that were hardly ever asked by communication scholars in the fifties and the sixties, were much more relevant to the unique problems and needs of the Third World nations. At least in Latin America, scholars contended that the problem was not one of maintaining the status quo but that of restructuring the socio-economic polity so that it could better serve humane development objectives. These, however, were not the dominant concerns of American communication scholars such as Schramm, Lerner, De Sola Pool and others in the fifties and sixties (Schramm, 1954).

The cure for the ills of underdevelopment was prescribed in terms of their knowledge and experience in the United States. Schemes which worked well for the Western nations were recommended to solve the problems in the developing nations. Thus, the Third World was told that more and more of the mass media was the solution for speedy modernization without ascertaining whether the mass media were actually needed in such numbers. This dubious argument was supported by the American-influenced Unesco's minimum standards for media development which recommended:

10 copies of the daily newspaper per 100 persons
5 radio receivers per 100 persons
2 cinema seats per 100 persons
2 television receivers per 100 persons

This was clearly the American notion of media development.

As Tunstall points out, 'typically only daily newspapers were mentioned although their relevance in rural areas of many poor countries is small, since a daily paper may in any case take several days to arrive from the nearest big city' (Tunstall, 1977: 211). The weekly newspapers and magazines were more relevant to the conditions in these countries and they also helped to conserve precious newsprint. Tunstall went on to point out that the Unseco figures for the electronic media were even more doubtful. 'The two cinema seats and two television sets per 100 population would obviously be concentrated in urban areas, whereas the five radio sets per 100 was too low to emphasize the possibility of making radio available to almost the entire population' (Tunstall, 1977: 212). In a nutshell, the Unesco recommendations considered socio-economic change in the Third World to be synonymous with the development of media hardware and software.

The hard-sell of Western communication models inhibited local ideas and planning more relevant to the conditions in the developing countries. To quote Tunstall again, 'for at least some nations in Africa and Asia an alternate set of targets might have stressed a high ratio of weekly papers and magazines per population, complete halt on cinema and television expansion, and a high ratio of radio sets to population... these are some possibilities among many—but the failure of Unesco to state such simple alternatives was a serious weakness' (Tunstall, 1977: 212). Thus, the Western communication models overvalued communication technology as a solution for social problems in the developing nations of Asia, Africa, and Latin America.

Critique of the Role of the Mass Media in Development

An implicit assumption running through the literature in the dominant paradigm was that the mass media (especially the electronic media) in developing nations carried a strong pro-development content (Rogers, 1969; Douglass, 1971). The argument went that increased exposure to mass media messages would obviously create the 'climate for modernization' in villages in the Third World (Lerner, 1958; Schramm, 1964). This view of the pro-development content of media messages was not entirely correct.

Larry Shore cited a substantial amount of research, done mostly on the content of newspapers and some on radio and television in Latin America, which suggested that consistently less preference was given to information relevant to development than to trivial and non-development oriented subjects such as sports or entertainment (Shore, 1980).

The main architects of the communication approach in the dominant paradigm such as Lerner (1958), Pye (1963), Schramm (1964), and Frey (1966) did not examine the relationship between the institutional structures of the media and their impact on the media content. Maybe, it was consistent with the underlying bias of examining the mass media devoid of their relationship to and with social structural factors. Thus, it could have been quite likely that messages preaching conspicuous consumption may have been a part of the larger construct of social-structural and economic dynamics that hindered humane development in the Third World (Fjes, 1976; Hamelink, 1983). In fact, Rogers (1976b: 135) made an astute observation concerning this phenomenon:

By the late 1960s and the 1970s a number of critical evaluations were being made of the mass communication role in development. Some scholars, especially in Latin America, perceived the mass media in their nations as an extension of exploitative relationships with the U.S.-based multinational corporations, especially through advertising of commercial products. Further, questions were asked about the frequent patterns of elite ownership and control of mass media institutions in Latin America and the influence of such ownership on the media content.

Even if governments in some developing countries actively promote a pro-development content in their mass media, it has to be viewed from the perspective of the total program structure constructed for each medium and the total time allotted to each type of program. For example, although the government in India is committed to rural development and carries rural programs which are clearly pro-development, the total percentage of such programs is very low. In 'home-service' radio programs, only 5.8 percent of total program time was devoted to rural programs while 40 percent of broadcast time was claimed by music and 24.8 percent by news (Government of India, 1979, 1982). There is here the anomaly of rural programs being pro-development but the total time accorded to such programs being rather insignificant.

Assuming that much of the media messages in developing nations are pro-development, there is still reason to be concerned about other factors. First, there is the question of selective exposure of the audience to particular media messages because, more often than not, such selectivity is towards messages which may not be pro-development. As Rogers observed on one of his visits to a village in a developing nation, 'the only radio in the village, owned by the president of the village council, was tuned to music rather than to news of the outside world' (Rogers, 1969: 96). Second, there is the question of comprehension of the media content even if the rural peasant chose to listen to pro-development programs. The absence of programming in regional language or major dialects, and the irrelevant content due to the largely urban control of media production in many developing nations make the message unsuitable for rural audiences (Masani, 1975). The development communication literature, due to its inadequate consideration of media message content (Vilanilam, 1979) and differences in their use and perception by the audiences, has made very little contribution to the understanding and solution of these problems.

In many developing nations, the mass media in their present form are not suited for the kinds of developmental tasks they have to perform and Western-originated examples and assumptions are irrelevant in the Third World situation (Eapen, 1975; Masani, 1975). An adequate response to the challenging task of rural development in developing nations would:

> involve a re-consideration of the structure of the broadcasting system, the location of transmitters and studios and the language and content of programs.... It is clear that unless policies are changed, the services expanded and decentralized there is little chance of the mass media playing a significant role in bringing about rural change (Masani, 1975: 2).

Revolution of Rising Frustrations

Lerner (1958) posited that by exposing individuals in developing nations to images of modernity and prosperity in the Western nations, the mass media could not only instill the modern values and behaviors but eventually help bring about a *revolution of rising expectations*. However, by avoiding a thorough examination of the social-structural constraints in developing nations, the scholars made faulty use of the mass media. By exposing people (through the mass media) to images of the West without the same conditions as in the West, individuals in the Third World were forced to behave irrationally (Fjes, 1976). For example, there was a serious imbalance in the want/get ratio. The mass media were successful in raising aspirations of people in the Third World but the governments were not capable of satisfying the new wants. Thus, what resulted was a *revolution of rising frustrations* (Lerner, 1958).

Knowledge Gap Hypothesis

In developing nations, the mass media—like other social institutions—can reinforce or increase existing inequities between the advantaged and disadvantaged sectors of the population. This 'increasing knowledge gap' first proposed by Tichenor and others (1970) remained largely unexamined in early communication research. They proposed the hypothesis that:

> As the infusion of mass media information into a social system increases, segments of the population with higher socio-economic status tend to acquire this information at a faster rate than the lower status segments, so that the gap in knowledge between these segments tends to increase rather than decrease (Tichenor et al., 1970: 159).

The existence of this gap does not mean that the lower status population remain totally uninformed or even absolutely worse off in knowledge, but rather that they become relatively lower in knowledge, thus giving rise to the *gap*

The authors posited several reasons for the knowledge gap to occur and widen with increasing media flow: (*i*) differential levels of communication skills (that is, persons with more formal education had higher reading and comprehension capabilities) between segments of the total audience; (*ii*) amounts of stored information or existing knowledge due to prior exposure to the topic (such receivers of communication were better prepared to understand the next communication); (*iii*) relevant social contact (there could be a greater number of people in the reference groups of the more advantaged sector, and these receivers may also have had greater interpersonal contact with other information-rich individuals); and (*iv*) selective exposure, acceptance, and retention of information (higher education could be related to greater voluntary exposure to communication). Thus, to the extent that the above factors were operative, the gap would widen as heavy mass media influx continued (Tichenor et al., 1970).

This knowledge gap could be socially significant. Differentials in knowledge could lead to greater tension in a social system, giving rise to greater disparities between different sectors of the population:

> In developing countries like India, most development benefits have tended to accrue to better-off segments rather than to the downtrodden for whom they may ostensibly have been intended. A much discussed case in point is the so-called Green Revolution that benefited the larger farmers and widened existing socio-economic gaps. Given their higher levels of knowledge, capital and social contact, it is not surprising that the 'haves' achieve greater effects from exposure to most interpersonal and mass media information sources (Shingi and Mody, 1976: 83).

Critique of the Models and Research Design

Critics pointed out serious problems with the conceptual underpinnings, the models, and the underlying assumptions of the mass media and modernization approach. For example, the scholarly work in communication and development in the fifties and sixties conceptualized the mass media as having direct and powerful effects on receivers in developing nations. This was essentially a recreation of the *magic bullet theory* of communication. However, the notion of an all-powerful media acting on defenseless receivers was tested extensively in the forties and fifties in the United States and was found wanting and discarded. Thus, we notice the recycling of rejected theories for analyzing the effects of the mass media in developing nations.

Much of the earlier research, especially Lerner's classic study in the Middle East, was done at the height of the Cold War between the United States and Soviet Russia. While the communist nations were criticized for their propaganda and indoctrination, the direct effects model of Western researchers was welcomed even though it attempted to manipulate people into discarding traditional values and behaviors and adopting *modern* ways (Golding, 1974). There were other inconsistencies in the underlying assumptions. For example, the 19th century concept of the *mass society* was overwhelmingly rejected in the West by the forties. The mass society concept stated that in an industrial society, people are isolated from each other, suffer anomie, and do not have meaningful ties to other individuals. However, by the forties it was shown that even within an 'impersonal' industrial society, people belonged to important social groups and had close interpersonal relationships with others in their subgroups. However, when turning to developing nations, researchers implied a mass society phenomenon wherein people, lacking significant group ties, were readily available for conversion by the mass media.

In the theories on modernization, the mass media were regarded as the independent variables. Was this an accurate assessment of the nature and role of the mass media in developing nations? Probably not. Beltran (1976) noted that a serious problem in mass communication models was to regard the mass media as playing an independent role in bringing about social change. However, other propositions were not tested adequately. It would have been equally probable to consider the mass media as a dependent variable, being affected by the variables such as the social structure, elite ownership of mass media institutions and their effects on media content, or the role of the mass media in helping to legitimize the status quo in Third World countries. Later studies showed the mass media as intervening variables in the process of change. The antecedent or independent variables were literacy, education, social status, age, and cosmopoliteness, while the dependent variables were empathy, achievement motivation, educational and occupational aspirations, innovativeness, and political awareness. Fjes argues that it could have been possible that 'the antecedent characteristics correlate directly with the consequent characteristics. A high degree of media exposure could very well be just another attribute of what is defined as a *modern* person' (Fjes, 1976: 11).

There were other methodological concerns. The partial correlations used to indicate the intervening nature of mass media exposure between the independent and dependent variables were not significantly different from direct or zero-order correlations. This raised questions on the intervening nature of the mass media variable. Also, as Rogers acknowledged, the correlational analysis did not reveal the time-order nature of these relationships. Part of this problem was the nature of correlational data and the abundance of one-shot cross-sectional surveys and the relative lack of experimental designs in development communication studies (Rogers, 1969).

While communication was conceptualized as a process, the models used failed to show that clearly. Early models of communication were one-way, top-down, and linear. Diaz-Bordenave (1977) called this the *transmission mentality*, a conceptualization that did not incorporate the transactional or the multidimensional nature of communication.

Problems with Operational Definitions

Operational measures for important concepts such as empathy and fatalism among the Third World peasants did not actually measure these variables. As Golding (1974: 47) noted:

> the scale of nine items Lerner used to measure empathy may or may not measure the ability to identify with other roles. His respondents were asked, 'what would you do if you were...?' in circumstances of counterfactuality. Furthermore, all questions require upward empathy of low-status actors.

In a study conducted by Gans (1962), American slum dwellers, whom he called *urban villagers*, were shown to score very low on empathy scales. Thus, Golding concluded that for the American slum dwellers as well as for the Third World peasant, such as Lerner's Balgat goatherd, 'the perception of massive structural constraints against upward mobility mitigates against "role empathy" far more than does an inert imagination' (Golding, 1974: 47). Thus, he concluded that empathy rather than being the cause of fatalism was actually the result of frustrated experience. Thus, operational problems with important concepts were largely due to the researcher's poor knowledge of the respondents and their cultural milieu. It was really the researchers who lacked empathy with their respondents and their cultures.

CRITIQUE OF DIFFUSION OF INNOVATIONS RESEARCH

The critique of the diffusion of innovations approach is categorized under three heads: (*i*) Theoretical biases in diffusion of innovations research; (*ii*) Conceptual and methodological biases; and (*iii*) Social-structural constraints to diffusion of innovations.

Theoretical Biases in Diffusion of Innovation Research

Communication Effects Bias

The predominant concern of communication research has been the effects of a particular source, medium, message or a combination of these elements on the receiver. Rogers noted, 'Much present-day communication research focuses on the effects of the source, message, or channel on change in knowledge, attitudes, and overt behavior of the receiver' (Rogers, 1969: 49). This explicit attention given to the general question of communication effects in the modernization process was also present in much of classical diffusion research. The communication effects orientation gave undue importance to the question of exposure to the mass media. 'Larger mass media audiences, accompanied by high levels of mass media exposure per capita, can be expected to lead those exposed to more favorable attitudes toward change and development, to greater awareness of political events, and to more knowledge of technical information' (Rogers, 1969: 101).

Inattention to Message Content

The obsession with effects of the mass media on behavior alteration through increased exposure gave little consideration to the content of the messages to which the audience was exposed. In fact, there was an implicit assumption that any kind of mass media exposure would lead to development:

> Nor does our measure of exposure consider the specific nature of the messages received from the mass media— whether musical, news, or technical content. It should be

remembered that exposure, not influence or *internalization*, of mass media messages is what is being dealt with here (Rogers, 1969: 101).

The methodology, therefore, in much of classical diffusion of innovations studies revealed a serious shortcoming. As no attempt was made to discover the type of media messages to which the audience was exposed, little or no attention was given to the content and quality of information, knowledge, and skills emanating from the messages. The corollary to this was that there was no attempt to investigate whether the content of the messages was internalized by the audience, i.e. if the messages were consumable, reliable, and efficient, leading to internalization of the message. The mass media exposure index was constructed thus: the respondents' indications of degree of exposure to each medium, in terms of number of radio shows listened to per week, and so on, contributing to form a standard score (Rogers, 1969). This quantitative approach to media exposure revealed nothing of the respondents' media message preferences: the respondent could have been listening to music, news, plays, talk, or even static noise from the radio set. The lack of the qualitative indication, therefore, made no measurement of what programs the respondent listened to on the radio or watched on television, whether these programs were pro-development, neutral, or anti-development in content, the quality and relevance of the programs, and differences in their use and perception (Golding, 1974).

The lack of adequate interest in the content of media messages and, consequently, individual or group differences in their use and perception led to a lack of interest in the second dimension of communication effects. Most diffusion of innovations studies focused predominantly on the first dimension, i.e. the behavioral dimension of communication effects. They posed such questions as: 'Has there been any effect of the media on respondents' behavior? If so, what has been the nature and direction of that effect on adoption behavior?' Very rarely did research seek to investigate another dimension on media effects on the audience: the cognitive dimension or what they know. Diffusion studies did not posit such questions as: Did the communication attempt have a relatively greater effect on the cognition of certain receivers than on others? Why? Whereas the first question asked about the level of communication effects on adoption behavior, the second question directed communication research to the differential levels of cognition among receivers and to the concern with knowledge gaps (Shingi and Mody, 1976). The lack of such focus, therefore, did not reveal to the early researchers the potential inequality media exposure could breed by creating 'knowledge gaps' among different sections of the audience, particularly the disadvantaged sections with a low socio-economic status (Tichenor et al., 1970).

Shallow Depth of Knowledge

The important dependent variable in most diffusion studies was adoption of non-traditional innovations by peasants. In the measurement of this consequent variable, however, most studies revealed methodological and conceptual weaknesses. Insufficient attention and treatment were given to the amount and depth of knowledge and skills the respondent possessed prior to the adoption decision. Shingi and Mody (1976) report that diffusion students substituted the broader concept of knowledge of innovations with the more easily measurable concept of awareness of new practices. The empirical definition of the awareness of an innovation was confined to '*Have you heard of ...*' types of queries and did not measure '*how to*' knowledge consisting of information vital for the efficient use of an innovation, and '*principles-knowledge*' dealing with the fundamental principles underlying an innovation. Thus, in the correlational analyses of diffusion studies the farmer variables were associated with this rather limited concept of knowledge of new practices with no measurement of the shallow depth of such knowledge or their conditional association with adoption. Shingi and Mody cautioned that 'the long-range competence of farmers to evaluate and adopt (or reject) future innovations is not directly facilitated by mere awareness of a great number of innovations.... In our opinion, the innovation-decision process is considered to be initiated not when the individual is merely exposed to information on the innovation but when he gains some understanding of how it functions' (Shingi and Mody, 1976: 95).

Conceptual and Methodological Biases in Diffusion of Innovations Research

The lack of innovativeness among diffusion researchers in

employing experimental and panel study designs in place of the familiar *post hoc* one-shot surveys gave rise to important conceptual and methodological biases (Rogers, 1976a): (*i*) A pro-innovation bias, (*ii*) Lack of a process orientation, and (*iii*) Neglect of causality. A discussion of these biases will be useful.

A Pro-Innovation Bias

An implicit assumption running through diffusion tenets was that adoption of non-traditional innovations would be advantageous to all potential adopters. While this assumption was true in a few cases, it could not, however, be justified in a majority of cases in the rural Third World where the innovations were clearly ill-adapted to local conditions (Rogers, 1976a; Roling et al., 1976). An example of the incompatibility of technological innovations with local practices was in the area of traditional subsistence farming in the rural Third World. Bortei-Doku (1978) noted that diffusion researchers arrived in peasant communities with a built-in bias toward Western ideals of agricultural practice with its orientation to permanent commercial enterprises concerned with plant population per unit area, planting distances, fertilizer use and other technologies primarily developed for single-crop systems. The mixed cropping and shifting agriculture practiced in developing countries were considered backward. In fact, the very nature of mixed cropping prevented easy application of scientific technological recommendations about planting distances, crop protection, and the application of fertilizers and pesticides. Thus, the peasants were persuaded to adopt the single-crop system with all its attendant technologies to ensure increased productivity. However, this innovation was not only incompatible with local conditions but also complex for the poor, illiterate farmers. If the small farmer was reluctant to adopt the innovation, it was not because he did not care to increase his productivity with the new techniques. Instead, there were many factors which served to perpetuate his practice of traditional farming:

> The truth of the matter is that traditional farm practices are based on the farmer's concept of the most efficient use of his land, given his available resources. Lacking financial resources not only to invest in cash crops but also to tide him

over till they mature and produce food-purchasing means for himself, his priority crops became those which guaranteed him his subsistence with minimum risk. To make sure he has a good supply in the early part of the growing season, he mixes his crops, planting, for example, early millet with some later maturing crop. Lacking the labor to clear and maintain large tracts of land, he farms on small manageable plots, mixing his crops to ensure himself self-sufficient variety.... Unable to obtain a loan to purchase a plough or hire a tractor for deep ploughing, he scrabbles the land with a hoe, dibbling corn on it with a pointed stick (Bortei-Doku, 1978: 4).

Thus, adopting the new innovation or adapting it to his traditional system was too risky for him to bear alone. Experimentation could lead to relative successes but then there was a greater likelihood of crop failure due to inadequate knowledge of application of modern technologies and methods.

A Step Forward or is it Backward?

New methods are not always better as illustrated by the failure of the Gezira Scheme in Sudan (*Wall Street Journal*, 1981). Before modern agricultural methods were adopted in this cotton growing area, the average yield was about five bales of cotton per acre a year. Now, the yield is about two bales per acre.

The *Wall Street Journal* notes that the problems began in the seventies when the government decided to increase the output at Gezira by adopting modern farming methods. Some of the innovations were the use of modern fertilizers, pesticides, crop rotations, and more frequent irrigation to improve fields. 'But the new farming techniques undermined the traditional balance in the Gezira. The initial dose of pesticides, for example, killed predators of the white fly but left the cotton crop more vulnerable than before. Worse, the Sudanese found themselves locked into ever-rising costs. Where they had initially planned only one spraying of pesticides annually, Gezira agronomists soon found it necessary to spray upto seven times a year. They didn't have enough money for the required crop dusting planes' (Wall Street Journal, 1981). There were other problems. The increased use of irrigation carried silt and other debris which choked the canals and ditches. Some of them were so full of mud and weeds that the simple gravity-flow system became ineffective. But the farmers could not afford the excavation equipment needed to reopen the choked canals.

The *Journal* neatly sums up the situation: 'That a step forward in technology should be followed by a step backward in production is an anomaly of economic life in poor countries such as Sudan, where the simple ways of the past sometimes work better than expensive new ways' (*Wall Street Journal,* 1981).

A discussion of the pro-innovation bias brings to the surface an aspect which has not received much attention from diffusion theorists: the painful contradiction between diffusion theory and its practice. Early diffusion research delineated the characteristics of the innovation itself which would affect its rate of acceptance (or rejection) by the potential adopter. Some of these factors were (as explained in Chapter 3): relative advantage, compatibility, complexity, divisibility, and communicability. Rogers, who coined these terms (1962: 124), underlined their importance:

It matters very little whether or not an innovation has a great degree of advantage over the idea it replaces. What does matter is whether the individual perceives the relative advantage of the innovations. Likewise, it is the potential adopter's perceptions of the compatibility, complexity, divisibility, and communicability of the innovation that affect its rate of adoption.

Yet, from some of the examples illustrated above it may be surmised that very limited attention was given in diffusion practice to the characteristics of an innovation before it was diffused and no study has looked into this anomaly. Therefore, the pro-innovation bias has been, in essence, the lack of a critical assessment of the innovation itself.

Absence of a Process Orientation

There was a misalignment between what the communication theorists defined and what the researcher actually measured. Though communication has always been conceptualized as a process in communication research, the research designs in diffusion studies mostly consisted of analyses of cross-sectional data collected through surveys at a single point in time (Rogers, 1976a). The dynamic process conceptualization of communication was thus obscured in this approach:

Very few communication research include data at more than one observation point, and almost none at more than two such points in time. So almost all communication research is unable to trace the change in a variable over time; it deals only with the present-tense of behavior. Communication thus becomes, in the actuality of communication research, an artificially halted snapshot (Rogers, 1976a: 209).

Mainstream diffusion researchers did not just obscure the concept of communication as a process. In fact, they distorted the concept of communication process itself. Contrary to the assertion of Rogers in the above quotation that research deals with the present-tense of behavior, diffusion research dealt not with the present-tense but the past-tense of behavior. In the correlational analyses, the dependent variable of innovativeness was measured with recall data about past adoption behavior. The diffusion research, therefore, went into the history of adoption behavior of the recipient and constructed, not an 'artificially halted snapshot', but an artificially constructed movie or biographical history of the adopter.

The pro-innovation bias coupled with an overwhelming use of *post hoc* survey design confined the focus of diffusion research to testing of strategies of *what is* or reaffirming current practice rather than *what might be* or testing alternative strategies. Since the innovation was thought to be good for the adopter and the present process of diffusion satisfactory, the survey design was used to replicate the status quo. There was no attempt to use field experimental designs and go beyond current practice to gain knowledge of effective means to reach an alternative, desired state (Roling, 1973; Roling et al., 1976).

Neglect of Causality

The terms 'independent' and 'dependent' variables, borrowed from experimental designs, were used incorrectly and ambiguously in correlational analyses. In an experimental design, an independent variable X could cause a dependent variable Y if, (*i*) X occurs before Y in a temporal sequence, and (*ii*) they co-vary. In most diffusion studies, as Rogers notes, the only aspect which was investigated was whether the independent variable co-varied with the dependent variable (innovativeness). The use of the *post hoc* one-shot survey design prevented the determination of time-order sequence between X and Y. Thus, it was seen that the dependent variable of innovativeness was measured with recall data about past adoption behavior whereas the independent variables were measured in the present tense. This virtually resulted in independent variables following the dependent variable of innovativeness in temporal sequence and yet leading to adoption of an innovation (Rogers, 1976a). In short, this was methodologically incorrect and impossible.

A discussion of the foregoing methodological and conceptual biases reveals the *post hoc* preoccupation of diffusion research with already diffused innovations. The diffusion tenets, Ascroft noted, 'provided researchers with few insights about strategies for 'pushing' the process, for 'causing' it to occur more rapidly, reliably, efficiently and completely' (Ascroft and Gleason, 1980: 3). The dearth of experimental designs in diffusion theory, therefore, gave rise to biases such as lack of process orientation, a pro-innovation bias and neglect of the issue of causality. This lack of an experimental approach in earlier research may perhaps be the reason for the theory being stunted.

In addition to these three biases, there are many more which have not been stated explicitly in diffusion literature.

Pro-Source Bias

While diffusion literature elaborately discussed the weaknesses, shortcomings or deficiencies of receivers impeding the adoption process, there was little or no research into the shortcomings and deficiencies of the source or initiator of the innovation. The source was considered to be faultless and blameless and any anomaly in the diffusion process was attributed to the recalcitrance of the receivers. There was even an explicit assumption that the source knew what kind of change was desirable for the adopter. This can be seen in the manner in which a change agent was defined: 'A change agent is a professional who influences innovation decisions in a direction deemed desirable by a change agency' (Rogers, 1969: 169). This pro-source bias had its roots in the influence of the dominant paradigm on diffusion research. The top-down, one-way, linear model of message flow in the dominant paradigm, by its very nature, supported the source against the receiver. Diffusion research, influenced as it was by the paradigm, could not overcome this bias.

In-the-Head Variable Bias

Much of diffusion research was preoccupied with such in-the-head variables of the receivers as empathy, familism and fatalism about which nothing much could be done. As Roling (1973) noted, such an orientation resulted in diffusion research dwelling at length on the relationship between variables which were not manipulable. Diffusion literature, partly because of its *post hoc* orientation, usually aimed at reaching conclusions about peasant communities instead of finding out methods and techniques of changing these communities. Use of over-time research designs and deciding what the goal of diffusion campaign was and working back from that point, would have revealed a number of other manipulable variables. One such variable, for example, was the knowledge variable, the lack of which was acting as a crucial constraint to adoption. However, much of the diffusion research chose to study non-manipulable variables in current practice and seldom about what would happen if one tried to change current practice (Roling, 1973).

Pro-Persuasion Bias

The preoccupation with effects, as illustrated in an earlier section, implied that the aim of communication research was to determine the persuasiveness of messages in changing the respondent's behavior for whatever purpose. This pro-effects and pro-persuasion bias was also inherent in much of diffusion research. An important task for diffusion researchers was to change the multitudes of ignorant peasants from a 'traditional' to a 'modern' way of life mostly through persuasion. However, by using the persuasion approach there was an implication that these peasants were resistant to change. This approach influenced a dichotomous categorization of respondents into the *persuasible* and the *recalcitrant*. An investigation of the analysis of adoption curves would show that those who were persuaded to adopt non-traditional innovations were literate with superior mental ability, they had higher social status, they had exposure to many channels of communication, and so on, while non-adopters comprised the resistant group which was open only to the most localite sources of information and generally ignorant of the process of modernization (Rogers, 1962). There is a logical inconsistency in this approach. How could a group which had little information on the new methods and generally ignorant of the modernization process be resistant? Logically, an individual can effectively resist a new idea or practice if he has sufficient knowledge about it and can logically and rationally argue against its acceptance. This pre-occupation with effects and persuasion, therefore, did not ensure that the receivers knew enough about the innovation to start with. Did the receivers understand what change was expected of them? Did they have sufficient information and knowledge to adopt a non-traditional innovation? Rather than such queries, an attempt was made to persuade people to change without checking if the prerequisites for that change were fulfilled. As illustrated above, those who were most resistant to change were also the most ignorant. Hence, the test of resistance cannot be made until the pro-persuasion approach is preceded by a pro-information strategy.

One-Way Message Flow Bias

On a macro level too, there were conceptual biases. The implicit assumption in diffusion research was that changes within developing nations occur exogenously. It was only through continuing contact with Western ideas and technology that nations of the Third World could become modern. This was the overall framework within which much of the work on communication and development occurred (Fjes, 1976). This assumption was reinforced by the dominant paradigm of development giving rise to the idea of a one-way, dependent relationship. This approach, to quote Rahim, 'has tended to block the researcher from seeing the reverse flow of ideas and innovations from the poor to the rich, from the less developed to the more developed, from the peasants to the technicians, administrators, and scientists' (Rahim, 1976: 224). Thus, in diffusion research there was not only a North to South [1] communication flow between nations, but even within a nation, there was a top-down message flow from administrators, scientists, and donor agencies, to rural peasants. Thus, in a nutshell, the flow of communication was from a Northerner to a North-like-Southerner[2] in the developing nations, and from him/her to the

[1] The industrialized democracies are termed *North* while most of the Third World nations are identified as *South*.
[2] The elite in Third World countries.

rural peasants. This one-way message flow, as explained earlier with the example of a multicropping agricultural system, could not see the virtue of traditional methods. Discussing multicropping traditional agriculture, an FAO report said: 'There are increasing indications that such systems should not be rejected wholesale as primitive and uneconomical. In fact, it appears that past research aimed at improving cropping systems had not shown enough attention to some of the techniques developed by small farmers, and that a scientific approach to such systems can sometimes give better results than the use of technology primarily developed for single-crop systems' (FAO, 1977). So, as Bortei-Doku (1978) pointed out, instead of finding ways to adapt new technology to existing patterns of farming, efforts were made to train a whole new generation of farmers through agricultural institutes. 'Such trainees, however, hardly ever returned to the farm to apply their new knowledge. They went instead in search of government jobs as field assistants and technical officers, leaving the problem of the development and improvement of traditional agriculture largely unsolved' (Bortei-Doku, 1978: 4). Instances such as these could have been avoided to a great extent in diffusion research had accommodated reverse flow of ideas and practices from peasants to scientists or donor agencies.

Flow of Innovations Can Be a Multi-Way Process

Flow of ideas and innovations can and has been a multi-way process. The cultural diffusionists cited numerous instances in human history of the flow of innovations between different cultures (Linton, 1936; Foster, 1962; Heine-Geldern, 1968). An excerpt from Linton (1936) brings home this point:

Our solid American citizen awakens in a bed built on a pattern which originated in the Near East but which was modified in Northern Europe before it was transmitted to America. He throws back covers made from cotton, domesticated in India, or linen domesticated in the Near East, or silk, the use of which was discovered in China. All of these materials have been spun and woven by processes invented in the Near East. He slips into his mocassins, invented by the Indians of the Eastern woodlands, and goes to the bathroom, whose fixtures are a mixture of

European and American inventions, both of recent date. He takes off his pajamas, a garment invented in India, and washes with soap invented by the ancient Gauls. He then shaves, a masochistic rite which seems to have been derived from either Sumer or ancient Egypt. Returning to the bedroom, he removes his clothes from a chair of Southern European type and proceeds to dress. He puts on garments whose form originally derived from the skin clothing of the nomads of the Asiatic steppes, puts on shoes made from skins tanned by a process invented in ancient Egypt and cut to a pattern derived from the classic civilizations of the Mediterrranean, and ties around his neck a strip of bright-colored cloth which is a vestigial survival of the shoulder shawls worn by the seventeenth-century Croatians. Before going out to breakfast he glances through the window, made of glass invented in Egypt, and if it is raining puts on overshoes made of rubber discovered by the central American Indians and takes an umbrella invented in Southeastern Asia. Upon his head he puts a hat made of felt, a material invented in the Asiatic steppes. On his way to breakfast he stops to buy a paper, paying for it with coins, an ancient Lydian invention. At the restaurant a whole new series of borrowed elements confronts him. His plate is made of a form of pottery invented in China. His knife is of steel, an alloy first made in Southern India, his fork a medieval Italian invention, and his spoon a derivative of a Roman original. He begins breakfast with an orange, from the Eastern Mediterranean, a cantaloupe from Persia, or perhaps a piece of African watermelon. With this he has coffee, an Abyssinian plant, with cream and sugar. Both the domestication of cows and the idea of milking them originated in the Near East, while sugar was first made in India... When our friend has finished eating he settles back to smoke, an American Indian habit, consuming a plant domesticated in Brazil in either a pipe, derived from the Indians of Virginia, or a cigarette, derived from Mexico....While smoking he reads the news of the day, imprinted in characters invented by the ancient Semites upon a material invented in China by a process invented in Germany. As he absorbs the accounts of foreign troubles he will, if he is a good conservative citizen, thank a Hebrew deity in an Indo-European language that he is 100 percent American (Linton, 1936: 326–27).

The neglect of a broad framework which considered diffusion of ideas and practices as a multi-way flow between individuals at the micro level and between nations at the macro level, has been, therefore, a serious conceptual and methodological weakness of diffusion research.

Network Analysis of Diffusion

The inadequacy of the monadic analysis in diffusion research of capturing the transactional and relational nature of communication between individuals led to an increasing focus on the possibilities of a network analysis. This approach was based on the convergence model of communication which defined it as 'a process in which participants create and share information with one another in order to reach a mutual understanding' (Rogers and Kincaid, 1981: 63). In the network approach, the communication relationship between two or more individuals constituted the unit of analysis (Rogers, 1976a; Rogers and Kincaid, 1981). The sample research design most likely was a total census of all eligible respondents in a system, rather than the earlier method of sampling scattered individuals in a large sample. Sociometric data about communication relationships was utilized besides the usual personal and social characteristics of individuals and their communication behavior used in the earlier monadic analyses. The data was then subjected to various types of network analyses to determine how social-structural variables affected diffusion flows in a system (Rogers, 1976a: 215):

> This advance allowed the data analysis of a 'who-to-who' communication matrix, and facilitated inquiry into the identification (*i*) of cliques within the total system and how such structural subgroupings affected the diffusion of an innovation, and (*ii*) of specialized communication roles such as liaisons,[3] bridges and isolates thus allowing communication research to proceed far beyond the relatively simpler issues of studying just opinion leadership.

The network analysis, it was hoped, would lead to a greater focus on understanding the role of social structures on diffusion flows, thus restoring its influence on communication behavior.

[3] Defined by Rogers as an individual who links two or more cliques in a system (Rogers, 1976a: 221).

The network approach was, essentially, a study of communication relationships within an arbitrary aggregate of individuals in a social system. If the monadic analysis with its individual-centered approach proved to be stultifying, why form a network which again is merely an arbitrary aggregation of individuals? Moreover, the aggregate of individuals constituting the network is not stable. It would be different in differing circumstances and cultures and, even within a given social system, it would change depending on the issues at stake. There are other problems with the network approach. There is an inadequate fit between the network analysis and the convergence model of communication which has guided this approach. The convergence model looks upon human communication as a dynamic and cyclical process but the communication network analysis is not yet in a position to investigate this over-time, dynamic nature of communication (Rogers and Kincaid, 1981). One of the major shortcomings of the network analysis has been its inability to describe the flow of influence at each point in time. Communication flows, as represented by the network structure existing at the time of data collection, are assumed to be stable over a decade after that date. This is a questionable assumption (Rogers, 1975). Also, the total census method restricts the size of the aggregate that could be selected as it is not feasible to handle a very large aggregation of individuals. The network approach is expensive, the analysis is complex and time-consuming, all of which again limits the number of people it can encompass. It is also impractical for the extension agent to carry out a network study since it would invariably require a computer to make all the complex sociometric configurations.

The dimensions of analysis in the network approach, as done until now, have been very limiting. Most of the data collected consists of soft variables—the 'who talks to whom' kind of individual communication variables. Unless economic, health, family planning, and other such systemic data is also included, it is not possible to get a total view of the different dimensions of development.

Social-Structural Constraints to Diffusion of Innovations

The classical diffusion model was originally conceived in the industrial countries of the West where the socio-economic, political, and cultural conditions were substantially different from those in Asia, Africa, and Latin America. Yet it was introduced in the Third World countries disregarding the nature of their overall social systems (Beltran, 1976; Diaz-Bordenave, 1976). The general assumptions behind the diffusion model as conceived in the developed nations were uncritically applied to the Third World nations leading to its becoming dysfunctional in the development process:

(*i*) communication by itself can generate development, regardless of socio-economic and political conditions, (*ii*) increased production and consumption of goods and services are the essence of development, and that a fair distribution of income and opportunities will necessarily derive in due time, and *iii*) the solution to increased productivity is technological innovation, irrespective of whom it may benefit and whom it may harm (Beltran, 1976: 18–19).

The neglect of social-structural and political factors in the diffusion of innovations produced negative results. For example, some researchers showed how diffusion practice actually widened socio-economic gaps between recipients of innovations.

Diffusion Tenets vis-á-vis Socio-Economic and Communication Gap

The role of diffusion practice in widening the socio-economic benefits and communication gap between individuals in the rural Third World, was discussed by Roling, Ascroft and Chege (1976). They contended that development agencies provided intensive assistance to a small number of innovative, socio-economically advanced, and information-seeking progressive farmers. The assumption was that innovations would ultimately trickle down to the other less progressive or traditional farmers. This strategy led to less equitable development.

In many developing nations, extension agents were in short supply and they reached only a fraction of farmers (McAnany, 1980a). This constraint, coupled with the progressive farmer strategy of diffusion practice, gave undue importance to opinion leaders. These leaders, who were actually the rich, educated, and progressive farmers, came into direct contact with extension agents. The basic tenet of diffusion research was that innovations would diffuse autonomously from progressive farmers to other members of the community. In reality, however, diffusion of innovations from the progressive farmers was mostly homophilous. Information, therefore, did not reach the subsistence farmers who were not integrated into their interpersonal networks of communication. Also, the messages which managed to reach the small farmers were usually distorted. This was largely due to the fact that diffusion research considered the innovation itself as the message. No effort was made to carefully construct messages to promote the innovation as it diffused, so as to prevent distortion. As Allport and Postman (1947) pointed out, messages lose fidelity very soon, so it may be unlikely that information received second-hand could provide as specific, detailed, and reliable information as messages received first-hand (Roling et al., 1976).

Diffusion practice benefited the advantaged sections of the rural populations because (Roling et al., 1976: 69–71):

1. Early adopters (usually the rich farmers) reaped 'windfall profits';
2. Having available funds relatively earlier than others permitted acquisition of additional resources when they were still relatively cheaper;
3. The adoption of an innovation usually required slack resources in order to adopt;
4. The focus on progressive farmers tended to make a fixed clientele over time;
5. Credit was provided to farmers who could provide collateral, so that costly and therefore profitable innovations could be more readily adopted by those who were relatively better off.

Thus, diffusion processes turned out to be imperfect equalizers of development benefits due to the unequal distribution of resources.

The pro-innovation bias of diffusion research implied that all innovations should be adopted by everyone because they were considered to be beneficial. But often research stations concentrated on developing innovations which benefited the progressive farmers. This was mainly because the farmer profiles available to the research stations were based on generalizations from a non-representative and purposive sample of progressive farmers with whom they usually came into contact (Roling et al., 1976). This process usually gave rise to irrelevant innovations handed down to the small farmers which could not be adopted. Thus, the progressive farmer strategy coupled with pro-innovation bias worked completely against the small farmer.

The diffusion process, in short, produced a vicious circle. Easier access to information by progressive farmers led to successes and greater efficacy which in turn led to more information-seeking and more successes. Lack of information access, on the other hand, led to relative failures and, therefore, less need for more information-seeking. The small, *traditional* farmer, crushed by forces from all sides over which he/she had no control, was obviously fatalistic, lacked aspirations, innovativeness, etc. 'Fatalism, mutual distrust, and so on, on the one hand, and modernity, information-seeking, and the like, on the other, may be actual consequences rather than causes of behavior' (Roling et al., 1976: 72).

From the foregoing analysis of the social-structural and political constraints to change, the knowledge gap, and the diffusion tenets in widening the socio-economic benefits gap, a fairly clear picture of the information environment of the rural poor is obtained. Clearly, an insufficient quantity of innovation information, knowledge, and skills is percolating to the disadvantaged sections of rural peasants either from the mass media or interpersonal channels of communication. There is a gross imbalance in the amount of information disseminated between the urban and rural areas, and, even within rural areas, between the elite and disadvantaged audiences. The quality of the information also leaves much to be desired. The innovations handed down to the rural poor are most often irrelevant and the information unreliable, and sometimes even negative to the adoption process. Invariably the source or the channel does not provide him/her with adequate and reliable information or may promote inappropriate innovations. In the light of these facts, it is obvious why the small or *traditional* farmer has been slow in adopting modern innovations.

SUMMARY

By the seventies it became increasingly clear in Asia and in Latin

America that socio-economic structural constraints diminished and even eliminated the influence of the mass media in overcoming problems of development. The process of development was not as straightforward and clear-cut as conceptualized earlier. And, the mass media, far from being the independent variable in the change process, were themselves affected by the extraneous factors. Much of the earlier communication research with its exaggerated emphasis on the individual-blame causal hypothesis to development problems, obfuscated the social-structural, political, and institutional constraints acting in concert against the individual's efforts to change.

Scholars contended that there was a benign neglect of social-structural and political constraints to development because the field of communication research was influenced by 'alien premises, objects, and methods'. The scientific knowledge, research, models, etc. that were exported primarily from the United States to developing countries, were best suited to the socio-economic, political, cultural, and structural arrangements in the United States of America: And, the US was no Third World. The mass media, in particular, were criticized for (*i*) their trivial and non-development content; (*ii*) for giving rise to a *revolution of rising frustrations* in developing nations; and (*iii*) for increasing the knowledge gap between the advantaged and disadvantaged sectors of the population.

The diffusion of innovations research was criticized for:

1. Its emphasis on exposure to the mass media by the audience and its inattention to the message content of the mass media. Such a focus did not reveal the potential inequality media exposure could breed by creating knowledge gaps among different sections of the audience;
2. Its pro-technological bias;
3. Pro-source bias;
4. Pro-persuasion bias;
5. One-way message flow bias; and
6. Its pro-progressive farmer bias. This led to an increase in the socio-economic and communication gaps between the progressive and subsistence farmers.

SECTION C

*Theoretical Framework for the
Eighties and Beyond:
From Empirical Positivism to
Qualitative and Normative Models of
Development and Communication*

Overview

The ferment in the field of development and communication during the seventies had useful consequences. The quantitative empirical positivism that guided thinking in the earlier decades was increasingly questioned and criticized. While the newer approaches did not necessarily discard the quantitative approach, there was a strengthening of the qualitative and normative modes of inquiry. Development priorities and standards became more contextual to needs and problems of individual countries or regions within them. While economic growth and industrialization were considered to be the goals of development in an earlier era, attention was now focused on other objectives as well: meeting specific needs of particular poverty groups; fulfilling such basic needs of people as health care, nutrition, sanitation, and shelter; placing emphasis on non-material indicators of development such as self-determination, self-reliance, and cultural autonomy; maintaining the ecological balance by protecting forests, water resources, air, ozone layer, etc.; and putting the spotlight on human rights—such as the right to free expression, right to communicate, and right to equitable employment and wages.

The roles assigned to communication also changed. The focus in the newer approaches was not just a top-down flow of information and ideas but co-equal knowledge-sharing between users and sources. Communication was now employed to conscientize the common people to their needs and problems; facilitate problem articulation; help in self-development efforts; foster cultural growth and autonomy; serve as a tool for diagnosis of a community's problems; and serve as an important vehicle in bringing about community participation.

Chapter 6

Alternative Development Paradigms: Emergence of New Theories of Third World Development and Role for Communication

> *No program will help small farmers if it is designed by those who have no knowledge of their problems and operated by those who have no interest in their future*
> —**Robert McNamara,** President of the World Bank, 1973.

It is a fact today that fewer and fewer individuals, families, and groups in a nation are consuming more and better goods and services. The consumption *basket* of the richest 10 percent of the people in a country, be it *developed* or *developing*, is very different from the *basket* of the poor majority. It takes more and more scarce resources to fill the rich persons' *basket* while their *baskets* themselves seem to be growing bigger. Dasgupta notes that in the United States (which constitutes about 5 percent of the world's population) the upper middle class has to control about 70 percent of the world's resources to obtain the *basket*. He asks: 'Can Asia, which comprises 80 percent of the people of the globe, and controls about 6 to 7 percent of the world's resources, ever hope to consume the basket?' (Dasgupta 1979: 5). This inequity is not dissimilar within individual nations. Dasgupta comments that in the United States the middle class, *developed* in terms of its consumption and control of goods and services, consumes substantially more resources than does the lower class. In India, an upper middle class child will similarly consume nine times more resources than a disadvantaged child in the same country. Thus, in a nutshell:

> While development creates wealth for the entire nation, it creates poverty for some people. The number of the latter is very large in the developing countries, whereas it is limited in the developed, affluent parts of the region: but the poor are there and the fact remains that development cannot help them. The forecasts are that as development gathers more momentum, the number of the underdeveloped will increase. It has, in fact, been increasing all these years (Dasgupta, 1979: 13). ·

The time has arrived to ask the fundamental question: Is the process of development associated with greater levels of poverty in nations?

DEVELOPMENT OF WHOM? AN ETHICAL PERSPECTIVE

The premise in the fifties, sixties, and seventies was that: when nations *develop* they can get rid of poverty. This may not be necessarily true. On the other hand it is in the *nature* and *method* of development (as it was conceptualized and carried out in the three earlier decades) to be associated with increasing poverty levels. The process of development cannot decrease the poverty of all but can certainly increase the affluence of a few. Some nations or individuals benefit from the development process. Their standards of living and consumption levels rise. However, for the majority of nations or peoples in them it is continued poverty (Dasgupta, 1982). Therefore, increasing development and decreasing poverty, while assumed to be synonymous and concomitant occurrences, is in actuality, not true. The relative state of the nations today and the stratification of people within them are indicative of this.

Reverse Protein Factories

More grain is consumed by livestock in the developed nations than is eaten by people in the developing world. About one-third of the world's grain—500 million tonnes—is used not to feed people, but to fatten livestock. And the proportion is increasing.

Feed grain use in the USSR, for example, doubled in a decade to 180 million tonnes by 1980.

There is another even greater irony in all of this. Easily the greatest number of the world's livestock are ruminants—cattle, sheep, and goats—which have very simple nutritional require- ments because they are capable of producing their own protein. Ruminants effectively have two stomachs. In the first, called the rumen, microbes digest all kinds of roughage. In the process, the rumen produces microbial protein that is then digested by the animal's true stomach to produce meat or milk. Cattle are usually fed grain simply to make them fat.

Certainly that livestock provides food for people, but it does so in an inefficient manner. To produce one kilogram of grain- fed beef requires about 8–10 kg of feed grain. Pigs require only four kg of grain to produce a single kg of pork, and chickens are better still, with a ratio of about two-to-one.

North Americans are the world's leading consumers of both meat and grain. The average American consumes about 800 kg of grain each year, but only about one-fifth of that is eaten directly—most of the rest is consumed in the form of meat or animal products. In the Third World, the average cereal con- sumption is about 200 kg per year, and four-fifths of it is con- sumed directly.

What this welter of statistics illustrates is a gross misuse of resources. Livestock are turned into 'reverse protein factories' by feeding them protein-rich grain, legumes, and fish meal in order to produce a rather smaller amount of protein in the form of meat. And by far the greater proportion of that meat goes in over-large servings to feed the people of the industrialized nations, the vast majority of whom consume far more protein every day than their bodies need.

Source: Bob Stanley, 'Feeding Folly?' *IDRC Reports*, 11,4, January 1983.

Dynamics of Development

In the seventies, realization dawned that development could no longer be viewed as just economic development, or in a more narrow sense, as 'economic growth'. When one talked of development, Seers (1977b) noted, the real indicators were decreases in the rates of poverty, income inequality, and unemployment. Another pertinent indicator would be the decrease in human suffering, as exhibited through physical violence and liquidation of poor masses.

Let us for a moment analyze the development process until the seventies from an ethical perspective. As examples of progress, we will select Brazil, an example of *successful* capitalistic development, and China, the *workable* socialist alternative.

Development for Whom?

Brazil set itself on the capitalistic path via the 'Brazilian Model of Development' after the military took over in 1964. The gains of this model were not insignificant. As Berger (1976: 155) noted:

> Nobody disputes that in recent years Brazil had achieved remarkable economic growth.... In 1965, the year after the military took power, the GNP growth rate was 3.9 percent. The rate increased in an accelerated fashion from year to year. In 1972 it reached 11.3 percent. Between 1964 and 1970 the GNP increased by 52 percent; in the same period industrial production increased by 69 percent.

The question is—who gained from this phenomenal growth, or, put another way, who suffered from this growth? Berger noted that there had been a rise in unemployment and not a fall. 'Thus, between the censuses of 1960 and 1970 the percentage of labor force in employment declined from 32.3 percent to 31.7 percent— not a dramatic decline, to be sure, but rather different from what one would expect during the unfolding of an economic miracle' (Berger 1976: 156). Also, the share of the national income reaching the top 5 percent of the people had increased from 29 per cent to 38 per cent (Berger, 1976). Weaver and Jameson noted that the top 5 million people had been receiving as much of the national income as the bottom 90 million. In fact, Berger asserted that the economic condition of the poor had declined not only relatively but also in absolute terms. Thus, for a large number of people in Brazil, the development process had further underdeveloped them.

The Case of China: Develop or Else...

The Chinese method of development has been widely acclaimed as a 'workable' model. From the limited information available, generalizations were made that in China, at the present time, there was no starvation. In other words, the index of the physical quality of life had significantly improved. Every person had a job and basic necessities such as good health care and housing. Further, there seemed to be an egalitarian distribution of the benefits of development.

However, when upholding this model as an example for other Third World nations to emulate, one must always assess the human costs of the model (Chu, 1987). Berger (1976: 168) noted: 'Anyone who looks at the record of the communist regime since 1949 with even a modest intention of objectivity will be impressed by the enormous quantity of human pain directly traceable to the actions of the regime. It is a record of death, anguish, and fear, deliberately inflicted upon the most numerous people on earth.' Since the communist victory in 1949, the regime had unleashed one terror after another, each one entailing physical suffering and liquidation (Berger, 1976): The Land Reform Movement (1951–52), The Suppression of Counter-Revolutionaries Movement (1951), The Thought Reform Movement (1951–52), The Three-Anti and Five-Anti Movements (1952), The Judicial Reform Movement (1952), Anti Hu-Feng Movement (1955), the Fulfillment of the Marriage Law Movement (1953), The Elimination of Counter-Revolutionaries Movement (1955), The Great Leap Forward (1958), and the Cultural Revolution (1966–68). Though exact figures are not available, Berger noted that people physically liquidated were in the region of one to five million, while the estimate of those who underwent physical suffering was between three and four million people.

For all those who marvel at the Chinese achievement—ranging from the White House in the United States to policy-makers in Third World nations—Berger posited an ethically distrubing question (1976: 176): 'Assuming that the Chinese people have more to eat today than they had before 1949, is this fact in any way due to the other fact that millions of their number were killed by the regime?' We do not know, but it might well be.

Brazil and China are not the only two nations where the poor majority have undergone great misery. Almost all over the world today (especially in the Third World) unemployment, income inequality, and poverty seem to be increasing. It is being realized that concomitant with development are other negative trends: a disproportionate share of the national wealth appropriated by a small elite, high rates of unemployment, and the inability of poor people to provide for their basic needs. To use a familiar cliche: the rich are becoming richer and the poor are getting poorer.

Policy-Maker and Theory-Maker:
A Grand Coalition

How did the process of 'development' emerge as a scheme producing deprivation and human misery, especially in the Third World? Did the policy-makers have a rationale rooted in the theories of socio-economic, political, and cultural development, or were they functioning in a theoretical vacuum? Evidently, the policy-makers were not acting in isolation. They seemed to have had the full support of the theory-makers.

Blaming the Victim

Blaming the victim is an ideological process, an almost painless evasion among the policy-makers and intellectuals all over the world. The generic formula of *Blaming the Victim*, Ryan (1976) writes, is in justifying inequality in society, by finding defects in the victims of inequality. According to him,

the generic process of *Blaming the Victim* is applied to almost every American problem. The miserable health care of the poor is explained away on the grounds that the victim has poor motivation and lacks health information. The problems of slum housing are traced to the characteristics of tenants who are labeled as 'Southern rural migrants' not yet 'acculturated' to life in the big city. The 'multiproblem' poor, it is claimed, suffer the psychological effects of impoverishment, the culture of poverty (Ryan 1976: 5).

As an ideology, *blaming the victim*, unlike the earlier conservative theories, did not put the spotlight on the victim's genetically inferior nature. Ryan commented that the new ideology, instead, focused on the victim's social origin. The shortcoming, however, was still located within the victim. The victim-blamer could thus criticize the social stresses that produced such 'defects' but yet turn a blind eye to the repeated onslaughts of the victimizing social forces on the individual. 'It is a brilliant ideology for justifying a perverse form of social action designed to change, not society, as one might expect, but rather society's victim' (Ryan, 1976: 8).

Social Darwinism

Darwin's work on evolution provided interesting material for social theorists such as Herbert Spencer and William Sumner. They interpreted, or rather distorted, Darwin's work to explain the survival of the fittest in the social arena. They argued very sincerely, Reich (1982) points out, that the state should not intervene on behalf of the poor. The Social Darwinists believed that such government interventions would have catastrophic results since they would interfere with the laws of natural selection. 'Spencer and his followers publicly deplored poor laws, state-supported education, regulation of housing conditions, and the protection of the consumer against dangers and deceptions. They also found anathema any state-enforced effort to achieve equality, even equality of opportunity, because evolution depended for its force on inequality' (Reich, 1982: 34).

All this cold-blooded rhetoric was not the product of demagogues or quacks. It flowed right out of the temples of learning and scholarship:

> It came directly from the lectures and books of leading intellectual figures of the time, occupants of professional chairs at Harvard and Yale.... It is important not to delude ourselves into thinking that ideological monstrosities were constructed by monsters. They were not; they are not. They are developed through a process that shows every sign of being valid scholarship, complete with tables of numbers, copious footnotes, and scientific terminology. Ideologies are quite often academically and socially respectable and in many instances hold positions of exclusive validity...such is the power of an ideology that so neatly fits the needs of the dominant interests of society (Ryan 1976: 22).

Social Darwinism, though a product of the last three decades of the 19th century, has not been totally discredited or discarded even a hundred years later. The victim-blamers, today, are talking about the same issue but using different terminology. Ryan comments that today's victim-blamers talk of cultural deprivation instead of the earlier notion of race and class differences in intellectual ability, and laziness has now been substituted with a new term: *culture of poverty*.

Culture of Poverty Recycled

From the notion of culture of poverty (Lewis, 1961) which included, among other things, provincial orientation, low formal participation, a lack of integration into national institutions, a strong present-time orientation, and inability to defer gratification and fatalism, it was a small theoretical leap to the 'subculture of peasantry'. Talking about the peasants in the Third World, Rogers (1969: 25) wrote: 'they possess certain traits that make them members of a "peasant culture" which transcends national boundaries.' He delineated the main aspects of this peasant culture: (*i*) mutual distrust in interpersonal relations; (*ii*) perceived limited good; (*iii*) dependence on and hostility toward government authority; (*iv*) familism; (*v*) lack of innovativeness; (*vi*) fatalism; (*vii*) limited aspiration; (*viii*) lack of deferred gratification; (*ix*) limited view of the world; (*x*) low empathy.

This exaggerated emphasis on the victim-blame causal hypothesis, as proposed earlier by Lerner, McClelland, Inkeles, Smith, and Hoselitz, among others, seemed to hold the individual responsible for all the attendant problems of development.

The dominant paradigm of development seemed to provide a blueprint for speedy 'development' for all those Third World nations stagnating in the backwaters of underdevelopment. As a paradigm, however, it was patently top-down. It reflected powerful political and corporate interests. This approach did not consider the question of equality in the distribution of the benefits of development. Little attention was paid to the fundamental contradictions of societies in developing nations where economic and political power are concentrated in the hands of a small elite and where large sectors of the population have no significant participation in the share of political and economic resources. Also, the dominant paradigm focused its attention on development constraints within a national state. Invariably, the reasons for underdevelopment were thought to be the social psychological makeup of individuals or the 'traditional' culture of peasants in the Third World.

Sustain the Status Quo

Much of the work in social policy planning, social action, and social theories has thus attempted to maintain the present inequality in societies. Blame-the-victim ideologists, the Social Darwinists, and the top-down experts of development, among others, strove to change the individual but leave the structure of dependence in societies intact. The intellectuals and the policy-makers had sought to legitimize the oppression and human misery caused by extreme inequality through *scientific* and *rational* explanations of subcultures: groups of individuals who are doomed to be backward because of their *cultural deficiencies*. In other words, the attempt has been to sustain the status quo in unequal societies and thus delay change.

Poverty can be viewed primarily as lack of money. According to Ryan (1976: 122–23), 'poverty is an economic status etiologically related to the absence of both monetary input and access to income generating resources.' Conceptualized thus the strategy to overcome poverty would be to bring every poor person above the poverty line through transfer of resources. Ryan argued that about 2 percent of the GNP in the United States would be sufficient for this purpose in that nation. However, poverty has not been perceived as lack of money. It is clearly the result of the *lower class culture* of the poor or the traditional culture of the peasants. The solution, therefore, is not distribution of resources. Instead, the spotlight is on how to change the 'way of life' of the poor. As Ryan notes, poverty is sought to be removed by the hard and wearying method of liquidating lower class culture and in that process liquidating the lower class.

Myth of Subcultures

Are the poor people or the peasants so different from mainstream society that they constitute separate and distinct subcultures? Are the perceived cultural differences imposed externally on these people or do they evolve from within these subgroups? These are some questions that need to be answered before arbitrarily subdividing populations into *culturally homogenous* categories. Ryan (1976: 127) warns that:

It is easy to be misled and to fall into the easy jargon of the day and call all kinds of minor phenomena cultures or sub-cultures. Consider a possible analogy: there are several million men who share certain traits, centering around an addiction to alcohol; they work irregularly, for example, show a high arrest rate, and also have high rates of family disorganisation.... On the basis of such findings, would we feel comfortable in talking about a culture or subculture of alcohol?

In fact, studies have been conducted to test empirically the hypothesis regarding differences in values, attitudes, and priorities between different class groups. These surveys have shown that there is no significant difference in any of these characteristics between different economic groups (Morgan et al., 1974). Similarly, studies in the Third World have shown that the peasants do not lack empathy or innovativeness or need achievement or any of the other psychological variables that epitomized the 'subculture of peasantry' (Ascroft et al., 1971; Roling et al., 1976).

A False Reality

Gunnar Myrdal reminds us that our conceptions of reality, though we presume them to be objective and scientific, are hardly value-free. On the contrary, they are basically opportunistic and systematically, though not consciously intended, falsify reality. He notes (1970: 3–4):

The fact that conceptions about reality, and ideologies and theories, are influenced by the interests as commonly perceived by the dominant groups in the society where they are formed, and that they so come to deviate from truth in a direction opportune to these interests, is easily seen and, in fact, taken for granted when we look back at an earlier period in history. But in our own intellectual endeavors we ordinarily preserve a naive non-awareness about such influences working on our minds—as, indeed, people have done in every earlier epoch of history.

Reviewing the role of communication media in social change one can notice the bias toward the interests of the powerful few. Research, particularly by Latin American communication experts, indicates how the media communicate the world view and values of the dominant classes in individual Third World nations and metropolitan centers (Diaz-Bordenave, 1980).

Communication systems are manipulated in all politico-economic systems: totalitarian, communist, dictatorial, military, religious, and capitalist to depict the *reality* of the central political and/or powerful corporate interests. The capitalist system is the only one that professes openly that it upholds freedom of thought, speech, and action and provides equal access to communication channels to all its citizens. This claim, however, is debatable. Diaz-Bordenave (1980: 14) comments:

> It is true that the manipulation of communication systems is not exclusive of capitalistic societies. Their true role, however, must be unmasked because in these societies the commercial media present themselves as the champions of democratic free expression, necessary for all citizens to judge the issues of the day, when in truth the media are the masters of distorted communication.

Mass Media: Tools of Exploitation

The main obstacles which hinder developing nations from attaining levels of *modernization* achieved in the West, have been ascribed to their *peasant culture* and *traditional* habits. The neo-Weberian concepts of *modernization* include the components of empiricism, rationalism, materialism, individualism, and universalism. The developing countries seem to lack all these qualities in their cultures, rooted as they are in sacred-value orientation, authoritarianism, and particularism. Therefore, underdevelopment in the minds of communicologists such as Lerner, Schramm, McClelland, Pye, and Rogers in the late fifties through the early seventies, was perceived as a cultural problem. The Third World needed to abandon its traditional cultures and support institutions if it wanted to taste the benefits of development. This kind of theorizing provided a tailor-made role for the modern media of communication. 'Out of this equation between development and re-education arose the all-important role given to the mass media by the communication approach. Nothing quite compared to the media of mass communication as instruments for the new education' (Krippendorff, 1979: 74). The interpersonal networks of communication were considered to be supportive of *traditional* structures and authority and hence were anti-development. The mass media, however, were free from such control. The question whether the mass media were instruments of exploitation, tools of a small coterie of elites, was not considered to be important. 'The ubiquity, standardization, and omnipresence of the mass media, which were found to be oppressive in the West, were the very features which recommended them in the historic mission to develop the Third World.... The approach showed scant regard for Third World audiences or for the possibility that it might conceivably have a vested interest in viewpoints and social attitudes' (Krippendorff, 1979: 74).

The Passing of Traditional Support Structures

The mass media, therefore, were considered to be harbingers of major change in the *traditional* Third World nations. Through *re-education* they were supposed to help the peasants in these nations cleanse themselves of their traditional values, attitudes, and cultural habits so that they could be anointed on the altars of modernity.

From an ethical perspective, what were the consequences of this role accorded to the mass media? The mass media attempted to wean people away from their *traditional* structures and habits and draw them toward the *modern* system. This process further impoverished the masses. The traditional social support structures that had provided security for thousands of years in the past were destroyed, and as Dasgupta (1979: 7) argued, the modern structures which replaced them protected the *very* process that disintegrated the networks and liquidated the social assets:

It must be remembered in this context that while development produces a certain amount of economic wealth and technological power, it also destroys a great deal of social resources that the societies concerned might have possessed before such development took place. The village society, the integrated kinship system, the caste, the large family, the church, the mosque, etc., might thus still provide a certain support to the poor which could be offered in a developed, industrialized society only by costly professional institutions and measures of social security. The granny at home, for example, is replaced today by the paid baby-sitter of the industrialized society, while the institution for the handicapped takes the place of the support that the extended network of relations might offer. As economic development takes place this 'social' wealth is destroyed.

An Ethical Perspective of Development

Ethics is defined in the dictionary as 'that branch of philosophy dealing with values relating to human conduct, with respect to rightness and wrongness of certain actions and to the goodness and badness of the motives and ends of such actions.' In this chapter, we have until now attempted to analyze the issues in development, noting the moral underpinnings of human actions in the theory- and policy-making realms. In the course of the reader's sojourn through the saga of development, or rather underdevelopment (as outlined in this chapter), a host of questions might have arisen. Let us examine a few of them:

1. **What is development?** This term, as denoted in the dominant paradigm, is an ethnocentric conception of what progress should be. It describes the type of modernization that has been achieved in the countries of West Europe and North America. Also, it has looked at development from a macro level.

Most of the earlier models defined development in rather narrow terms. They viewed development as economic growth obtained through greater industrialization and accompanying urbanization. Development performance was thought to be described through measures such as the GNP and per capita income levels.

Missing in this definition was the need for a more broad-based definition of development. Any discussion of development must include the physical, mental, social, cultural, and spiritual development of an individual in an atmosphere free from coercion or dependency. Also, greater importance would need to be given to preserving and sustaining local traditional cultures and other artifacts as these are usually the media through which the people at the grassroots structure their reality of the world around them. Local cultures in the developing nations, quite contrary to some deeply-held notions, are not static. The fact that they have survived centuries of hostile alien rule speaks volumes for their dynamic nature. As a development tool, these cultures can generate solutions to many of the problems at the grassroots due to their deep knowledge of the social-cultural ethos of the people. To talk, therefore, of uprooting local cultures is not only naive but also ethically indefensible.

2. Development at what level? Much of the work has been at the level of the nation-state. Even research at the micro level has been concerned with bringing the nation, or some region, as a whole into modernity.

Missing in this was the conceptualization that different individuals and groups require different strategies for development. If development is not to create greater misery for a large body of humanity at the periphery, then we need a process by which not only the *mythical* concept of nation is developed but the disadvantaged masses are also helped to overcome their wretched existence.

Poverty and Development

Development and poverty can and do coexist. In the case of individuals, development and poverty do not have to coexist, but nations are not individuals. The popular notion is that development and affluence are synonymous while poverty and underdevelopment are concomitant processes. The notion is that when nations *develop* they can get rid of poverty. This is not true. On the other hand, it is in the *nature* of the development process (as it is being carried out and conceptualized today) to cause greater poverty. Second, it is the *method* of development process that causes poverty.

Fewer and fewer individuals are consuming more and more. The consumption basket of the richest 25 percent of the people in a nation, be it developed or developing, is very different from the basket of the poor majority. It takes more and more to fill the rich person's basket and the baskets themselves seem to be getting bigger and bigger. The present development process cannot make the poor person's basket as big as the rich person's. Very few people are going to acquire bigger baskets.

On the other hand, it is more likely that fewer people will end up with smaller baskets or no basket at all.

The poor people in the world consume a fraction of the earth's resources. Development cannot and will not increase the consumption levels of these people to the level of the few rich because adequate resources for that are not available.

Increasing development and decreasing poverty are two different processes. By accelerating development (as conceptualized in the dominant paradigm), one is not necessarily decreasing poverty. Chances are that one may be increasing poverty. In order to decrease poverty one needs also to decrease affluence. However, poverty per se is not negative. In fact, it is a relative term. It is human misery that is negative and should be eradicated. It is the eradication of human misery which should be the objective of development practitioners. We have to index what constitutes basic necessities for a healthy and productive life and provide them.

Source: A talk by Professor Sugata Dasgupta at the International Center, University of Iowa, 1982.

3. **Who determines whether and when the definition of development**—excluding or including certain problem definitions—**is acceptable or unacceptable?** The elites in every nation have always had the prerogative of deciding what the country needs. As shown in the earlier part of this section, this is inappropriate. In many Third World countries today, economic and political power are concentrated in the hands of a small elite. In such circumstances, any definition of development by the elites will be in a direction opportune to their interests.

Missing in this approach was participation by people at the grassroots. People who are the objects of policy need to be involved in the definition, design, and execution of the development process. While this idea has been raised very often, it has not been adequately operationalized. How would it be possible to bring about effective participation of the masses at the grassroots in the development process? One useful method would be to consider the creation of viable institutional structures at the interface between the agencies of the government and the 'anonymous' masses wherein they could be actively involved in all issues that concern their welfare. Participation, in such a bottom-up orientation, would need to be broad-based. The concept of participation as favored by the bottom-up strategies, such as the participatory communication systems and intermediate technologies, was narrow: achieve the cooperation of the masses in adopting better health care practices, increase agricultural production, etc. True participation, however, as discussed, would go beyond such goals as higher productivity and better health habits, to bringing about conscientization of the masses on their extremely unequal social and spatial structures.

4. Who reaps the benefits of development and who bears the risks? Any policy that continues to exploit the masses at the cost of the rich and powerful is morally indefensible. What is needed in future is a more egalitarian distribution of benefits and risks of development across all social and economic classes. Perhaps the Western model as enunciated in the dominant paradigm is inappropriate for the Third World nations. This model which emphasized capital-intensive technology and centralized planning of development gave an unequal advantage to the elites. An alternative model that stresses labor-intensive approaches and decentralized planning of development with effective local people participation would be more appropriate to conditions in the Third World.

5. What are the moral implications at the policy-making level? Policy-makers, on the basis of their own actions, should refrain from increasing human misery. The focus needs to be on humane development, i.e. to reduce human suffering and not increase it. Berger (1976: xiii) succinctly describes some of the implications at the development policy-making level:

Most political decisions must be made on the basis of inadequate knowledge. To understand this is to become very gingerly toward policy options that exact high human costs.

The most pressing human costs are in terms of physical deprivation and suffering. The most pressing moral imperative in policy making is a calculus of pain.

What is badly needed today is such a self-examination by every intellectual and policy-maker concerned with development.

ALTERNATIVE CONCEPTIONS OF DEVELOPMENT IN THE SEVENTIES

The concept of development changed quite drastically in the seventies. There was a move away from the earlier technologically deterministic and GNP-centered definitions to alternative conceptions that were more qualititative. Everett Rogers (Rogers with Shoemaker, 1971) who was criticized for his earlier definition that stressed industrialization and economic growth and neglected other human factors, summarized the newer concept of development thus:

> a widely participatory process of social change in a society, intended to bring about both social and material advancement (including greater equality, freedom, and other valued qualities) for the majority of the people through their gaining greater control over their environment (Rogers, 1976b: 133).

Denis Goulet, a political economist, saw development as (1971: xx):

> freeing men from nature's servitude, from economic backwardness and oppressive technological institutions, from unjust class structures and political exploiters, from cultural and psychic alienation—in short, from all of life's inhuman agencies.

In another context, Goulet (1973) explicated in detail his ideas of *real development*. This description of development was holistic and included a clean environment, growth with equity, provision of basic needs such as food, shelter, education, and medical care, meaningful employment and relationships with others, and a harmonious relationship between culture and change.

Wang and Dissanayake (1984a: 5) emphasized the protection of nature and culture. They defined development as:

> a process of social change which has as its goal the improvement in the quality of life of all or the majority of people without doing violence to the natural and cultural environment in which they exist, and which seeks to involve the majority of the people as closely as possible in this enterprise, making them the masters of their own destiny.

The new definitions of development were pluralistic and indicated several new goals for meaningful and real development in the Third World (Rogers, 1976c; Hedebro, 1982).

1. Equity in distribution of information and other benefits of development: The emphasis was placed on the poorest of the poor, those living in urban slums and backward rural areas. The widening hiatus between the advantaged groups and the disadvantaged had to be closed. *Growth with equity* was the clarion call of the seventies.

2. Active participation of people at the grassroots: The objective was to involve the input of people in activities that were ostensibly set up for their benefit. This not only *liberated* the people from a *spiral of silence* but also ensured that development plans and decisions were relevant and meaningful to the recipients.

Paulo Freire was a vigorous exponent of the idea of *participation for liberation*. Freire (1971) and Illich (1969) were severe critics of the Western educational systems in Central and Latin American nations, which they considered irrelevant to the real problems of these countries. Instead, the alien educational systems made the people passive and uncritical of the existing inequity in their societies. For Freire, education and communication have to be participative and receiver-centered. Rather than being top-down, the educational process has to be dialectic, helping people to understand the world around them and liberating them from the oppressive tyranny of a world view created by the elites to serve their own ends.

3. Independence of local communities (or nations) to tailor development projects to their own objectives: The reliance here would be on local human skills and material resources, thus fostering greater self-reliance in development and, importantly, leading to freedom from external dependency.

4. Integration of the old and new ideas, the traditional and modern systems, the endogenous and exogenous elements to constitute a unique blend suited to the needs of a particular community: This approach would not consider the local culture as something to be discarded but instead it would benefit from the native wisdom to come up with a unique syncretization best suited to the tasks at hand.

The Socialistic Experience

Curiously, the realization that the development effort in the Third

World nations following the Western paradigm of development was rather sluggish, synchronized with the news of China's success story. Following its own development model, the People's Republic of China had made tangible gains in the areas of health, family planning, and agriculture, and achieved equity among its people in the distribution of development benefits. Thus, China, at the very least, showed the rest of the Third World that it was possible to develop without following the Western model of development.

The Chinese model is rooted in the concept of socialism. There is no private ownership of the means of production. All factors of production are owned by the state, the party, or a cooperative. Objectives and goals are set by a collective of individuals such as a commune, and the individual is required to work for the collective good. Mao Zedong, the Chinese leader in the sixties, believed that China's greatest strength was its human power living in villages. So, the development model was labor-intensive and rural-based. In addition to this, the party succeeded in mobilizing people to work for the declared goals through a unique system of communication involving the mass media and interpersonal channels working with organized groups and party functionaries.

Tanzania and Cuba are other examples of success stories in an otherwise desolate landscape of Third World development (Hedebro, 1982). A major achievement of Julius Nyerere, the then President of Tanzania, was to involve the people in development decision-making (Nyerere, 1968). Through the establishment of *Ujamaa* villages, Tanzania achieved, to a great extent, decentralized and popular participation of the people in activities that were important and relevant to them. Cuba, on the other hand, achieved very impressive gains in spreading literacy among its people living in rural areas with the voluntary participation of its citizens.

While China, Tanzania, and Cuba achieved some measure of success in their development objectives, it must be remembered that each of these nations has a unique philosophy of development. All three countries believe that society and people need to work together to achieve goals that are for the common good. Clearly, it is a model based on socialist principles. It is unlikely that other Third World nations could follow their example unless they also imported their political philosophies and social organization (Hedebro, 1982). The development efforts of the People's Republic of China and India are often compared. But, India is a democratic country and believes in individual choice and freedom whereas China (as events in 1989 clearly demonstrate) does not necessarily believe in these ideas. For example, India has not achieved the same success as China in population control in spite of the fact that India was the first developing country to embark on a family planning policy at the highest political level. Thus, the ineffectiveness of the Indian family planning drive is not due to ineffective communication strategies or the lack of willingness on the part of the government, but rather, the unpopularity of the program itself. Another important reason is the divergent political philosophies of these two large nations. India, under its democratic form of government, has always believed that the individual has the freedom of choice. Therefore, unlike China, India cannot mandate couples to limit their families to just one child. Thus, as Rogers (1987) points out, 'the success of the development programs that are unpopular with the people rest mainly on a strong government authority, rather than on the role of communication.' The same argument of diametrically different political philosophy and social organization may be extended to other areas of development where China has done particularly well relative to India. However, regardless of the non-transferability of the Chinese or Tanzanian models, the lesson learnt in the early seventies was that it was possible for a country to embark on a successful path using its own unique paradigm of development.

Intermediate Technology

In the early seventies there was a strong reaction against the high technology (especially the capital-intensive variety), massive industrialization, urbanization, and the centralized economic planning features incorporated in the dominant paradigm of development. On the one hand, the success of nations such as China that advocated decentralized and labor-intensive techniques, and on the other, the widening socio-economic gaps created between groups of people by high technology and capital-intensive innovations such as the Green Revolution in the Punjab, India, and the

Philippines, provided impetus to efforts seeking alternative models of development. Schumacher's thesis *Small is Beautiful* (1973) provided one such alternative. This English economist advocated an intermediate technology that exploited local knowledge, resources, and techniques. He was especially concerned about the rural poor and unemployed in developing countries who were bypassed by the modernization drives of those nations. In fact, Schumacher believed that development planning put too much emphasis on capital-intensive industrialization and neglected small-scale rural enterprises. 'Schumacher's case is a very strong one in favour of a technology which improves labor productivity, uses local resources, minimizes the use of non-renewable resources, and produces goods intended for local markets. It is in essence small-scale, self-help development' (Weaver and Jameson, 1978: 78).

The appropriate technology idea had several advantages. It attempted to:

1. Create employment in rural areas where most of the people live;
2. Use local skills, material, and financial resources, thus leading to lesser dependence on external sources;
3. Maximize use of renewable resources;
4. Be compatible with local cultures and practices; and
5. Satisfy local needs and wishes (Dunn, 1978: 5).

In short, Schumacher's ideas were conducive to self-reliant development at the village level.

Basic Needs Approach

Another consequence of the disenchantment with the trickle-down idea of development was a focus on basic needs: those necessities that are absolutely essential to maintain a decent quality of life. The usual indicators of development such as the gross national product (GNP) and per capita measures did not give adequate information on the quality of life of individuals at the bottom of the socio-economic ladder in developing nations. Early proponents of the basic needs idea were Mahbub Ul Haq and Holis Chenery of the World Bank, Paul Streeten, a development economist, and James Grant of the Overseas Development Council.

The basic needs approach, a concept of eliminating some of the worst aspects of poverty, has drawn support from a variety of sources: the World Bank, the International Labor Organization (ILO), United Nations Economic and Social Council, the United States Congress, and many national governments. Paul Streeten (1979: 48) summarized the main objectives of this approach:

1. Provide adequate food and clean drinking water;
2. Provide decent shelter;
3. Provide education;
4. Provide security of livelihood;
5. Provide adequate transport;
6. Help people participate in decision-making; and
7. Uphold a person's dignity and self-respect.

Thus, this approach emphasized both basic, fundamental needs of people and a respect for human rights. However, since basic needs may be met in ways that deny basic rights, and human rights may be practiced in ways that may reject basic needs, Streeten added one more human right: the socio-economic right to international resources. This included: the right to universal primary education; the right to adequate food and health standards; the right to equitable employment; and the right to minimum wages and collective bargaining.

Several attempts have been made to address the basic human needs problems in a quantifiable way (Grant, 1978). One measure that has been developed by the Overseas Development Council is the PQLI: the Physical Quality of Life Index. This index incorporates data on three factors—life expectancy at age one, infant mortality, and literacy—into a single composite index which has a low of zero and a maximum of 100. Morris (1979: 4) pointed out that while the PQLI does not measure important qualitative indicators such as freedom and justice, it does attempt to measure how basic life-sustaining social needs of individuals are met by their societies. It is possible to use the PQLI to compare any changes between nations or between ethnic, regional groupings within nations. Grant supports the idea of using life expectancy, infant mortality, and literacy as indicators of the quality of life (1978: 9):

A major advantage of consolidating these three indicators in the PQLI is that such a composite index usefully summarizes a great deal of social performance. It also encourages consideration of the interrelatedness of the policies that bear on each aspect of development and thus favors the emergence of broadly rather than narrowly conceived strategies of development. Use of life expectancy or infant mortality alone, for example, all too often leads to the mistaken conclusion that these problems should be left for medical practitioners alone to resolve. Together, however, the three indicators provide important information about how the benefits of development are distributed—about how well the worst aspects of poverty are being eliminated.

The basic needs approach, then, is a micro analysis attempting to eradicate the worst kind of poverty among the poorest of the poor in developing nations. All the objectives in the basic needs paradigm are equally important and it needs a broad-fronted implementation.

Integrated Rural Development

In 1973, Robert McNamara, President of the World Bank, delivered a bell-wether speech calling for *New Directions in Development* to overcome what he perceived to be a stalemate in development approaches (World Bank, 1973). The centerpiece of these new directions was a proposal for what he termed *integrated rural development*. This new orientation emphasized that all existing constraints to socio-economic development be tackled simultaneously. The movement in the seventies, therefore, tended to be a *broad-fronted approach* to development planning. Multilateral and bilateral agencies such as the FAO, IBRD, USAID, and several national governments put together multipackage programs to overcome external constraints.

McNamara distinguished between relative and absolute poverty. While relative poverty underlined the inequity in the distribution and consumption of resources between and within nations, absolute poverty meant a life degraded by denial of basic human necessities. He proposed reorientation of development policies from mere economic growth to equitable distribution of the fruits of economic growth. This meant a switch from GNP targets to meeting basic needs of the poorest of the poor. Some of the necessary measures to meet this goal of basic needs were:

Acceleration of land and tenancy reform;
Better access to credit;
Assured availability of clean water;
Expansion of extension services and applied research;
Greater access to public services;
Organizational changes and new forms of rural institutions;
Popular participation in development decision-making;
Involvement of local leadership in program planning;
Decentralization of authority to rural communities.

Local Organization for Development

In the dominant paradigm, the informational value of communication to individuals was given more emphasis whereas the organizational value was virtually ignored. However, some scholars point out that exogenous information will not affect a community unless it organizes the people and starts a process of autonomous development (Hornik, 1988). Roling put forth the hypothesis that the rural poor are improverished because they lack power over anything. He argued for changing power relationships in the social system and increasing the countervailing power of the rural poor in relation to other groups (1982: 9):

Reward systems ensuring creation of opportunities for the rural poor, and especially self-sustaining linkage relationships, can only be created when the rural poor involved acquire power over opportunity-building systems. The latter must somehow be accountable to the former.

How could the poor at the grassroots acquire the countervailing power and make the system at the top accountable to them? One effective method suggested is the formation at the grassroots of strong organizations capable of articulating and protecting the interests of the peasants and others residing on the periphery. Discussing small-scale self-help development projects (SHDP) in rural Kenya, Barkan and others (1979) noted that these organizations have, on many occasions, forced the center to enter into a bargaining relationship with the periphery, or some parts of it. Reviewing the findings of eighteen case studies on local organizations in Asia, Uphoff and Esman contended that there is a strong empirical basis for concluding that local organizations are a necessary condition for speedy rural development, particularly the kind that brings about higher productivity and improved welfare of the majority of rural people. They noted that, 'those cases in which there was more organization reaching down to the local level, accountable to the local people, and involved with rural development functions have accomplished rural development objectives more successfully with respect to the available resource base than have those with less rural organization' (Uphoff and Esman, 1974: xi). Some of the successful development objectives they cited were higher agricultural productivity and better rural welfare, i.e. health, nutrition, education, security, employment, political participation, and equity in income distribution. Barkan et al. (1979: 31), discussing the role of the SHDPs in Kenya, pointed out the following achievements:

1. They produced a net transfer of resources from the center to the rural areas;
2. They appeared to foster a more equitable distribution of wealth within local communities;
3. They marshalled local initiative and entrepreneurial skills in ways the State could not do by itself;
4. Most importantly, they provided an organizational infrastructure at the grassroots without which the development of the rural poor was unlikely to proceed.

Fostering Inequities

While local organizations could extract greater resources from the center and lead to greater equity in rural areas, they could also lead to greater inequality. Certain groups in the rural areas could acquire a disproportionate share of material goods and services. Also, local organizations could help some leaders become very powerful, giving rise to local elites in areas where there were none before. Certain organizations could initiate the beginning of new class formations in rural areas. And, it is also possible that powerful local organizations could exacerbate regional inequality between different communities on the periphery of the national political economy.

Uphoff and Esman (1974: xviii) describe some criteria that could eliminate (or at least reduce) the shortcomings pointed out above:

1. Local organizations should be linked to higher level decision centers by multiple channels: This would enable the organization to achieve the benefits of specialization in communication and also to enjoy alternative avenues of influence. Also, this would prevent the dangers of single channels being blocked or monopolized by vested interests;

2. Sanctions on leadership: In order to get best results, the sanctions need to be balanced from the top and from the bottom. Leaders could be made accountable to their communities through elections, participation in rural projects, public meetings and such other activities. They could be made accountable to the center by making them conform to guidelines and standards enforced by auditing, inspection and regular informational controls;

3. Equity in distribution of assets and income: This is a very crucial issue, politically sensitive but nevertheless very important. Relatively more equitable distribution of assets and income is an important condition for extensive rural development and effective local organization.

While effective local organizations do have positive effects in bringing about more autonomous development, they require a political commitment from the governments and other power bases. As Uphoff and Esman (1974) caution, the governments must be committed to the idea of equitable rural development through local organizations which would entail significant transfer of resources from the center to the periphery. This may not be easily forthcoming in all countries.

Re-emergence of Culture in Development

Since the seventies, there has been renewed interest in studying and pointing out the positive role of local culture in social change. The old paradigm has been criticized for the way it conceptualized the role of culture. Theorists, in the dominant paradigm, held the stereotypical view that culture was necessarily in conflict with modernization. This view seemed overly abstract and unreal (Gusfield, 1971; Wang and Dissanayake, 1984a). On the contrary, several examples were provided of the symbiotic relationship between culture and change:

In Japan, for example, industrialism and feudal social structure united to produce a unique pattern of economic development. Obedience to the family and to the Emperor, lack of vertical mobility, and subordination of the individual to the community usually associated with tradition, have played a crucial role in stimulating the Japanese economy. Its success compares favorably with that of more conventional modern societies (Wang and Dissanayake, 1984a: 8).

Wang and Dissanayake (1984a) posited that culture was essential not only to provide a context to development and change but also to maintain a certain degree of continuity. Denying the role of culture would deny the continuity that it has provided during all periods of change and thus deny history to the people or nations involved.

Increasingly, there was a call for a new paradigm of development which was more open-ended and flexible than the deterministic and prescriptive models of the fifties and sixties. Among other things, the new paradigm needed to reconceptualize the role of culture in change. Local cultures in developing nations, quite contrary to deeply-held notions of 'modernizers', were not static. The fact that they survived centuries of hostile alien rule under colonial regimes was a measure of their dynamic nature. Wang and Dissanayake (1984a) reinforced the view of culture as an open system in constant interaction with other elements in a society undergoing change. The local culture was constantly exchanging information with its external environment, interacting with other components in the system and thus continuously changing. In short, the culture was acting upon the environment, and at the same time, being acted upon by it.

Wang and Dissanayake (1984a) provided examples of how culture and tradition could in fact be employed in social development efforts. In India, Mahatma Gandhi used traditional cultural symbolic systems to propagate new ideas, behaviors, and values among the masses. He used his stature as a holy man to bring about several social reforms. Another example is the *Sarvodaya*

Shramadana Movement in Sri Lanka. This experiment which was started more than twenty-five years ago makes active use of traditional forms and philosophies of communication to meet user needs in the rural and other areas where the problems exist. Unlike the earlier development strategies that adopted Western models, this movement fosters a radical rethinking of the issues and problems of development, drawing on traditional philosophies, local resources, and skills to confront and ameliorate problems. Dissanayake outlines the philosophy of development of this movement: 'It is based on self-reliance, self-development, grassroots development, popular participation, maintenance of ecological balance, and the importance of culture in social development' (Dissanayake, 1984: 46).

The Sarvodaya Movement is a self-help organization, currently with development programs in more than 2.500 villages all across Sri Lanka. Essentially, it is an approach where local culture is considered as a facilitator of development rather than as an obstacle to social change:

> Rather than blindly following the developmental scenarios that have been written in the West... the architects of the Sri Lanka Sarvodaya Movement are engaged in a timely and arduous endeavor to formulate and put into practice a development strategy springing from the deepest currents of the culture that permeates society (Dissanayake, 1984: 39).

Kantowski (1980) notes that the *Shramadana* camps foster spiritual development of both the individual and the group. The development of the individual personality is brought about by the emphasis on four Buddhist principles: kindness, compassion, sympathetic joy, and equanimity. Similarly, four Buddhist principles guide group behavior: sharing, pleasant language, joint work, and equality.

All these principles are put into actual practice through *Shramadana* or labour-donating camps. Dissanayake (1984) notes that in these camps important village activities such as laying of roads, construction of schools, community centers and rural housing schemes, repair and construction of irrigation channels, and clearing land for agriculture, are performed through the active voluntary participation of local people. The other activities of this self-help, bottom-up development approach include: training in agri-

culture-related activities, development of local arts and village industries, training of village pre-school teachers and health workers
(Ratnapala, n.d.).

Dissanayake compares the Buddhist model of communication as
used in the Sarvodaya Movement with the typical Western or
Aristotelian model (schematically represented in Table 6.1). The
model emerges as an interactive, two-way process, bringing out
the dynamic nature of communication, whereas the Western model
uses the static, top-down, one-way, transmission model of Berlo
(1960). Thus, in every way, the Sarvodaya Self-Help Movement
represents a refreshingly new approach to development when
compared to the centralized top-down techniques used in Sri
Lanka and other developing countries. In short, as Ariyaratne
(1987) aptly notes, the approach attempts to do no violence to the
local culture or the spirit of the individual, family or village.

TABLE 6.1
Western and Buddhist Models of Communication

Aristotelian Model	Buddhist Model
1. Emphasis on communicator	1. Emphasis on receiver
2. Influence a key notion	2. Understanding a key notion
3. Focus on control	3. Focus on choice
4. Emphasis on outward process	4. Emphasis on both outward and inward processes
5. Relationship between communicator and receiver asymmetrical	5. Relationship between communicator and receiver symmetrical
6. Stress on intellect	6. Stress on empathy

Source: Dissanayake (1984:49). 'A Buddhist Approach to Development'. *In* Wang
and Dissanayake (eds.), *Continuity and Change in Communication Systems*. Copyright Ablex Publishers. Reprinted by permission.

NEW ROLES FOR COMMUNICATION IN DEVELOPMENT

In the fifties and sixties, mass communication was considered the
prime mover in social development. Information was thought to
be the missing link in the development chain. Mass media such as
the printed channels and the radio were saddled with the important task of spreading information as widely as possible among the
people. Government authorities, subject experts, and extension

agents would go on the radio or visit villages lecturing to people on how to have smaller families, increase their agricultural yields, or live healthier lives. Communication flows were hierarchical, one-way, and top-down. People were regarded as passive receivers of development information. All this changed in the seventies.

Communication in Self-Development Efforts

The idea of self-development gained popularity in the seventies. In other words, user-initiated activity at the local level was considered absolutely essential for successful development at the village level. Thus, the emphasis was not so much a top-to-bottom flow of information and messages from a government official to a mass audience, but importantly, bottom-up flows or communication between people. People had to discuss together, identify their needs and problems, decide on a plan of action, and then use a specific medium of communication and an information data base most appropriate to their needs. Thus, while the mass media were

---

Audio Cassette Forum Bridges Communication Gap

How does an organization with offices widely scattered in rural areas increase the level of participation of its members and build group solidarity without the members ever leaving their doorstep? After experimenting with radio broadcasts, a monthly magazine, bulletins, etc. and finding them ineffective, CALFORU, a central cooperative in Montevideo, tried audio cassettes. What was needed was an instrument and a method to allow two-way communication so that local units could be part of the decision-making process. More active participation of the member groups would increase their sense of belonging and commitment to the organization. It would also bring forward prospective new leaders to renew managing committees that were growing stale.

Audio cassettes were found particularly suited for a two-way exchange of information. One side records the first part of the dialogue and the other, if the cassette is reversed, is used by the group to whom it is sent to express their ideas. In short, the Cassette Forum works as follows: All participating groups periodically receive a collective cassette (i.e. same message to all of them) recorded on one track, and dealing with a problem, a consultation or a proposal involving a subject of interest to all of them. Each group listens, comments upon and discusses the problems raised. Once a conclusion is reached, the group records the opinions of its members and proposals on the other track and returns it to the coordinating center. The coordinating team listens to all responses, analyzes them, decodes them and organizes them. They then become the basis for a new collective cassette. The next collective cassette always begins with a report to groups which sums up the replies received on the previous cassette. The voices of the participants themselves are transcribed, reproducing exactly what they said, and recorded. Thus, all groups are informed about what the others think; each one listens to the ideas and proposals of others and can compare them with its own. The original responses are sent back to local units so that they can hear themselves speaking their own voices. This establishes a relationship between groups. An opportunity is provided for dialogue, exchange of experience, reflection and discussion about their common problems and possible solutions. Decisions may be made democratically with the participation of all those affected by them.

This method is being used successfully by several organizations in Brazil, Ecuador, Venezuela, Colombia and Uruguay.

Source: Mario Kaplun, 'The Cassette that Talks Back', *IDRC Reports*, Vol. 14: 3,4, October 1985.

necessary, they were not sufficient for the tasks at hand. The emphasis was not on big media but appropriate media. Along these lines, Havelock (1971) suggested a *problem-solving* model which put the spotlight on the needs of users and their own diagnosis of their problems. In this model, the needs of the users were studied intensively, as also how they went about solving their problems. The need for information, then, was the prerogative of the user at the village level rather than some authority at the top.

The ensuing discussion on the role and place of communication in social and behavioral change is radically different from the postulates of the dominant paradigm of development. Early communication models implied that the mass mediated information was absolutely essential regardless of whether or not it was needed. Communication processes took place in a social and cultural vacuum and environmental variables were not given any consideration at all (McQuail and Windahl, 1981). This was a trifle strange because models in the sociology of mass communication had indicated, as early as 1959, that mass communication is but one social system among many others in a society. Riley and Riley (1959) had shown in their model that mass communication should be regarded as an important social process among other equally salient social processes. While the mass media affected individual and society, they were themselves influenced by other environmental variables (Figure 6.1).

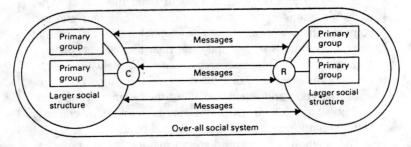

C = Communicator   R = Receiver

Figure 6.1: Riley and Riley Model (1959:577).
SOURCE: 'Mass Communication and the Social System'. *In* R.K. Merton et al. (eds.), *Sociology Today: Problems and Prospects*. © Robert Merton, Sociology Dept., Columbia University, New York. Reprinted by permission.

Self-development implied a different role for communication from what was conceptualized and operationalized in the dominant paradigm. Development agencies still had to perform a service function in terms of collecting technical information but it was no longer prescriptive. Communication flows were now initiated in response to articulated needs of the users. Several examples may be provided of successful self-development efforts. The Indian experiment with Radio Farm Forums is a case in point. The radio station provided an organized listening group in a village with useful information on agriculture and other related matters. This was the top-down component of information flow. However, the members of the listening group were the final deciding authority. They discussed the new information, its relevance to their needs and problems, and then decided to seek more information, if necessary. Thus, horizontal flows of communication were very important and any help requested was clearly at the initiative of the user (Masani, 1975).

Again, in Fogo in New Foundland, Canada, the income from once lucrative fishing business was all but destroyed. There was a flight of young people out of the village. The residents decided to act on their own using a loaned portable video recorder from the Canadian Broadcasting Corporation. They initiated discussions and debates of what the problems were and what ought to be done, all of which was taped. The people then viewed the tape and collectively decided a plan of action and with external help made their village prosperous again (Schramm, 1977). The Fogo process was replicated with some success in Ramghat *panchayat* in Surkhet district, Nepal. Here, a video camera was used to facilitate participation of women in issues of interest to their community (Belbase, 1987).

In Tanzania, there was useful information exchange between the users and subject-matter experts. When villagers in the Arusha region decided to construct latrines in their villages, they borrowed relevant audiotapes from the local communication center, which helped them with expert knowledge from the project authorities (Hedebro, 1982). Thus, Hedebro points out, in this project, the idea was not to persuade the people to do something specific at the initiative of the source but rather to let the users decide what ought to be done and then seek expert information, if necessary, on their own.

Rogers (1976b: 141) summarized the chief roles of communication in self-development efforts:

1. Provide technical information about development problems and possibilities, and about appropriate innovations, in answer to local requests, and

2.Circulate information about the self-development accomp-
lishments of local groups so that other such groups may profit
from others' experience and perhaps be challenged to achieve
a similar performance.

The role of the mass media, then, in the self-development
efforts was of a catalyst in change rather than the sole cause.
Importantly, the communication channels initiated a dialogue
between the users and the sources, helping them to 'talk together'.
Schramm (1977: 3) summarized it very succinctly:

Only when communication can build itself into the social
structure, is it going to show any real hope of extensive results.
Only when media channels can mix with interpersonal channels and with organization in the village, are you going to
have the kind of development you will like.

The communication system in the People's Republic of China is
a good example of this model. The mass media in this country
work with and through a complex web of interpersonal channels
and groups, feeding people with information they need and at the
same time carrying feedback to the party cadres.

Role of the Folk Media in Development

The newer concepts of development that were discussed in an
earlier section emphasized, among other things, the re-emergence
of culture as a facilitator of development, the integration of traditional and modern systems, and an active participation of people
at the grassroots in development programs. This change of focus
put the spotlight on indigenous channels of communication or the
folk media which were relegated to relative oblivion in the
dominant paradigm of development. The folk media seemed to
incorporate all of the newer concepts of development. They were
products of the local culture, rich in cultural symbols, were intimate
with the people at the grassroots and highly participatory, and they
had great potentiality for integration with the modern mass media.
Randall Casey (1975: 1) gives the reader a flavor of the thinking in
the seventies *vis-à-vis* the folk media:

There is ... an emerging realization that traditional elements of today's societies possess communication channels that can serve as means to stimulate rural development, and which are compatible with mass media and extension workers. These channels, are folk media which use the local idioms and are people-based.

In the early seventies, several international conferences addressed the idea of using folk media to promote development: the Expert Group Meeting sponsored by the International Planned Parenthood Federation and Unesco in London (1972); the New Delhi Seminar and Workshop on Folk Media sponsored by the Unesco and the Indian Ministry of Information and Broadcasting (1974); and the East-West Communication Institute Seminar on Traditional Media in Honolulu (1975).

Folk Media

The folk media consist of a variety of forms: folk theatre, puppetry, story-telling forms, folk dances, ballads, and mime. They have served as vehicles of communication and entertainment in Asia, Africa, and Latin America for centuries: 'Through the use of dialogue, action, music, song, and dance the stage has presented a vitally important view of the cosmos which has implanted basic beliefs and behavior patterns in rural audiences' (Van Hoosen, 1984: 127). Wang and Dissanayake (1984: 22) define folk media as a 'communication system embedded in the culture which existed before the arrival of mass media, and still exists as a vital mode of communication in many parts of the world, presenting a certain degree of continuity, despite changes.' Ranganath (1975: 12) defines the traditional media as 'living expressions of the lifestyle and culture of a people, evolved through the years.' These definitions reiterate the origin and nurturing of the folk channels in and by the richness of the indigenous culture.

The traditional uses of the folk media were primarily for entertainment, social communion, and religious activity. However, many flexible folk forms have lent themselves as vehicles of persuasive communication wherein modern messages exhort the audience members to limit the size of their families, live in harmony with their neighbors, lead more healthy lives, etc. For a long time, however, the traditional media did not enjoy this attention by development specialists. In the dominant paradigm of development, anything that

Old Zheng Shops For Shoes

The power of story-telling to make a point is demonstrated in this allegory which comes from the classical Chinese ·text *Han Fei Zi*. The moral of this story is that people should place more faith in actual practice than in old rigid values or prescriptions.

In the land of Zheng lives Genius Zheng
But everyone calls him Zheng Dum-dum.
He's stubborn and his temper's not very sweet,
He won't even try on a shoe unless he's measured his feet!
Now, one day he's going to buy some shoes,
But he takes out the measure before he goes.
He measures the height of the top of his feet,
Then the arch, and the width, and the length to his toes,
And carefully he writes 9.876 inches down on a sheet—
He always buys his shoes by the size.
Then he puts his note on the table top.
And steps outside, and locks the lock.
He walks ten miles on his own two feet
And comes to town on East Main Street.
They're selling shoes in the market place
And old Zheng heads over there, making haste.
Pairs and pairs of brand new shoes,
He picks out a pair that he can use.
Then old Zheng reaches in his pocket only to realize,
'Oh no! I forgot to bring the size.
Without a size, I can't buy shoes,
I'd really feel just like a twit
If I bought 'em and they didn't fit.'
So he hurries on back out of town,
Going home for the size that's written down.
He's all worn out and wet with sweat and gasping, he is really beat,
He's walked so hard that blisters have popped up under his feet.
When he left, the sun was at high noon,
When he returned, you could already see the moon.
He walks up, and looks around, and the shoe market's already closed down!

Old Genius Zheng can only stand and stare at the empty
market square.
Someone says: 'Old Zheng, your temperament's hard to beat—
Why didn't you just try the shoes on your own two feet?'
'But how can you buy if you don't have the size?
Just having feet isn't good enough', Old Zheng replies.
People in the old days were strange, you say?
I saw someone just like him only yesterday.

Source: Jan Walls, 'Satire: On the Road to Change', *The
IDRC* Reports, 12: 2, July 1983.

was even remotely connected with the indigenous culture was to be
eschewed. Since the traditional media were extensions of the local
culture, they were regarded as vehicles that would discourage modern
attitudes and behavioral patterns and instead reinforce cultural values
of the community. Moreover, Lerner (1958) had predicted that the
direction of change in communication systems in all societies was
from the oral media to the technology-based mass media. Also, the
mass media were hailed as indices and agents of modernization. Thus,
all resources in Third World nations were devoted to the strengthening and growth of radio and television. The period from the fifties
to the seventies, therefore, was characterized by benign neglect of
the traditional media.

The fall of the dominant paradigm in the seventies could not have
occurred sooner for the folk media. The newer concepts of development
such as self-help, grassroots participation, and two-way communication, led to a re-examination of the advantages of the traditional
media as vehicles for information, persuasion, and entertainment
of the rural masses. Clearly, the folk media have several advantages:
they are part of the rural social environment and, hence, credible
sources of information for the people. They command the audience
as live media and are ideal examples of two-way communication. They
have proved useful in generating grassroots participation and a dialogue between the performers and the audience. Many of the folk
media formats are flexible, thus facilitating the incorporation of
development-oriented messages in their themes. This renders the
traditional communication media useful and credible channels for
promoting planned change. Also, they are relatively inexpensive and,
in almost all cultures, command rich and inexhaustible variety both

in form and theme. The timeless traditional media, therefore, present inexhaustible alternatives in form and theme for experimentation in communication (Ranganath, 1980).

Critical Issues in Using Traditional Media for Development

There are some important concerns in using the folk media for development. First, a crucial issue at hand is the insertion of development-oriented messages into the content of a folk form. This is a delicate task requiring intimate knowledge of the nature of traditional communication channels (Mane, 1974). Ranganath (1980) cautions that preparation of a book of basic data, or a comprehensive account of all the known traditional media in a particular region/country should be given the highest priority. Unfortunately, this kind of research on the traditional media is lacking in most Third World nations (Wang and Dissanayake, 1984b). In the book of basic data, Ranganath (1980) suggests, the following characteristics of every folk form should be recorded under these categories:

a) Form (audio, visual, audio-visual)
b) Thematic content
c) Flexibility in accommodating development message
d) Cultural context

In terms of flexibility, Ranganath (1980) points out that it is possible to categorize all the media as: rigid, semi-flexible, and flexible. The rigid forms are usually ritualistic and very religious and reject all foreign messages. Some examples are: *Yellamma* songs, *Vydyarakunitha* (both of south India) and Chinese revolutionary opera (Ranganath, 1980; Chiao and Wei, 1984). The semi-flexible media might permit the limited insertion of foreign messages through certain characters or situations. Examples here would be rural dance drama such as *Yakshagana* of south India, leather puppetry such as *Wayang Kulit* of Indonesia, and religious forms such as *Jatra* of India. The flexible media provide unlimited opportunities for inserting development messages. Examples would be puppet drama such as *Wayang Orang* (Indonesia), ballads such as *Lavani* and *Gee Gee* of India, *Chamsoun* of the UAR, some forms of theater such as *Katha*, *Bhavai* and *Tamasha* of India, *Kakaku* of Ghana, and the Caribbean *Calypso*.

More scientific research needs to be done to categorize all the folk media in terms of the above criteria: form, theme, and flexibility, before being used as vehicles to carry development-oriented messages. Otherwise, there is a danger of harming the folk form and the inserted message (Ranganath, 1980). One example is the *Yellamma* songs, a rigid form. The songs are popular with devotees of Yellamma, the goddess of worship. Research showed that the devotees were poor and had large families:

> It was considered that these songs could be harnessed to carry pre-determined messages on various aspects of the population theme... the field reaction to the message-bearing medium was disturbing; it even became hostile... the new content of the songs to them was not merely incongruous but sacrilegious (Ranganath, 1980: 21–22).

Thus, while the folk media have great potential in communicating development-oriented messages to rural audiences, they should be . employed judiciously. And this requires intimate knowledge of the various folk media.

Another important issue deals with the integration of the folk with the mass media. This could work to the mutual advantage of both: it gives the folk media a wide geographical spread while providing the mass media with a rich array of information and entertainment themes. However, there are dangers to both media if proper methods of integration are not used. A case in point is an experiment conducted in Taiwan of integrating bag puppetry with television (Wang, 1984). Like other folk media, the popularity of once famous bag puppetry was on the decline, mainly due to the competition from television. However, by adapting it to fit the needs of television, there was a revival of this ancient Chinese folk form. Television, too, benefited from this since it was able to draw a record number of viewers who were interested in watching the puppet shows (Wang, 1984). However, in the long run, bag puppetry was changed so much to fit the needs of television that it lost its original character. The extempore dialogue was replaced by a written script, the traditional Chinese language gave way to popular slang, Chinese classical music was replaced by a hybrid of Chinese and Western rock music, and even the symbolic face-painting of the puppets was de-emphasized (Wang, 1984). Soon, televised bag puppetry was no longer the medium that attracted people to it. The changes had done serious harm to the form and theme of bag puppetry.

However, adaptation need not necessarily change, destroy or reduce the original popularity of a folk form (Chander, 1974; Chiranjit, 1974). There are several examples of successful integration: Indian television and commercial films have successfully integrated elements of folk theatre, songs, and dances (Agrawal, 1984; Krishnaswamy, 1974); Iran's *Barnameh* has been successfully adapted to radio and television; *Kakaku* of Ghana has become a successful serial over radio and television; and the Caribbean *Calypso* is a hot favorite on the stage, in films, and on television (Ranganath, 1980). In fact, integration of the folk media may be necessary to legitimize television among rural viewers and, perhaps, inevitable for the future of the waning folk media. Efforts, however, should be made to preserve the originality of each folk form (Yount, 1975).

Bridging Gaps through Development Communication Strategies

By the early seventies it was fairly clear that the social-structural constraints on development did not often yield to the indirect influences of the media. Realization dawned that there was much more to development than just communication and information (Rogers, 1976b). All this pointed to the fact that the main barriers to development in many parts of the Third World, particularly Latin America, may be mainly structural and not primary informative and that a basic restructuring of society might be needed to make the diffusion of innovations more functional in the development process (Beltran, 1976; Diaz-Bordenave, 1976; Rogers and Adhikarya, 1979; McAnany, 1980b).

However, social-structural change, desirable as it is, is difficult to achieve. Such a basic change in society needs political and ideological commitment and popular participation by a majority of the people. This kind of commitment is not easily forthcoming in many developing nations as the structures continue to support the status quo (McAnany, 1980a; Gran, 1983). There are some approaches, however, that can be useful in narrowing the socio-economic hiatus in development through communication strategies, despite the absence of major structural changes at the macro level.

Narrowing Gap through Redundancy

A communication experiment conducted by Shingi and Mody (1976) refuted the findings of Tichenor and others (1970) that the media increase socio-economic inequities among their audiences. In their study, they discovered that the media (in this case, television) could narrow the socio-economic benefits gap, but this would require using proper communication strategies. The main finding of the study indicated that those sections of the audience (i.e. the lower socio-economic status groups) which were high on ignorance before the programs, gained most in absolute terms from the television programs, although they still had a little less knowledge than the higher-knowledge audience prior to exposure.

The researchers called this the 'ceiling effect'. By selecting messages that were redundant or had little potential value to the large farmer, the media could narrow and even close—rather than widen—the communication effects gap. The significance of this study was that it proved that the knowledge or communication effects gap is not inevitable. In fact, the gap could be narrowed if appropriate communication strategies are used in diffusion activities (Shingi and Mody, 1976: 97):

1. Low knowledge and other small farmers should be encouraged to see television shows and given access to a receiver set;
2. Message content should be simple and easily understandable to non-elite audiences. Technical jargon, if any, should be simplified and sources of high credibility and understandability should be utilized;
3. The salience, appeal, and presentation of information should be such that lower-knowledge audiences could 'catch-up' with higher-status counterparts who would probably find lesser value and interest in such messages due to its redundancy and 'ceiling effect'.

These strategies, however, would need to be built into a flexible, on-going development support project, and such a venture would have to be institutionalized. One-shot approaches to development communication, the Indian Satellite Instructional Television Experiment, for example, may not result in any significant behavior change among receivers. Such ventures which provide intensive information support for a short period and are then discontinued, can be likened to the analogy of sending a child to school for a short while then taking him/her out but still expecting the child to retain all that he/she learnt. What is necessary is an institutionalized, on-going, and flexible strategy.

Overcoming Pro-Literacy Bias

A great majority of the people of lower socio-economic status (SES) in the Third World are illiterate. Yet, there have been few effective strategies in development communication research of communicating innovations to an illiterate audience (Rogers and Adhikarya, 1979). All strategies and innovations presuppose literacy and some level of knowledge or formal education (Melkote, 1984), which are by themselves innovations to the rural and urban poor.

Thus, most development benefits have accrued to the large farmers and other elite groups since they possessed the necessary prerequisities such as adequate literacy, education, and previous knowledge of innovations for exploiting the new information, methods, and techniques (Shingi and Mody, 1976; Gaur, 1981). This pro-literacy bias has acted as a major constraint to the diffusion of information to the preliterate audiences. It has prevented strategies of percolating information, knowledge, and skills to an illiterate audience which, incidentally, forms the bulk of the population in rural areas. Meanwhile, it has led to easier information access for elite groups in the urban areas.

The pro-literacy bias can be defined as the tendency of a source of communication to encode messages in terms of symbols, either written, printed, or verbal, which imply literacy and numeracy skills on the part of receivers even when they are known to lack both skills. In an earlier investigation of communication strategies of the World Bank-sponsored Training and Visit Extension system in south India (Melkote, 1984), the present author identified several symbols in extension messages to illiterate farmers that required knowledge of the native language as used by the literati, knowledge of English, the Western calendar, weights and measures in the Metric or Imperial systems, statistical terms such as averages, percentages, means, and technical terms in agriculture, agronomy, and agrobiology.

If the objective is to reduce socio-economic status and knowledge gaps between people in the developing nations, it is absolutely essential that the pro-literacy bias be identified and removed from all development-oriented communication strategies.

Tailored Messages

Access to the media has been a crucial constraint among the lower socio-economic status (SES) audiences in rural areas of the Third World. When a development agency decided to address these audiences, an important task, therefore, was to increase their exposure through better access to the media. The treatment of the messages, however, was exactly the same as that meant for higher SES audiences (Melkote, 1984). Rogers and Adhikarya (1979) caution that the lower SES groups are very different in their education, belief systems, decision-making patterns, communication habits, etc. and that the messages meant for the high SES groups may not be equally effective with them.

Therefore, while the main message content could remain the same, the message quality, i.e. relevance, design, and treatment, should be tailored to the lower SES groups. This communication strategy would require formative evaluation of the audience such as the preparation of audience profiles and needs-assessment studies, preparation of prototype materials and pre-testing them before they are mass produced.

Rogers and Adhikarya (1979) maintain that the lower SES groups are different in their education from their higher SES counterparts. However, the actual fact is that in much of the Third World, the rural media audiences with low SES have no formal education at all. They constitute a different sample altogether and any message designed for them cannot make any prior assumption of literacy, education, previous knowledge, etc. It is imperative that the pro-literacy bias that permeates extension strategies be overcome if development messages are to have any effect on lower SES groups.

It is not practical or feasible for these people to learn everything about an innovation through one or two instructional radio or television programs or a couple of visits by the field extension agent. Diffusion of an innovation, therefore, especially to lower SES groups, will need to adopt a sequential approach, with message content built according to the level of complexity of innovation and comprehension of receivers. Also, the communication content will need to be tailored to cater to peasants with different levels of cognition of innovations.

The Tetu Extension Project in rural Kenya successfully adopted such a 'gradual stages' approach to the diffusion of agricultural innovations (Ascroft et al., 1971). To start with, in the first stage the peasants were taught simple useful techniques such as row cropping, equal spacing, contouring, and weeding. None of these innovations involved any complex technology. Once the farmers had learnt these innovations and were comfortable using them, the diffusion process moved on to the second stage. Here, the farmers were told how to harvest crops and dry them. Still no complex, overhauling innovations were introduced. In the next stage, the farmers were given hybrid seeds and taught techniques of thinning and applying fertilizers and insecticides. It was only in the last stage that concepts of farm management and administration such as bookkeeping, a careful re-arrangement of plots and growing a balanced set of crops were introduced. Such a sequential adoption process, spanning a couple of years, helped people with the lowest SES to successfully adopt complex innovations. In the absence of a diffusion strategy such as the one utilized in the Tetu Extension Project, it would have been almost impossible for the illiterate or the semi-literate farmer to successfully adopt a complex innovation such as the miracle rice or the hybrid maize which requires fourteen explicit steps to be followed in order to obtain a good crop yield. Conceptually there is only one innovation (i.e. hybrid seed), but empirically there are about fourteen different innovations. Each step in the adoption process is, in fact, a separate innovation by itself. Thus, besides the hybrid seed, there are a whole host of practices which are new and complex to the farmer. It is important, therefore, that diffusion strategies be sequential and over-time, introducing one innovation at a time and breaking up the content to suit the illiterate farmers. Also, the strategy would have to be institutionalized, for example, through the establishment of schools such as farmer training centres, and provide assistance on a permanent basis to the farmer if they are to have any significant impact on rural communities.

Assessing Audience Needs

The classical diffusion of innovations perspective, influenced as it was by the dominant paradigm of development, considered the process of communication to be linear, one-dimensional, and one-way. In this process, excessive weight was given to the source of communication rather than the receiver, usually leading to inequality in the communication process, particularly in development programs (Rogers and Adhikarya, 1979). Diaz-Bordenave (1976) reports that emphasis in agricultural communication has been on communicating pro-innovation messages to farmers, instead of finding out what they need. There have been very few needs-assessment studies of poor peasants.

Thus, in development communication research, there was no clear idea of the bottlenecks to development that poor peasants faced. And, since there was little two-way participatory communication, there were few channels by which development agencies could understand and appreciate the frustrations of peasants in their attempts at adopting innovations.

Therefore, there is a great need for effective and reliable needs-assessment studies of intended audiences. If feed-forward information is encouraged through a two-way participatory process of communication, the communication process could lead to a narrowing of the socio-economic benefits gap.

At the present time, the political and ideological commitment and popular participation by a majority of the people is not easily forthcoming for such a basic change in society. However, it is possible for development workers and communication practitioners to work within structural constraints and help reduce widening socio-economic and status gaps between people.

By assessing the needs of lower SES groups, tailoring messages and communication strategies to the needs and capacities of these groups, overcoming the pro-literacy bias, and reducing knowledge gaps, it may be possible to achieve beneficial social outcomes. Thus, if the productivity of poor peasants is increased and the socio-economic benefits gap reduced through effective strategies such as those outlined above, there is a good possibility of achieving more equitable development even in the absence of major socio-structural changes at the macro level.

Development through Television
Entertainment Programs

In the seventies, the idea of using television as an instructional/ development medium appealed to both administrators and development experts because of its immense potential in propagating useful ideas and practices. The Satellite Instructional Television Experiment (SITE) launched in India in the mid-seventies broadcast instructional television programs to remote villages in India. However, research studies later showed that most viewers prefer television entertainment shows to educational programs. Two examples illustrate the trend toward increasing the entertainment content of television programs (Rogers, 1987):

1. In American Samoa, an educational television system introduced in 1967 now serves as a channel for broadcasting American entertainment shows;
2. The transmitter in Kheda district in Gujarat, India, that produced local development programs was closed down in the mid-eighties when the audience switched to viewing the Ahmedabad television station when it started to broadcast national programs (mostly entertainment) into Kheda district.

In many developing countries today, there is a general trend toward increasing commercialization of television channels. This means that the emphasis on entertainment programming will become more pronounced. A silver lining in this dark cloud may be the marketing of development-oriented entertainment programs. Therefore, pro-development *soap operas* may have an important potential for development communication (Rogers, 1987). A soap opera is a television serial with a gripping story (not necessarily development oriented) and a host of characters that have the audiences glued to the television set. In the United States, such day-time serials are called soap operas because the sponsors of such programs are usually companies producing detergents and other household cleaners (Singhal and Rogers, 1989).

The idea of a soap opera with a pro-development theme originated in Peru in 1972 with the show *Simplemente Maria* which told the rags-to-riches story of a slum girl who achieved financial success through her proficiency and hard work on her Singer sewing machine

(Singhal and Rogers, 1988). Inspired by the success of the Peruvian soap opera, the Mexican commerical television network *Televisa* produced six development-oriented soap operas between 1975 and 1981. One of the shows called *Ven Conmigo* dealt with adult literacy while another called *Accompaname* stressed family planning (Singhal and Rogers, 1988). According to Singhal and Rogers (1988: 111), 'Pro-development soap operas in Mexico promoted knowledge and values to the viewing audience so that these individuals could better understand the reality of their social problems, and seek possible solutions.' Following the example of Mexico, the Indian television authority experimented with *Hum Log*, a soap opera dealing with social problems in contemporary Indian society. This show too became very popular with Indian viewers leading to sentimental protests when it was finally taken off the air in 1985 after running 156 episodes (Singhal and Rogers, 1988).

The success of both Mexico and India with their pro-development soap operas is prompting other developing countries (such as Kenya, Nigeria, Egypt, Brazil, Pakistan, Bangladesh, Turkey, Thailand, Indonesia, and Zaire) to adapt this entertainment strategy to their specific needs (Singhal and Rogers, 1988). Therefore, the use of pro-development, commercially-sponsored soap operas on television channels in several Third World countries will have important policy implications and, at least in the near future, will need close and careful evaluation of their positive effects.

New Communication Technologies for Development

An interesting phenomenon from the mid-seventies has been the growth of communication technologies and their applications in development activities. The United States and several West European countries have already become information societies, i.e. a country in which the production, processing, and distribution of information software and hardware are the main activities (Rogers, 1986).

Communication technologies include, among others, television broadcasting, video cassette recorders, computers, satellite communications, telephony, teleconferencing, and audioconferencing. There has been a significant proliferation of each of these technologies in the developing countries in the last fifteen years. The SITE in India, the Palapa Experiment in Indonesia, use of video in several developing countries, and experiments with satellite-based rural telephony in Peru and India are only some of the examples of the wide dissemination of new technologies in the Third World. Scholars have argued quite emphatically in support of these new technologies *vis-à-vis* the development of Third World countries: telecommunications have been considered a spur to economic development (Maitland Commission, 1984; Jussawala, 1985), rural telephony has been recommended to eliminate the isolation of villages (Hudson, 1984), while satellites and computer technology have been suggested to link 'industry with markets and raw materials, the organization of political and social movements, and democratically oriented decision making' (Stover, 1984: 87). Just as there are many supporters of new technology, there are many skeptics who do not buy the rosy and optimistic picture. Their skepticism is not directed against the capabilities of the new technologies to bring about the desired outcomes described above— that is not doubted at all. Rather, they are skeptical about the socio-cultural, political, and economic contexts in developing countries that may effectively prevent the achievement of positive outcomes as seen in the Western countries (Jayaweera, 1987a).

Can information technology lead to healthy national development? Yes, provided the recipient society is patterned along the lines of Western countries: affluent, economically self-reliant, rich in technological skills, with strong social and political institutions ensuring its citizens freedom of expression, participation in public affairs, right to independent thought, genuine participatory communication, attention to basic needs, and so on. This is a far cry from the situation that exists in the majority of Third World countries, where a small coterie of individuals has cornered a disproportionate share of economic and political power, where the social and political institutions perpetuate inequality among people, and where the superpowers are more interested in supporting puppet dictatorships and autocratic regimes than in encouraging a genuine government of the people.

Another criticism of the new technologies is their highly capital-intensive nature. Their production requires highly specialized skills and only a few countries have that degree of skill (Stover, 1984). Moreover, developing nations acquire this new technology chiefly through transnational corporations which are more interested in making profits than in encouraging development (Schiller, 1981; Stover, 1984). Therefore, the desperate technological dependence of most Third World countries on the developed nations, the costs of technology, and the stranglehold of multinational corporations on the flow of technology are some of the crucial constraints that will effectively block the growth of viable, relevant, and self-reliant information technology in the developing nations (Smythe, 1985; Schiller, 1986; Lent, 1987; Reddi, 1987).

The great optimism about the potential of telecommunications and other new technologies for development is, in many respects, similar to the crusade in the fifties and sixties for the introduction and spread of the mass media in developing nations. Exposure to the mass media, it was believed, would cleanse individuals in the Third World of their traditional values, attitudes, and cultural habits, anointing them on the altars of modernity. Yet, today, despite widespread adoption of the mass media, the plight of the urban and rural poor in developing nations has become, if anything, somewhat worse than it was in the sixties. In the absence of drastic changes in the international and intranational economic and political structures, one wonders whether the case of information technology will be any different.

SUMMARY

The early seventies may be considered a watershed in the literature on communication for development. Scholars, researchers, and administrators became increasingly restive with the notion of *development* and its progress in the preceding two decades. Ironically, the plight of the very poor in the developing nations had not improved significantly since the sixties. In fact, the situation seemed to have deteriorated.

The concept of development changed quite drastically. There was a move away from the earlier technologically deterministic and GNP-centered definitions to alternative concepts that were more qualitative. They stressed: (*i*) Equity in distribution of information and other benefits of development; (*ii*) Active participation of people at the grassroots; (*iii*) Independence of local communities to tailor development projects to their own objectives;

(*iv*) Integration of the old and new ideas, the traditional and modern systems to constitute a unique blend suited to the needs of a particular community.

There were other interesting developments in the mid-seventies. The opening of China to the rest of the world showed that it was possible for a country to embark on a successful path using its own unique model of development. Also, the success of nations such as China that advocated decentralized, labor-intensive techniques provided impetus to efforts seeking alternative models of development. Schumacher's idea of *Small is Beautiful* provided one such alternative. Another consequence of the disenchantment with the trickle-down idea of development was a focus on *basic needs*: those necessities that are absolutely essential to maintain a decent quality of life. Finally, there was a renewed interest in studying the role of culture in social development.

The role accorded to communication in the development process also changed significantly. Communication was used increasingly in self-development activities. The idea of self-development gained popularity in the seventies. In other words, user-initiated activity at the local level was considered absolutely essential for successful development at the village level.

The newer concepts of development such as self-help, grassroots participation, and two-way communication led to a re-examination of the advantages of the traditional media as vehicles for information, persuasion, and entertainment of the rural masses. Clearly, the folk media have several advantages: they are part of the rural social structure and, hence, credible sources of information to the people. They have proved useful in generating grassroots participation and a dialogue between the performers and the audience. Many of the folk media formats are flexible, thus facilitating the incorporation of development-oriented messages in their themes. However, more research needs to be done on (*i*) identifying flexible folk forms for inserting development-oriented messages, and (*ii*) integrating the folk with the mass media in such a way that it does not destroy or change the original popularity of a folk form.

Research in the seventies also suggested relevant communication strategies for narrowing the socio-economic hiatus between people in developing countries despite the absence of major structural changes at the macro level. Some of these strategies were:

1. To narrow the communication gap between those high and low on socio-economic status by building redundancy in communication messages. The researchers called this as the *ceiling effect;*
2. To identify and overcome the pro-literacy bias in development communication strategies; and
3. To tailor messages to the needs and interests of the lower socio-economic groups.

The growth of new communication technologies in the late seventies and early eighties added a new dimension to development communication activities. Several scholars have argued that technologies such as satellites, rural telephony, telecommunications, and computers will usher in a new era of development in Third World countries. However, several other scholars are more cautious of the positive effects of new technologies, given the inhospitable socio-economic, political, and economic contexts in developing nations.

Chapter 7

Another Development :
Strategies for Participation and
Communication in the Eighties

> *He alone is a friend who helps us to think about our problems on our own*—A grassroots activist interviewed in *Development*, 1984, vol. 2: 47.

T he decade of the eighties was a time for stocktaking. While the *optimistic* fifties and sixties were replaced by the *counter-revolution* of the seventies, in the eighties scholars and administrators reviewed communication for development theory, development projects, and information programs to assess their contribution (or lack of it) to overall development in Third World countries. The conclusions reached have not been positive. Robert Hornik, in a comprehensive review of development communication activities in agriculture and nutrition since the fifties, concluded that of the several thousand current educational programs employing communication technology and 'given the available data about audiences reached, practices changed, benefits achieved, and long term institutional survival, we can assume that most of them fail' (Hornik, 1988: 14).

FAILURES IN THEORETICAL CONCEPTUALIZATION

An important explanation for the apparent failure of development communication projects is the underlying theoretical conceptualization of the role of information: communication scholars have blithely assumed that most problems of development may be solved by throwing information at them and not doing anything else (Hornik, 1988). This has been explained in earlier chapters but a reiteration is necessary to analyze the problem of weaknesses in theory. Many of the problems of development have very little to do with information and are caused more by structural inequities and lack of resources.

Evaluations of development activities in the eighties have revealed that there are not one but several time-sequenced development goals ranged like high hurdles from the immediate to the ultimate. Scholars have also identified a number of constraints found to be acting in such a way as to curtail achievement of these goals and many of these were not information related (Ascroft, 1985).

Ultimate Objective

All development strategies had the ultimate goal of raising the quality of life in the rural areas. Quite often, this was also interpreted as raising the standards of living of the rural people. But, it was realized that this goal was too ultimate and comprehensive. There were a number of other subgoals which were more immediate and needed to be met in order to achieve the ultimate objective of raising the quality of life. These goals could be listed in descending order and would constitute long-term and immediate objectives of any development strategy.

Long-Term Objectives

The quality of rural life could be improved by achieving all of the following objectives:

1. Increased incomes from sources within rural areas in agriculture, commerce, and industry;
2. Improved levels of social, physical, and mental well-being, such as better health, nutrition, and sanitation practices; smaller families; eradication of social injustices; land reforms; ensuring freedom of religion, speech, association, and political participation; provision of leisure and entertainment facilities like constructing community entertainment centers,

holding village fairs, providing radio, television, and other entertainment shows; and,

3. Increased self-generating development of rural people through increased self-determinism, self-reliance, and capacity to sustain continuing growth and development.

All these objectivès were still distant and more immediate goals needed to be fulfilled in order to meet the objectives listed above.

Immediate Objectives

These would constitute:

1. Raised levels of surplus marketable or reinvestment output in agricultural, commercial, and industrial enterprises in rural areas;

2. Increased wage employment in public works and private enterprises;

3. Improved public services such as extension, training, education, social, health and nutrition services;

4. Increased decentralization through effective field staff and local people participation in decision-making and project development.

Most of these objectives are usually attained to some extent due to the already existing methods and facilities in rural areas. The important issue is how to achieve these objectives to a greater extent than would seem possible with existing techniques. In diffusion research, it was assumed that these objectives—agricultural productivity, for example—were not achieved simply because the technological innovations they expounded were not available or adopted in rural areas. Hence, diffusion research recommended replacing traditional methods with technological innovations rather than improving the existing techniques and methods.

Most often, the existing methods do not need wholesale replacement. Usually, these methods are unable to raise productivity beyond an optimum level due to several constraints, the removal of which is beyond the control of peasants.

Constraints To Rural Development

1. *Lack of an effective system for delivering knowledge and skills* to the rural folk prevents them from taking advantage of productivity-increasing and, therefore, income-generating techniques and technologies;
2. *Lack of an effective system for delivering financial and material inputs* to small-scale farmers leads to non-implementation of recommendations for improving their enterprises;
3. *Inadequate market development* prevents farmers from having a guaranteed outlet and a fair price for their surplus produce;
4. *Infrastructure underdevelopment* deprives the farmers the means of conveying their produce to markets or of communication needed by them to make informed entrepreneurial decisions. (Also includes inadequacy of other facilities such as electricity, domestic and irrigation water schemes, education, health, and other social welfare amenities);
5. *Lack of employment opportunities* in rural areas for the rural landless or those with farms too small to occupy them full time results in decreasing levels of income generation; and
6. *Lack of people involvement* in designing, planning, and executing their own development leads to non-adoption of productivity-increasing innovations.

Seen in the light of the development objectives on the one hand and constraints upon goal achievement on the other, it becomes obvious that overcoming the constraints is, in effect, the most immediate goal to achieve. Without the prior removal of these constraints none of the other objectives: ultimate, intermediate, or immediate, are likely to be satisfactorily attained. To the development worker in the field, these six factors are suggestive of the kinds of constraints that would need to be removed in some concerted fashion if development goals are to be given greater likelihood of attainment. That the action should be concerted cannot be overemphasized.

The existence of formidable structural and resource-related constraints does not necessarily mean that there is no role for information in development activities. Hornik points out that

(1988: 156) 'knowing that failure to innovate is *sometimes* economically explained, is not evidence that it can *always* be explained economically. There is counter evidence that supports the notion that worthwhile change is possible, given fixed resources.' ' For example, inequity of nutritional status within families is open to non-income and information-based interventions. In countries such as India and Nicaragua, studies showed that additional incomes were not used for nutritional improvement even when there was a clear need to do so (Hornik, 1988). Thus, it is possible to improve nutritional status of mothers and infants or agricultural productivity of farmers through information-based interventions even when other resources remain constant. Further, there are other situations when communication can have great potential for change and adaptation (Hornik, 1988):

1. When the environment changes quite rapidly (example: change in food prices, migration, population explosion, revolutions, and natural disasters) and current behavior may not be adequate to deal with the changed circumstances;
2. When new resources are introduced: such as new credit opportunities, new products such as hybrid seeds or soy milk product, and improved technologies (like ORT).

If indeed there is some potential for communication activities in development, why have current programs using both conventional approaches and communication technology failed to realize their objectives? Does the fault lie with the receiver for not adopting the innovation? While the *victim blame* theories succeeded in explaining the problems in the fifties and sixties by pinning the blame on the receivers, today Hornik (1988), Ascroft (1985) and a majority of other scholars concur that the problem lies with the way information programs/projects are conceptualized, designed, and delivered. There is very little information flowing to the beneficiaries and much of it is not relevant to their needs and problems:

Available studies suggest that conventional information distribution channels are typically weak. They may reach a small proportion of the potential audience and they carry information that is either dated or unresponsive to the needs of the audience. Agricultural extension agents are too few, have too little research and logistical support, and are too rarely rewarded for successful work with farmers. Health and nutrition education is most often a burdensome additional activity for predominantly curative health services; ambitious outreach programs atrophy with time (Hornik, 1988: 157–58).

Studies conducted by Melkote (1984) and Vallath (1989) point out serious problems with extension messages in agricultural projects. Messages were laced with a pro-literacy bias making them quite unsuitable to the illiterate small-scale farmers.

Another reason why communication projects have failed to help the very poor is the top-down and authority-driven nature of these programs. 'So long as the *targets* of development efforts depend on an elite's paternalistic willingness to do good, to spend resources for the benefit of the powerless, little good will be done. The answer is to be found in small-scale efforts run for and by the beneficiaries, called *participatory* programs' (Hornik, 1988: xii). Perhaps we are again seeing failures in theory. Too much emphasis has been placed on informational value to individuals and very little importance given to the organizational value of communication for communities. There is much more benefit in treating a community as the unit of manipulation rather than individuals since many innovations are beyond the resources of individuals (Hornik, 1988).

The remainder of this chapter, then, is divided into two sections. In the first section, the concept of *participation* is comprehensively discussed. It will be shown how participation may be operationalized in development communication projects. Some problems in message construction in extension projects will be addressed and participatory message development models that may be used to overcome message- and source-related biases will be described.

In the second section, the concept of *Development Support Communication* (DSC) is introduced. It will be shown how this concept is used to bridge communication gaps through co-equal knowledge-sharing between *beneficiaries* and *benefactors*. However, DSC as conceptualized in this book, goes beyond just message transmission. It should really be seen as a management information function. Finally, a model for multidisciplinary training of students for DSC work will be described.

ANOTHER DEVELOPMENT: STRATEGIES FOR PARTICIPATION AND COMMUNICATION

Development priorities have changed over the last ten years. There has been a subtle shift from the positivist-instrumentalist approach of the modernization paradigm toward a model that is less quantitative, and more qualitative and normative (Rogers, 1987). In this paradigm, priorities are more contextual to the needs and problems of individual countries (or communities) than the universal applicability of earlier paradigms (Servaes, 1985; Mowlana and Wilson, 1988). As Jacobson points out, it signifies a period in which nations (or areas within them) are expected to set their own priorities, goals and standards which may be unique to their problem-situations (Jacobson, 1989). Jan Servaes (1985) defines this as *multiplicity in one world*.

This new paradigm of the eighties, sometimes termed as *Another Development*, is pluralistic and does not have the authoritarian characteristics of the earlier modernization paradigm. The new approaches focus on both human and economic concerns. Consequently, increased attention is being paid to basic needs of people, health, nutrition, ecology, structural transformation, and participatory democracy.

Sustainable Development: New Watchword for the Nineties

The World Commission on Environment and Development has defined sustainable development as 'meeting the needs and aspirations of the present generation without compromising the ability of future generations to meet their needs' (Brundtland, 1989: 14). This idea of sustainable development will become an important conceptual and practical framework for all development activities in the nineties and beyond. Importantly, it puts forth the view that promotion of the environment and economic development are not separate issues. For a very long time now, economic progress and growth were assigned the highest priority and the resulting environmental sacrifices were considered inconsequential.

As Williams posits: 'It was this underlying premise which largely marginalized the save-the-environment efforts of the past two decades, with the resulting cumulatively more serious threats to life support and global systems which we face today' (Williams, 1989: 8). Today, the human race faces enormous challenges to its very existence: reckless destruction of rain forests; carbon emission of fossil fuels and the consequent warming of the earth's climate; land, water, and air pollution; damage to the ozone shield, etc.

The Worldwatch Institute has set the year 2030, a mere forty years away, as the amount of time humankind has to transform itself into a socio-economic polity which can sustain itself indefinitely. If humankind continues to pursue policies that endanger our fragile planet, the Worldwatch Institute predicts that ecological disaster and economic decline will be concomitant and causal processes resulting in societal disintegration (*The Blade*, 1990).

Neither the developing nor the developed countries are solely responsible for the present state of affairs. The developed nations will need to focus their attention on reducing and finally eliminating contamination of our planet by 'harmful and inefficient exploitation of energy, misuse of chemicals and uncontrolled disposal of toxic wastes' (Williams, 1989: 7). The developing nations, on the other hand, ought to focus their energies on halting the destruction of natural resources, limiting the population explosion, and not imitating the Western model of growth and development which has, until recently, ignored the fragile ecosystem of planet Earth. Perhaps this is easier said than done for many Third World countries which can now afford and have access to technologies to *enjoy life* like the Westerners have over the past few decades. The irony is that these technologies may be harmful to the environment.

Williams suggests that the top priority now should be to 'help developing countries build the local capacity to integrate sustainable resource policies and management into their development programs. Assistance should be offered for assessment of environment impact and adoption of strategies for natural resources conservation.' The developed countries will need to take a hard look at life styles of their people which are marked by wasteful consumption of resources and attempt to build environmental concerns into their industrial and economic policies. As Gyan-Apentang (1988) posited: 'Between the East and the West, the science that produced space travel and nuclear weapons should be able to create an environment-friendly alternative life-style.'

Focus on Community Participation

The eighties have witnessed an increasing recognition within national governments, multilateral agencies, and non-governmental organizations of the importance of the social aspects of development. Areas of greater interest have been the issue of participation of intended beneficiaries in the planning and implementation of projects, the inclusion of social analysis into development planning, and the consideration of gender issues in development project planning and policies (Bamberger, 1988).

There have been several factors that have provided impetus to addressing the importance of community participation in development activities:

1. There has been some evidence in World Bank projects in rural and population/health areas of the positive impact of community participation on project efficiency;
2. Local and national governments are finding it increasingly difficult to manage adequately the innumerable development projects and programs, thus paving the way for a more prominent role for non-governmental and community organizations;
3. Non-governmental organizations and several United Nations agencies such as UNICEF and ILO have made it their development objective to *empower* the underprivileged populations by giving them greater control over resources and decisions in projects and programs affecting their lives;
4. There has been a greater sensitivity to gender issues. The special needs and problems of women need to be taken into account in project design and management (Bamberger, 1988: 2).

Operationalization of 'Participation'

Ascroft and Masilela (1989) point out that the concept and process of participation are poorly defined and internally inconsistent, abstract, and ambiguous in the social sciences. Attempts at operationalization of this term range from 'those which are thinly-veiled reincarnations of the dominant paradigm—the *participation-as-a-means approach*—to those which genuinely represent the case for the basic needs paradigm—the *participation-as-an-end approach*' (Ascroft and Masilela, 1989: 12).

The participation-as-an-end approach has received support from scholars and administrators alike (Tehranian, 1985; Alamgir, 1988; Bamberger, 1988; Diaz-Bordenave, 1989). They argue that participation must be recognized as a basic human right. It should be accepted and supported as an end in itself and not for its results (Kothari, 1984). The need to: think, express oneself, belong to a group, be recognized as a person, appreciated and respected, have some say in crucial decisions affecting one's life, etc. are as essential to the development of an individual as eating, drinking, and sleeping (Diaz-Bordenave, 1989). And, participation in meaningful activities is the vehicle through which the needs described above are fulfilled. Diaz-Bordenave (1989: 3) puts it across cogently: 'Participation is not a fringe benefit that authorities may grant as a concession but every human being's birthright that no authority may deny or prevent.'

The participation-as-a-means to an end approach could be seen along a continuum: ranging from attempts at mobilization of the populace to cooperate in development activities to *empowering* the people so that they may articulate and manage their own development. In the former approach, the people may not be expected to participate in identifying the problem or designing a development program. In such situations, participation by the people is very shallow, reduced to a process whereby people are externally manipulated to serve the ends of authorities in charge of such programs (Nair and White, 1987; Ascroft and Masilela, 1989; Diaz-Bordenave, 1989). Participation as a process of empowering the people, though politically quite risky to higher authorities, is the ideal consequence of participation. Here, the individuals are active in the development programs and processes, they contribute

---

A Grassroots Tree Planting Campaign

In one part of Tijuana in Mexico, the neighborhood name *El*

Florido represents a hope and not a reality. El Florido is not very *florido* (in bloom). On the contrary, although the soil is fertile, El Florido winds through dry, bald, desert hills. One of the homes here, owned by a woman named Alejandra, stood out from the rest; it had a nice garden with many small, healthy trees, bright flowers and vines spiraling around the porch.

The community was interested in reforestation of their area. They set about doing this in their own unique way. Alejandra was invited to work with members of the *Taller,* a grassroots communications workshop, to create a photomural. She agreed to host a meeting, invited other women from her neighborhood and jointly they planned on constructing a photomural. Alejandra and her friend decided what to photograph. The message was communicated through a basic juxtaposition of two images: a photograph of houses on barren hills with no green in sight next to a photo of a healthy green tree in front of a house with a garden. Under the first picture was written *Asi Esta* (This is how it is), and under the second picture was written *Asi Puede Ser* (This is how it could be).

The group also used photographs to illustrate gardening techniques designed to make more efficient use of costly and scarce water. Then the group met to edit the photographs, to write the text, and lay out the mural. The group decided on several slogans: *Luchemos por un Florido...'Florido'* (Let's Work for a Community...In Bloom); *Transforma lo Seco en Verde, lo Triste en Alegre* (Transform the Dry into Green, the Sad into Happy), etc. The photomural was then stapled to the bulletin board in the market place during a Sunday morning community meeting.

Evaluating the impact of the mural was not just a matter of counting the number of neighbors who signed the mailing list at the market place or the number who came to subsequent meetings. Instead, the biggest impact the mural had can best be seen in the process of creating it. This experiment proved to be an effective catalyst for organizing the community. Alejandra, her neighbors, and members of the *Taller* entered into a productive dialogue concerning the lack of trees and gardens in their community. They discussed the campaign's benefits, shared water-saving techniques, and decided how to pitch the campaign to other members of the community. Also, while shooting the photographs, they were actively investigating community problems and explaining their efforts to neighbors. Soon, a reforestation committee was formed. Members of this committee visited government authorities to solicit participation in the government's tree-donation program. After a few months, a truck arrived in the neighborhood to distribute 200 small trees, now firmly planted in El Florido's soil. Committee members also organized a pilot project in family gardening. They obtained technical help from specialists working for a local development agency. Fifteen families have planted model organic vegetable gardens. And, these families will continue to spread their knowledge throughout their community.

Source: Philip Decker, 'Grassroots Communication: Lessons From a Tree-Planting Campaign', *Development Communication Report*, No. 65, 2, 1989, pp. 1–4.

ideas, take initiatives, articulate their needs and problems, and assert their autonomy (Ascroft and Masilela, 1989). An important issue here deals with the often conflicting aims of development project efficiency on the one hand and empowerment of the beneficiaries on the other. Many bilateral and mutilateral donor agencies employ participatory approaches to achieve project efficiency (Bamberger, 1988). Thus, the success of participatory approaches needs to be examined in terms of the overall objectives of the government and the donor agencies: social justice or economic growth and development. Bamberger (1988: 6) does not see such a dichotomy. He posits that:

efficiency and empowerment objectives are complementary stages in a long-term evolution strategy. Advocates of this approach argue that empowerment is a longer-term objective that first requires the strengthening of community institutions, which is best achieved through organization of small and then increasingly larger projects. If this approach is valid, tracing an increasing degree of community empowerment with each successive project should be possible.

Participatory Research

The participatory research model is built upon the pluralistic *multiplicity in one world* paradigm described earlier (Servaes, 1989). It involves the input of individuals at the grassroots in defining and planning development goals and strategies. Participatory research calls for:

> upward, transactive, open and radical forms of planning that encompass both grassroots collective actions and large-scale processes. This kind of planning and research is centrally conceived with human growth, learning processes through mobilization, and the basic aim is to involve the people under study cooperatively in the planning and research process, with the planner or researcher as a facilitator and participant (Servaes, 1989: 17).

A Little Bit of Self Help Goes a Long Way

The example of how native Indian people in Canada solved a problem important to their community shows how ordinary people are capable of generating the knowledge necessary to guide their action.

In the sixties, health and social service professionals identified a widespread crisis in native family life. Alarming numbers of parents were evidently failing to provide adequate care and supervision of their children. The response of government-supported social agencies was to remove the children from the circumstances of neglect and place them in foster care outside the communities, where they typically remained until the age of 16 or 18.

Social science researchers interested in this phenomenon noted that child neglect, with subsequent child removal, was occurring most frequently in communities where the shift away from a hunting and fishing life style had taken place without complementary integration into an urban-oriented, industrial economy. Mental health clinicians observed that the deficiencies in parenting were occurring in families where the parents themselves had been deprived of adequate socialization because of confinement in residential schools throughout their formative years, a practice that had largely been abandoned by the seventies.

There were also studies documenting a correlation between foster care experience and conflict with the law, suicide, and other symptoms of mental distress in native youth and young adults. Although these research findings gave a partial explanation of what was happening, they did not result in action to institute new economic strategies or to stem the tide of further family disruption.

It was the initiative of native political leaders that established child welfare reform as a national native priority in 1983. This was the culmination of a participatory research process, carried out primarily in an oral mode, which began in local communities and gathered momentum over several years. Local actions had protested adoption practices that permanently removed native children from tribal membership. Influential chiefs, who had themselves lost children or other relatives to adoption, foster care, and suicide, were outspoken in their criticism. A film and study reports on the issue were produced and widely circulated. Nation-wide hearings of a federal government committee on native self-government provided a forum in which the breadth and depth of concern became evident.

By 1983 there was a consensus among native people and assent in government agencies that wholesale removal of native children from their families and communities had to stop and that family support measures had to be initiated. Local leaders demanded that social agency personnel be accountable to local authorities. Alternative care facilities in the community began to be identified. Health education, carried out by health aides recruited from the community and aimed particularly at young, often single parents, was promoted. Study circles and workshops on nutrition, family violence, alcohol abuse, and parent-child communication were convened. Competent parents and elders knowledgeable about traditions of child rearing were sought out as resources.

At present, local communities in many districts are banding together to establish family and child service agencies. These agencies assume legal responsibility for protecting the welfare of children, which, native people declare, has always been their right and their responsibility, even though it was taken over for a time by outsiders.

Source: M.B. Castellano, 'Collective Wisdom, Participatory Research and Canada's Native People', *The IDRC Reports*, 15, 3, July 1986.

The characteristics of participatory research may be described as follows (Kronenburg, 1986: 255):

1. It rests on the assumption that human beings have an innate ability to create knowledge and that this is not the prerogative of 'professionals';
2. It is an educational process for the participants in the research program as well as for the researcher. It involves the identification of community needs, awareness regarding constraints, an analysis of the causes of glitches and the designing and execution of solutions;
3. There is a conscious commitment of the researcher to work for the cause of the community. Thus, the traditional scientific principle of neutrality is rejected in this research;
4. It is based on a dialectical process of dialogue between the researcher and the community. Dialogue provides a framework which guards against manipulation from outside and serves as a means of control by the community over the direction of the research process;
5. It is a problem-solving approach. The aim is to discover the causes of problems and mobilize the creative human potential to solve social problems by changing the underlying conditions to those problems;
6. Its major asset is its heuristic value. The close cooperation between the researcher and the community fosters an atmosphere in which all participants analyze the social environment and formulate plans of action.

Some scholars consider the new participatory strategies as 'organic' and 'human' and contrast it with the earlier mechanistic models (Servaes, 1989). The main characteristics of these ideal-typical extremes are summarized in Table 7.1.

TABLE 7.1
Organic and Mechanistic Models for Research and Policy

Mechanistic Model	Organic Model
Motive for cooperation:	
People need to be helped (Charity)	People can help themselves (Empowerment)
Assumptions about target group:	
They lack abilities and resources	They have the ability to

to develop themselves (They are helpless)	develop themselves (They can be mobilised)
Attitude toward problems: Problem-solving	Problem-posing
Attitude toward participation: Means to achieve ends	A never-ending process
Objective of policy makers: Implementation of project objectives	Striving toward a common vision and understanding of self-development
Learning relationship: Teacher knows all and student knows nothing	Everybody has something of interest to share
Valuation of knowledge: Western knowledge is superior	Traditional knowledge is equally relevant
Agent of change: Policy-maker or researcher	People themselves
People seen as: Targets, objects	Subjects, actors
Leadership position: Project leader	Coordinator, animator, facilitator
Selection of leaders: Appointed by higher authorities	Preferably selected by people themselves
Leadership qualifications: Decision-making, management, authoritative	Cooperation, delegation, receptive, adaptability
Media used: Mostly mass media	Integrated media use
Communication process: Top-down, one-way	Bottom-up, two-way
Organisational structure: Hierarchical, vertical	Horizontal, two-way
Design criteria: Productivity and economic growth	Needs and criteria for well-being formulated by people themselves
Approach to work: Execute tasks	Listen to people, facilitating

Mode of Communication:
Monologue, consultation   Dialogue

Planning format:
Blueprint, project approach   Open-ended, process approach

Time perspective:
Short-term   Long-term

Initiative for evaluation:
By funding agency or   By people themselves
higher authorities

Type of solution:
Symptom curing;   Aimed at elimination of root
evolutionary change   causes; structural change

Source: Jan Servaes. 1989: 18–19.

Distortions and Constraints in Participation

First, there is a certain ambiguity regarding the conceptualization and operationalization of participation. It has different meanings for different people. Participation could mean *empowerment* of the people for some, while for others it could signify the manipulation of the populace to carry out goals set from the top. Or, it could signify conscientization of the masses to the world around them or it could be false participation where the people are co-opted to maintaining the status quo. It could be used to promote social justice in a society or to bring about economic development and greater efficiency to development programs. Participation could be at the local or national level (Diaz-Bordenave, 1989; Jacobson, 1989).

Second, there are several constraints that may prevent effective and meaningful participation of the people at the grassroots (Alamgir, 1988: 99):

1. Inhospitable political climate in the host society;
2. Inadequacy of local leadership and organization;
3. Authoritarian structure that prevents democratic decision-making;
4. Isolation and alienation of the poor and the powerless;
5. Unequal access to factors of production;
6. Inadequate government policies or financial support;
7. Lack of support for participation of women;

8. Inadequate infrastructure for generating true participation (i.e. horizontal and vertical linkages between self-help organizations).

Participation and Communication

If communication was important in modernization theories, it is an integral part of participatory development approaches. The range and role of communication in participatory approaches is much more complex and varied. This section and the next will sketch the present thinking on ways in which participation and communication are conceptualized and operationalized. The communication approaches, unlike in the modernization theories, vary depending on the normative goals and standards set by the host communities.

Grassroots Dialogic Forums

If development is to have any relevance to the people who need it most, it must start where the real needs and problems exist, i.e. in the poverty-stricken rural areas, urban slums, etc. People living in such peripheries must be encouraged to perceive their *real* needs and identify their *real* problems. To a large extent, these people have not been able to do so due to a lack of *real* participation in development strategies ostensibly set up to ameliorate their problems. Alternative communication strategies such as the bottom-up approach have often turned out to be mere cliches lacking in substance.

Some of the newer approaches favored active participation of peasants and others at the grassroots in developing nations. On the surface, these signaled a positive departure from the earlier overly top-down, prescriptive approaches. However, the structure of elite domination was not disturbed. Diaz-Bordenave (1980) noted that in these new approaches, the participation that was expected was often *directed* by the sources and change agents. In these so-called bottom-up approaches to development, people were induced to participate in self-help activities, but the basic solutions to local problems were already selected by the external development agencies. The participation of the people was directed because, often times, the aim of development projects was to achieve the cooperation of the masses in increasing agricultural production, achieve better formal and non-formal education, etc. Thus, people at the grassroots were co-opted in activities which, in the long run, would make consumers of them for industrial goods and other material comforts. Participation, therefore, was a means to an end: the end being greater dependence of the masses on a market controlled by the elites, both national and international (Diaz-Bordenave, 1980). True participation, however, should go beyond such pragmatic goals as higher productivity, better health habits, higher education, to social and political action by masses at all levels. The goal of participation efforts should be to facilitate *conscientization* of peasants on the extremely unequal social, political, and spatial structures in their societies. It is through conscientization and collective action that peasants could be made to perceive their *real* needs, identify their *real* constraints and plan to overcome problems.

It was Paulo Freire (1971) who first introduced the concept of conscientization. He was disappointed with educational systems in Brazil and Chile and advocated 'its replacement with a more liberating type of communication education that would contain more dialogue and would be both more receiver-centered and more conscious of social structure' (Diaz-Bordenave, 1976: 46). Freire argued that in the traditional pedagogical systems, the receivers were supposed to be uncritical and passive, ingesting the world view of the elites and then perceiving their problems and needs in terms of the elite-dominated rationality. Freire argued that in the pedagogical system he proposed, the receiver would be liberated from his/her mental inertia, penetrate the ideological mist imposed by the elites and perceive the realities of his/her existence (Diaz-Bordenave, 1976: 46). He called this process conscientization. Armed with *new* knowledge of their existential situation, the peasants could then come up with a plan of action that would liberate them from their dependent and exploited status.

Freire used a photograph, a picture or a drawing to represent the existing reality. A discussion was then initiated which sought to conduct an autopsy of the existing realities and encouraged the participants to question why things were as they were, what could be done to rectify the situation, etc. In other words, communication channels were used in this approach to generate a dialogue, to help people talk together and understand each other. Communication was thus a vehicle for *liberation* from mental and psychological shackles that bound peasants to their existing situations. In many ways, communication was performing its true function: *communicare* or build commonness.

New Communication Functions of Participatory Media

Another Development considers participation by itself as central to the development process. Increased participation of the people as enabled through interpersonal and group communication, the indigenous communication channels or the mass media are seen as synonymous with individual and social development (Jacobson, 1989). All this indicates new functions for communication in development. Diaz-Bordenave cites some of the new functions for communication media that may contribute significantly to a participative society (1989: 11):

1. Help in the development of a community's cultural identity;
2. Act as a vehicle for citizen self-expression;
3. Facilitate problem articulation:
4. Serve as tools for diagnosis of community's problems.

Until now, the mass media have served largely as vehicles for top-down persuasion or as channels to convey information from experts/authorities to the people. To rectify this situation, many national governments in Asia, Africa, and Latin America have incorporated indigenous communication media (i.e. folk media) to increase the effectiveness of communication and to bring about greater participation of rural and urban poor in the development process (Wang and Dissanayake, 1984b). However, the use of alternative media such as the indigenous communication channels has not made a significant difference in the basic role of communication. When using either the mass media or the folk channels for development, an issue that should be of critical concern is: communication for what purpose? As in the mass media, the traditional communication channels too may be used to dictate the views and prescriptions of the dominant class, legitimize an unfair socio-economic system, and thus maintain a status quo in an unequal society. Or, the folk media could be employed to conscientize the masses on the unjust structures in their society and encourage them to seek social transformation. Thus, regardless of the media employed, the overall design of the communication strategies will have a lasting impact on the goals. Ross Kidd (1984) and Van Hoosen (1984), through their comparative analyses of organizations using the folk media to promote development in Asia and Africa, highlight crucial issues involving design of communication strategies. They posit that folk media channels could be one-way, top-down, and used to co-opt the masses to the prescriptions from above, or they could be used just as effectively to encourage social consciousness and critical awareness of their audiences to their existential situations. Kidd compares the Song and Drama Division (SDD) of the Ministry of Information and Broadcasting, Government of India, with Action for Cultural and Political Change (ACPC), a self-help group of educated Harijans (a socially oppressed group) in Tamil Nadu, India, to highlight the differences between the top-down and grassroots models.

Song and Drama Division (SDD). The SDD is controlled either by the central government from the nation's capital city or by the respective state governments. The chief role of the SDD is to use the folk media such as theater, mime, and song and dance to modernize people's attitudes and behaviors (Parmar, 1975). Basically, the SDD acts as a publicity unit informing the people about services and programs made available by the government and then, via the folk media performances, persuade the audiences to accept the *modern* ideas and change their attitudes and behaviors accordingly. The model is top-down and highly prescriptive. The program content and topics have to be approved by decision-makers at the highest governmental levels. The process resembles the *banking* exercise (Freire, 1971) wherein exogenous ideas are deposited into the heads of passive receivers. Kidd (1984) posits that there is a consistent philosophy and rationale behind this communication framework. The SDD accepts:

> the modernization framework of transforming the traditional sector through introducing modern inputs. This provides the rationale for their 'banking' approach. The poor are poor because they are 'backward' or 'traditional'. It is up to the modern sector to overcome traditional ideas and bad habits and replace them with new ways of thinking and behaving. This is necessarily a one-way approach because the poor have

nothing to contribute to the interaction, being 'ignorant' and 'backward'. Their role is simply to absorb new information, attitudes, and habits (Kidd, 1984: 117).

The SDD performs the valuable function of creating awareness among the rural people of new services and programs provided by the government specifically for their benefit. The folk performances also provide useful information on such topics as a balanced diet or where to get a loan. However, the underlying bias is to entirely blame the receiver for his/her backwardness. The skits usually point out that a person is backward because he/she has too many children, or is lazy, does not eat healthy food, maintain hygienic surroundings, etc. While some of these reasons may indeed be true they reflect only one dimension of the reality. Often, there is another aspect to reality:

These easy slogans fail to address, for example, (a) the economic circumstances (needed for labor and old-age security) forcing people to have large families (b) the issue of transportation itself (c) the exploitation of rickshaw pullers (d) the red tape and corruption involved in getting a development loan (e) the underlying political economic conditions which often leave people without any diet, let alone a balanced diet. Instead of giving a broader picture of people's material conditions, the political-economic structures creating those conditions, and the obstacles they face in taking individual or collective actions, an easy technical solution is offered (Kidd, 1984: 119).

Thus, while the masses are encouraged to engage in self-help activities by providing them with information of new services and programs, the larger aim is to persuade them to take on a compliant role in an inequitable socio-economic system.

Action for Cultural and Political Change. A question that begs for an answer is: self-help to achieve what? If people are locked into an oppressive and inequitable socio-economic and political structure, is self-help going to be used to achieve minimum gains while maintaining the status quo in society or is it going to be employed for social transformation?

Action for Cultural and Political Change (ACPC), an organization of Harijan agricultural laborers in Tamil Nadu, India, believes in social transformation. It is a popular organization run by the peasants in which drama occupies a central part of a socio-economic and political transformation process involving conscientization, organization, and struggle (Kidd, 1984). For the ACPC, 'the cause of poverty and underdevelopment is not the inadequacies and ignorance of the poor; it is the structural relationships which keep the poor powerless, subservient, and exploited' (Kidd, 1984: 118). Thus, their 'backwardness' is more a symptom rather than the cause of their wretched state. Organizations such as the ACPC consider the conventional strategy to development as the 'Band-Aid' approach: a situation where the wounds of soldiers returning from a war are treated with band-aid and they are sent right back to fight the war. What the ACPC is attempting through their people's movement is to do something about the 'war' which is producing so many wounded soldiers. This organization does not see any merit in the conventional approach to development where the victims of an inequitable and unjust structure are given token benefits in the form of handouts (i.e. band-aids) to temporarily relieve their misery and then promptly sent back to accept a compliant role in the structure which produced their misery in the first place.

The organizing process of the ACPC consists of a number of stages: (*i*) getting into, accepted, and grounded in an area; (*ii*) adult education and literacy classes; (*iii*) leadership training and action committees; (*iv*) cultural action programs and mass meetings; and (*v*) struggle and movement (Kidd, 1984: 107). Unlike the conventional development approach which is essentially an exercise in top-down propaganda and bureaucratic paternalism, controlled and run by development planners, the ACPC approach is a self-reliant, people's movement at the grassroots. The main vehicle of conscientization, organization, and struggle is the drama. The plays

> grow out of the situations, experiences, and analysis of the actors who are themselves villagers. They aren't handed centrally produced, prepackaged scripts and told to perform. They create their own dramas out of their own collective analyses of their immediate situation and the deeper structures in which they are embedded. This is a genuine expression of the people (Kidd, 1984: 117).

As stated earlier in this chapter, the ACPC approach is a fine example of how people living in the periphery perceive their *real* needs and problems through active participation in the development strategies. Through reality-based village plays, the peasants are encouraged to develop a critical awareness of the realities of their situation, identify *real* constraints, and plan collectively to overcome problems. What we see here is a self-reliant, grassroots movement that truly understands its *real* problems and is attempting to achieve its goals.

The ACPC is not the only village-based group doing such work. Several grassroots community groups in the Philippines such as *Kulturang Tabonon Sa Debaw* of Davao and the *Kabalaka Mobile Theater* also advocate dramatic conscientization (Van Hoosen, 1984). These groups are attempting to bring awareness amongst the villagers of some of the socio-political factors affecting their lives. Other notable examples of participatory grassroots movements include the *Bhoomi Sena* movement in India, the *Mother's Club* in Korea, the *Ujamaa* in Tanzania, and several community groups in Colombia, Mexico, Brazil, and Chile.

The approach described above illustrates effective ways of using the folk media to mobilize people at the grassroots. The concern, however, is: how feasible or practical is it to stimulate such grassroots movements all over the countryside in the developing countries given the prevailing socio-economic and political structures in these nations? It is very likely that vested interests may feel threatened by the activities of grassroots development efforts to change the status quo. Examples from Brazil and Mexico where physical force was brought on grassroots development groups attests to this fact (Shaull, 1971; Van Hoosen, 1984).

However, the bottom-up approaches described in this chapter provide an effective framework of action for the people at the grassroots. They help them to perceive and articulate their needs and expectations and strive to achieve their objectives through collective action. Such grassroots movements will be close to the indigenous culture, using it as a facilitator of development rather than working against it as in the top-down, exogenous models. Also, Rahman (1981: 43) notes, 'participation is a process whose course cannot be determined from outside—it is generated by the continuing praxis of the people, i.e. by a rhythm of collective action and reflection. This is what makes the process people's own as opposed to the people being mobilized, led or directed, by outside forces.' However, it is paradoxical that such efforts may cause an adverse reaction from vested interests whose power may be threatened, leading to legal, administrative, and physical interventions to stop such 'subversive' movements.

Knowledge-Sharing on a Co-Equal Basis

Leading scholars in development communication are now arguing for communication between the *benefactor* and the *beneficiary* where each side has an equal chance of influencing the other. The communication model that is envisaged for this would allow for exchange of information, ideas, etc. between equals. The emphasis is on knowledge-sharing rather than top-down transmission of information and teaching (Ascroft et al., 1987; Ascroft and Masilela, 1989).

The communication model that would be set up for this kind of interaction would, of necessity, be sender- and user-oriented. It would incorporate, among other things, multiplicity of ideas, decentralization, deprofessionalization, deinstitutionalization, symmetrical exchange with interchange of roles between senders and receivers. This orientation of the new communication model, contrary to the oligarchic communication models of the fifties and sixties, is fundamentally two-way, interactive, and participatory at all levels (McQuail, 1983; Servaes, 1985). The pluralistic nature of this model fits well with the *multiplicity in one world* paradigm; it also implies a more dialectic mobilization, thus complementing the Friere approach.

Communication on a co-equal basis is ethically correct and practically more relevant and useful. By promising a more democratic forum for communication it supports the *Right to Communicate*, a basic human right recognized by the United Nations charter affording access to communication channels to all people at the national, local, and individual levels. Practically, it is important too. By allowing a symmetrical exchange of ideas between senders and receivers, it provides access to the storehouse of useful information and ideas of people at the grassroots. Some development agencies have benefited from such knowledge. Alamgir (1988: 98) notes that 'the International Fund for Agricultural Development has found that much that is innovative in rural development stems from the traditions and practices of the poor themselves, who have experience in the demands of survival in a harsh environment.'

However, in development communication the experts and policy-makers have neglected to listen, understand, and incorporate the innate wisdom and knowledge of the rural and urban poor concerning the environment in which they are very familiar (Alamgir, 1988). The diffusion of innovations research reinforced the stereotype constructed earlier by modernization theories that the rural people in developing nations had little useful knowledge or skills to contribute to real development and much of it was either irrelevant or trivial.

In the eighties, however, development scholars began to rediscover the complexity, depth, and sharpness of rural people's knowledge:

> Rural people's knowledge is often superior to that of outsiders. Examples can be found in mixed cropping, knowledge of the environment, abilities to observe and discriminate, and results of rural people's experiments. Rural people's knowledge and modern scientific knowledge are complementary in their strengths and weaknesses. Combined they may achieve what neither would alone. For such combinations, outsider professionals have to step down off their pedestals, and sit down, listen and learn (Chambers, 1983: 75).

In this section, an attempt is made to document the range and depth of rural people's knowledge. This may serve as countervailing power to the presumed superiority of the outsider's knowledge. While Chambers (1983) documents indigenous knowledge in several areas such as ecology, climate, agriculture, animal husbandry, botany, and zoology, the emphasis in this section will be on just a few:

Farming practices. Many traditional practices of farmers such as mixed cropping, shifting cultivation or sparing tillage were considered backward and unscientific. For example, the bias of outsiders was in favor of mono-cropping and anything that did not fit their model (such as mixed cropping) was condemned. Agricultural scientists now recognize the several advantages of mixed cropping.

Environmental knowledge. Chambers (1983) notes that the rural people have an extremely keen sense of observation and their knowledge about their environment is very detailed. For example, an average !ko bush woman in Africa can recognize and name 206 out of 211 plant types in her environment, and in the Philippines the knowledge of the Hanunoo cultivators outnumbers by more than 400 types the grouping of the taxonomical species of the local flora by botanists. Another area of knowledge is soil and land types. Peasants have a very intimate knowledge of the soil and are able to identify soil fertility through observation of color and texture and able to distinguish pH levels by tasting the soil.

When it comes to climate as well, local knowledge is very strong. In Kenya, for example, the farmers have their own theories of correlation between lunar phases and rainfall and they have used this knowledge while sowing seeds. While the meteorological office disbelieved the local 'folklore', scientific data has proved the strong correlation between lunar phase influences and rainfall patterns (Chambers, 1983).

These examples, while certainly not exhaustive, serve to document the fact that there is a vast storehouse of knowledge among the rural people on soil types, climate, humidity, weather-related animal behavior, farming practices, etc. that have been generally neglected and ignored by the experts.

Knowledge-sharing on a co-equal basis will mobilize the large knowledge resource in rural areas that has been underutilized in development enterprises.

Model for Knowledge-Sharing

Nair and White (1987) propose a transactional communication model that would complement Ascroft's idea of co-equal knowledge-sharing. In their typology matrix, 'transactional communication is a dialogue, wherein sender and receiver of messages interact over a period of time, to arrive at shared meanings. The transactional process is a two-way persuasion process where the development communicator and target group are expected to talk over their differences, giving and taking, and finally arriving at a consensual agreement' (White and Patel, 1988: 7).

Nair and White (1987) have developed a typology of participation from the perspective of the receiver in Figure 7.1

In this typology matrix, the authors describe three levels of participation (high, quasi, low) between the source and receiver of development communication which may be further subdivided into nine role typologies as indicated in the nine cells (Nair and White, 1987):

1. High participation is involved, active, creative with continuous interaction and dialogue. Power is shared between the communicator and receiver.
2. Quasi participation is less intense, less creative and has less dialogue.
3. Low participation suggests little dialogue, no meaningful involvement and no consciousness of the need for change.

The nature of participation is described by the individual cells in the matrix. As before, the perspective is that of the receiver (Nair and White, 1987: 37):

1. Ideal (High TG/High DC): The source and receiver are in continuous contact and working as co-equal partners in the development effort, making decisions regarding the implementation, jointly assessing the outcomes, etc. However, this is an ideal situation and occurs rarely in reality due to the unequal power structures and inequitable distribution of resources in many Third World nations.
2. Active (High TG/Quasi DC): Here the receiver is slightly more active than the communicator who assumes a supportive and facilitative role.
3. Bottom-up (High TG/Low DC): Due to the very low involvement of the communicator, the receiver may lack access to external information sources. Also, the high activity could be chaotic due to a lack of coordination with the source.
4. Passive (Quasi TG/High DC): Here the source would be the dominant partner in the interaction. The receiver's role is passive.
5. Transactional (Quasi TG/Quasi DC): This is the most important cell in the typology. Interaction would involve a constant give and take between the source and receiver.
6. Elective (Quasi TG/Low DC): In this cell, the users would make use of indigenous knowledge and select issues critical to their progress. There is very little involvement of the communicator.
7. Top-down (Low TG/High DC): All decisions, information, and action would flow from the experts, administrators, etc. A sense of apathy and powerlessness would prevail among

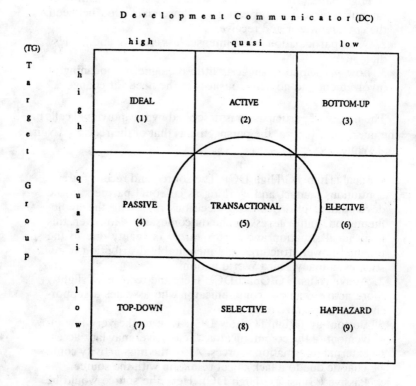

Figure 7.1: Participation Matrix (Receiver Perspective)
SOURCE: Nair and White (1987:37). Figure from *Media Development* 34 (3).
   Reprinted by permission.

the receivers. Development efforts would continue only so long as external direction was present.
8. Selective (Low TG/Quasi DC): As in the previous cell, the communicator is the dominant partner here, selecting issues, laying down the development agenda, etc.
9. Haphazard (Low TG/Low DC): Development effort here is random or accidental, maybe even chaotic.

Nair and White (1987) posit that the transactional typology (cell 5) provides an atmosphere that is best suited for knowledge-sharing on a co-equal basis between the source and the receiver. Unlike the ideal typology (cell 1), it is achievable and realistic since there is a slightly lower level of expectation from the transaction. They point out that in this environment 'there would be an optimum amount of synergistic dialogue, joint decision-making and participation in all communication processes' (Nair and White, 1987: 37).

Operational Impasse in Knowledge-Sharing

The participatory communication approaches in the previous sections suggested a conceptualization that argued for a democratization of the development process and communication channels so that farmers and others in rural areas with a rich knowledge of their environment could interact on an equal footing with technical experts in agriculture, health, family planning, etc. However, this has been held in check by an operational impasse—the absence of a common language of communication:

> On the one hand, peasants lack the necessary education-based communication skills to engage their industrialized benefactors in useful discussion. Benefactors, on the other hand, seem to lack interest in mastering the tradition-based communication systems of those they seek to help (Ascroft and Masilela, 1989: 14).

Field studies in the late sixties and seventies (Kishore, 1968; Sandhu, 1970) and in the eighties (Melkote, 1984; Vallath, 1989) have indicated a serious communication constraint in development projects in the Third World. Vallath (1989) in a study of the World Bank-sponsored Training and Visit project in Karnataka, India, showed that the agricultural experts were not successful in achieving

---

Pro-Literacy Bias in Extension Radio Messages

Research in communication fidelity (Melkote, 1984; Vallath, 1989) has shown that the language in all extension media, including radio, is needlessly complex and technical. The farmer has to confront a host of unfamiliar names of pesticides, chemicals, fertilizers, seed varieties, etc. and complex instructions on a variety of crop cultivation techniques. To give an idea of the language style used on the radio, a typical instruction to a farmer on how to protect his crop from a pest is reproduced below:

> Bugs and gum insects which suck the sap from the leaves and green insects which eat the fruits cause damage to the green gram, black gram and other pulse crops. They should be observed and controlled. 25 percent Thiamosein or 30 percent Dimethoate at the rate of 750 milliliters or 620–750 milliliters of 25 percent Methyl dimesein should be mixed in 500 liters of water per hectare and sprayed on the crop to control the gum insects. To control the green insects, 375 milliliters of Dichlorophos or 1250 milliliters of 50 percent Malathion or 875 milliliters of 35 percent Endosulphon should be mixed in 500 liters of water and sprayed on the crop (an English translation of *Polam Panulu*, a Telugu broadcast to farmers, 11 July 1983).

In the above, all chemicals are listed using their generic scientific names making it almost impossible for an average farmer to pronounce and remember them. The instructions presume sophisticated literacy and numeracy skills on the part of farmers even though the majority had had no formal education at all.

The treatment given to radio broadcasts is not conducive to effective communication. Radio is a good medium for communicating experience but unsuitable for communicating names and numbers. An examination of this and other radio scripts reveals an indiscriminate use of highly technical terms and complex instructions packed into programs of very short duration. The variety, nature, and quantity of information and facts conveyed are excessive for a medium that caters to the human ear.

isomorphism of their communication content with user-farmers. There was not only a low level of comprehension of extension messages but also a great variablility in comprehension of extension messages among farmers.

In another study (Melkote, 1984), this author examined extension media such as pamphlets, posters, booklets, and radio scripts used in an extension project in India and found that they were laced with pro-literate terms even though the target farmers were illiterate. For example, messages were laced with names of weights and measures unfamiliar to a majority of farmers: milliliters, liters, meters, square meters, centimeters, percentages, hectares, etc. Names of calendar months were of the unfamiliar Western calendar rather than the Hindu calendar. In short, the language in all media, including radio, was needlessly complex and technical. An important finding in this study was that high education levels of farmers were significantly related to high comprehension of extension messages, thus reflecting a *pro-literacy bias*. It was evident that the treatment accorded to extension messages served better those farmers who possessed high literacy and numeracy skills and had other characteristics similar to the extension officers (Melkote, 1984).

Participatory Message Development Strategies

A discussion of the operational impasse in knowledge-sharing indicates that message-related and source-related biases must be removed from development communication strategies and attempts made to achieve a high and uniform comprehension of messages among receivers. This would, at least, help the source to explain that the variance in the decisions of user-receivers to accept or reject innovations was not due to lack of comprehension. The rationale underlying this argument is that uniform and adequate comprehension of development messages is a necessary condition for effective decision-making by receivers. Thus, message construction and comprehension have important effects on the process of diffusion of information attempting to produce behavior alterations among recipients. Future research and practice in development communication will need to give greater attention to message strategies, i.e. selection of elements, design, structure, code, and treatment of messages so as to increase their fidelity among receivers.

There is another important area for research and practice. This falls within the general area of *bottom-up* communication but focuses on an aspect never researched before: treatment of messages for source comprehension of receiver intentionalities (Ascroft and Melkote, 1983). Just as top-down communication needs to focus on message design and treatment for adequate, uniform, and accurate receiver comprehension, researchers and practitioners ought to examine ways of enabling the voice of recipients to be encoded in messages which would need to be structured and treated for accurate and uniform comprehension by the source, ranging from the change agents to high-level administrators within the project and donor agencies.

Nair and White (1987) suggest a participatory message development model wherein the receivers (or the target group) and the source contribute their knowledge, creativity, energies, etc. as co-equal partners. Hopefully, this would remove the egregious biases inherent in the present top-down development messages and lead to formulation of more effective communication messages and strategies. In Figure 7.2, Nair and White (1987) attempt at describing a micro-level message construction model which provides an opportunity for participation by receivers.

They point out that in this model, '+' indicates involvement, '−' indicates non-involvement, and '<>' indicates transactional communication between the receivers (TG) and development communicator (DC). Also, the necessary steps in message construction are outlined within the four major phases of message development. Three levels of participation are described. These are ideal types, and in reality 'it is likely that the extent of participation will fall at mid-points on the continuum most often, but in some situations the target group (TG) will dominate and in others the development communicator (DC) will dominate' (Nair and White, 1987: 38).

The participatory message development model shown in Figure 7.2 was operationalized successfully and adapted for video communication in two case studies conducted in Washington county, New York state, and Sonori village in Maharashtra, India. Many of the assumptions of transactional communication between the receivers and the communicators, discussed earlier in this chapter, were supported in these case studies. Thus, the Nair/White model of participatory modes in message development provides a useful conceptual and operational framework for the communicators and receivers to work as co-equal partners in message definition, design, construction, and evaluation.

Participation in Message Development

Phases of Message Development	Participation Level						
	Low		Medium			High	
	TG	DC	TG		DC	TG	DC
PHASE I : DEFINE							
• identify target audience	+	+	+		+	+	+
• define problem	+	+	+		+	+	+
• assess needs	+	+	+		+	+	+
• map alternative solutions	+	+	+		+	+	+
• select innovative solution	+	+	+		+	+	+
PHASE II : DESIGN							
• plan strategies	−	+	+	◇	+	+	−
• define content	−	+	+	◇	+	+	−
• select communication forms	−	+	+	◇	+	+	−
• create format/package	−	+	+	◇	+	+	−
• plan message support	−	+	+	◇	+	+	−
• integrate media	−	+	+	◇	+	+	−
PHASE III : PRODUCE							
• plan production	−	+	+	◇	+	+	−
• produce media	−	+	+	◇	+	+	−
• post-production	−	+	+	◇	+	+	−
• field test prototypes	+	+	+	◇	+	+	+
• package media and support materials	+	+	+	◇	+	+	+
PHASE IV : EVALUATE							
• disseminate messages	+	+	+		+	+	+
• solicit feedback	+	+	+		+	+	+
• conduct evaluation	+	+	+		+	+	+
• define needs of TG	+	+	+		+	+	+
• redesign media packages	+	+	+	◇	+	+	+

Figure 7.2: Source and Receiver Participation in Message Development
Source: Nair and White (1987 : 39). Figure from *Media Development* 34(3), 1987. Reprinted by permission.

Development Support Communication

The emphasis on greater participation of the beneficiaries in the development process in general, and in message development in particular, has led to a reorientation in the study and operationalization of the role of communication in development activities. There is a shift from 'the concept of development communication (DC) with its emphasis on top-down, big-media centered government-to-people communication to development support communication (DSC) focused on co-equal, little-media-centered government-with-people communication' (Ascroft and Masilela, 1989: 3). A concomitant development is the emergence of a new development professional: the development support communicator, who mediates between the technical experts and their beneficiaries. This person is required to help the beneficiaries interact with the technical personnel, administrators, etc. as co-equal partners. Thus, the new horizontal axes provided by development support communicators will counterbalance the vertical axes of development communication involving the technical change agents.

The development communication model and development support communication model are compared in Table 7.2. A similar table was also generated by Jayaweera (1987b).

Models for Development Support Communicator

In an earlier section, an operational impasse was discussed: the absence of a common language of communication between the administrators and technical experts on the one hand and receivers on the other. Scholars and practitioners of development support communication are now focusing attention on this communication constraint inherent in many development projects. The objective is to construct communication models which could presumably make development communication messages both comprehensible and relevant to the capacities and needs of user-receivers. In these proposed models, the development support communicator has the job of *bridging the communication gap* between the technical specialists with expertise in specific areas of knowledge such as health matters and agriculture, and the users who may need such

TABLE 7.2
*Comparison of Development Communication (DC) and
Development Support Communication (DSC) Models*

Development Communication	Development Support Communication
Source: University-based	Development agency-based
Structure: Top-down; authoritarian	Horizontal knowledge-sharing between benefactors and beneficiaries
Paradigm: Dominant paradigm of externally directed social change	Participatory paradigm of an endogenously directed quest to maintain control over basic needs
Level: International and national	Grassroots
Media: Big media: TV, radio, and newspapers	Small media: video, film strips, traditional media, group and interpersonal communication
Effects: To create a climate of acceptance by beneficiaries for exogenous ideas and innovations	Create a climate of mutual understanding between benefactors and beneficiaries

Source: Ascroft and Masilela, 1989: 16–17.

knowledge and its specific applications. The development support communicator is expected to translate technical language and ideas into messages that would be comprehensible to users.

Ascroft and Brody (1982) have adapted the ACB model of Westley and MacLean (1957) to describe systematically the role of a development support communicator. The model is depicted in Figure 7.3.

In this model, designed originally to explain the role of mass media in society, the **X's** on the left are the different stimuli in the environment or items of information. 'A' is an advocacy role and he/she selects and transmits messages from these stimuli (**X's**) to 'B'. 'B' needs the information about his/her environment to help satisfy needs and solve security problems. The inclusion of the 'C' role in the model makes it relevant to the proponents of the DSC

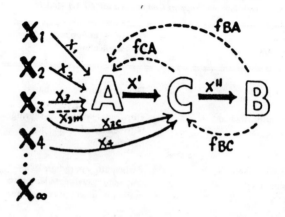

Figure 7.3: Westley and MacLean Model of Communication
SOURCE: Westley and MacLean (1957:35). 'A Conceptual Model for Mass
Communication Research'. *Journalism Quarterly* 34:31-38. Reprinted by
permission.

concept. 'C' is in constant interaction with 'B' through feedback
loop 'fbc' and with 'A'. 'C' understands the needs and problems of
'B'. He/she selects, transmits, and interprets the information 'B'
needs. Thus, 'C' extends B's environment and helps satisfy his/her
needs and/or problems. The placing of 'C' between 'A' and 'B'
makes the model useful in highlighting the importance of the DSC
practitioner. If 'A' is thought to be the technical expert and 'B' the
recipients or the beneficiaries, then 'C' describes very articulately
the role and function of a development support communicator.

However, the communication of messages from the technical
experts should not be at the expense of shutting out ideas and
perspectives from the receivers. This would make the idea of DSC
dysfunctional. Ascroft and Brody (1982: 30) warn that in many
development projects,

> The bottom line is that DSC personnel are no more than the
> mouth-pieces of development, doing the bidding of develop-
> ment planners as best they can, performing wherever and

whenever possible a more sophisticated, technologically-bound service than is within the capability of the average samaritan.

Thus, the DSC practitioners while attempting to improve the efficiency and effectiveness of sources of development aid, may not necessarily be promoting the interests of the recipients of that aid. The role of the DSC practitioner, therefore, will have to be expanded to facilitate the popular participation and action required for rural development. Beneficiaries should have greater access to communication media, not just as receivers but also as sources and actors.

The model proposed by Diaz-Bordenave (1989) provides such a pro-active role for beneficiaries. In his model, the farmers are assigned the role of key protagonists of agriculture and agricultural development. Thus, they are no longer passive 'adopters' of proffered innovations but 'demanders' of technological innovations. In Figures 7.4 and 7.5, Diaz-Bordenave's model and the model used in the dominant paradigm for diffusion of innovations are presented together to show the role and position of the beneficiary *vis-á-vis* the benefactor.

Diaz-Bordenave (1989) notes that in Colombia farmers are asked to appoint their representatives on government boards of agriculture and also participate in research alongside scientists and extension agents. All these changes in the paradigm would render communication as a tool for dialogue and involve the user-receiver as a participant in problem-identification, problem-articulation, and problem-solving.

Beyond 'Just Message Construction'

The importance of constructing effective development message strategies cannot be overemphasized. However, the task of message construction or transmission from the sources to receivers or vice versa is a micro-level objective of DSC. At the macro level, the DSC subfield is concerned with effective organization of a development program (Agunga, 1985).

Woods (1982) emphasizes the social system analysis employed by DSC. He posits that it is extremely important to consider carefully

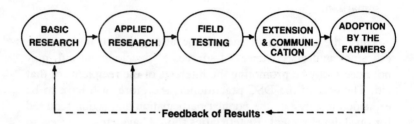

Figure 7.4: Pro-Source Model Used in the Dominant Paradigm
SOURCE: Diaz-Bordenave (1989).

Figure 7.5: Pro-Active Role for Beneficiaries
SOURCE: Diaz-Bordenave (1989: 6).

all the different development support organizations that are likely
to impact on the project and then examine their communication
needs, problems, and interests before planning intervention strategies. Childers (1976: 87) echoes similar ideas. He describes DSC
as a:

discipline in development planning and implementation in
which more adequate account is taken of human behavioral
factors in the design of development projects and their
objectives. Then, on the basis of a behavioral analysis and the

development of a feasible design, the requirements for technical human communication are built into that project as part of its own plan of operation and as a part of its budget.

Thus, these development scholars and practitioners conceive DSC as a management information function. It takes a holistic examination of development project goals, design, methodology, budget, linkages, etc. to ensure success of the overall program (Agunga, 1985). Thus, DSC has a dichotomous goal structure. As far as the beneficiaries of development are concerned, DSC is used to mobilize, organize, and train them so that they may participate effectively with the experts and government authorities. For the sources of development or benefactors, DSC can be used to execute better management strategies, hire and train development support communicators in effective communication skills, coordinate the various user-agencies, and generally ensure that the development program does not suffer from glitches. Thus, DSC would include administrative and management skills besides communication (Agunga, 1985). This calls for an interdisciplinary training of DSC personnel.

University of Iowa Model in DSC

The University of Iowa program in DSC is one of the select few that takes a multidisciplinary approach to training its students. The Iowa program suggests a triadic model of interactive development support as shown in Figure 7.6. The three broad domains of knowledge relevant to development are: (*i*) Areas of technical assistance; (*ii*) Contextual knowledge of Third World communities; and (*iii*) Contributions of several social science disciplines to the development effort (Ascroft, 1985).

The triangles at the top of Figure 7.6 represent the totality of techniques and technologies which form the nucleus of development work: commerce and industry, food and agriculture, health and sanitation, infrastructure and institution-building, and population and family planning. These triangles are superimposed on each other so that all share a common base, which in turn is the rectangle that describes any Third World society's development context. The shaded area on top represents common knowledge and information of existing techniques and technologies available for transfer to any given community (Ascroft, 1985).

Triadic Model of Interactive Development Support

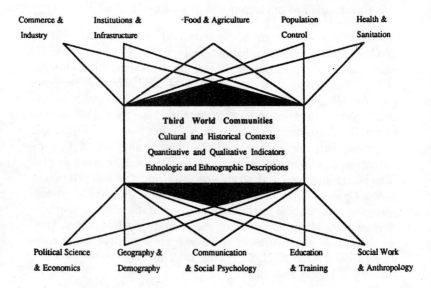

Figure 7.6: Triadic Model of Interactive Development Support
SOURCE: Ascroft (1985:14).

The rectangle in the center describes the contextual knowledge necessary about the host society. This would comprise the history and culture of the community, ethnologic and ethnographic descriptions, and qualitative and quantitative indicators of development.

The triangles at the bottom of the Figure describe the different social science disciplines that contribute to development problem-solving. Ascroft (1985: 13) points out that:

a major obstacle... consisted of whether communication was being narrowly conceived of as a discipline in its own right or broadly regarded as a summary term to stand for all the behavioral social sciences. Judging by the qualifications of those who eventually filled most of the professional DSC positions, the broader view has so far prevailed to the point where mention is frequently made of the *communication social sciences*. Usage of communication in this way has tended to mask the fact that each behavioral social science, not just communication, has a development support role to play.

The triangles at the bottom indicate the social science disciplines participating interdependently with each other, each with its own independent as well as its overlapping contributions to development support problem-solving. All these triangles together represent the total knowledge and skills necessary for *development support*. The shaded area at the bottom indicates the common base shared by the different disciplines and is thus potentially the area of maximum interdisciplinary interaction.

The Iowa triadic model organizes and relates systems relevant to the development process. It describes the interconnections between the different knowledge systems which have previously not been too clearly perceived. According to Ascroft (1985: 15), the components in this DSC model making up the triad include:

1. **The natural sciences,** including the extension system, responsible for determining suitable techniques and technologies promising of satisfying Third World basic needs; for technical demonstrations and instructions; and for participating in diffusion campaigns.
2. **Third World communities** responsible for critically evaluating development proposals intended to benefit them; for clarifying their needs and wants to government and other benefactors; and for participating in the determination of the nature and trajectory of their own development.
3. **The social sciences** responsible for generating participatory decision-making systems between the other two members of the triad; for bridging gaps of language and culture between them and, hence, for ensuring two-way comprehension of development proposals and Third World reactions and counter-proposals; and for designing and mounting campaigns for making development proposals and information common knowledge to intended audiences.

Thus, the concept of DSC is broader in scope than Project Support Communication (PSC), a term used in certain United Nations agencies. DSC does not have to be confined to a project situation. DSC, very broadly, deals with the training of communication specialists who can help in the planning, design, development, and execution of messages and communication strategies geared to some development objective. The communication could be from project administrators to recipients or vice versa, or communication between project administrators themselves. The DSC person could act as the agent of the project administrators or some such authorities, an agent of the users, or both.

Conclusion

Contemporary development communication literature is placing a great deal of emphasis on grassroots participation. While the dominant paradigm of the sixties has not yet completely vanished, it is less dominant, at least among scholars and researchers. A new paradigm, *Another Development*, has been proposed by several development scholars. This new paradigm is pluralistic and does not suffer from the authoritarian overtones of the dominant paradigm. In this approach, communities are expected to set their own priorities and standards which may be unique to their problem situations. The new approaches focus on human and economic concerns. Therefore, greater emphasis is being given to basic needs of people and participation of beneficiaries in development programs set up for their benefit.

The role of communication in participatory approaches is more complex and varied. Unlike in the dominant paradigm, the exact nature and role of communication in *Another Development* will depend on the normative goals and standards set by the host communities. Communication in the new approaches could help in the development of a community's cultural identity, act as a vehicle for people's self-expression, or serve as a tool for diagnosis of a community's problems.

.The communication models being proposed in the new approaches are both sender- and receiver-oriented. Such models would allow for knowledge-sharing on a co-equal basis rather than be a top-down transmission of information and persuasion. The DSC model, which would complement these approaches, has also been extensively discussed.

While participatory approaches hold great promise for more equitable and relevant development, the idea of participatory development is still only an *approach*. We do not yet have a full-blown theory of participation. Since the definitions of participation vary and development contexts may also be different in different communities, cross-cultural generalization and application may be inappropriate.

A task for the nineties would be to come up with a set of core ideas and principles of participation and communication, and an operational framework so that the ideas expressed in this chapter may find concrete application in different contexts.

References

Abraham, Francis. 1980. *Perspectives on Modernization: Toward a General Theory of Third World Development.* Washington, D.C.: University Press of America.

Abramovitz, M. 1956. 'Resource and Output Trends in the United States since 1870'. *American Economic Review* 46: 5–23.

Adelman, I. and **C.T. Morris.** 1973. *Economic Growth and Social Equity in Developing Countries.* California: Stanford University Press.

Agrawal, Binod C. 1984. 'Indianness of the Indian Cinema'. *In* G. Wang and W. Dissanayake (eds.), *Continuity and Change in Communication Systems*, pp. 181–92. New Jersey: Ablex.

Agunga, Robert. 1985. 'Development Support Communication as a Diffusion Strategy'. Unpublished paper. University of Iowa, Iowa City.

Alamgir, Mohiuddin. 1988. 'Poverty Alleviation through Participatory Development'. *Development* 2/3: 97–102.

Allport, G. and **Leo Postman.** 1947. *The Psychology of Rumor.* New York: Holt.

Ariyaratne, A.T. 1987. 'Beyond Development Communication: Case Study on Sarvodaya, Sri Lanka'. *In* N. Jayaweera and S. Amunugama (eds.), *Rethinking Development Communication*, pp. 239–51. Singapore: Asian Mass Communication Research and Information Center.

Arkes, Hadley. 1972. *Bureaucracy, Marshall Plan, and the National Interest.* New Jersey: Princeton University Press.

Ascroft, Joseph. 1985. 'A Curriculum for Development Support Communication'. Prepared for the Universities in Pakistan for a Development Communication Workshop held at the University of Punjab, Lahore, 1–11 July 1985.

Ascroft, Joseph with **Robert Agunga, Jan Gratama,** and **Sipho Masilela.** 1987. 'Communication in Support of Development: Lessons from Theory and Practice'. Paper presented at the seminar on Communication and Change. The University of Hawaii and the East-West Center, Honolulu, Hawaii.

Ascroft, Joseph and **Alan Brody.** 1982. 'The Role of Support Communication in Knowledge Utilization: Theory and Practice'. Paper presented at the conference on Knowledge Utilization: Theory and Practice, East-West Center, Honolulu, Hawaii.

Ascroft, Joseph and **Gary Gleason.** 1980. 'Communication Support and Integrated Rural Development in Ghana'. Paper presented at the 30th International Conference on Communication, Human Evolution and Development of International Communication Association, Acapulco.

———. 1981. 'Breaking Bottlenecks in Communication'. *Ceres*, No. 80, 14(2): 36–41.

Ascroft, Joseph and **Sipho Masilela.** 1989. 'From Top-Down to Co-Equal Communication: Popular Participation in Development Decision-Making'.

Paper presented at the seminar on Participation: A Key Concept in Communication and Change. University of Poona, Pune, India.

Ascroft, Joseph and **Srinivas Melkote**. 1983. 'An Ethical Perspective on the Generation of Development Communication Research Useful to Policy Makers and Practitioners'. Paper presented to the 33rd annual conference of the International Communication Association, Dallas.

Ascroft, Joseph et al. 1971. 'The Tetu Extension Pilot Project'. *Strategies for Improving Rural Welfare*. Occasional Paper 4. Nairobi, Kenya: University of Nairobi, Institute for Development Studies.

Ascroft, Joseph (coordinator). 1973a. 'The Overall Evaluation of the Special Rural Development Program'. Occasional Paper 8. Nairobi, Kenya: University of Nairobi, Institute for Development Studies.

Ascroft, Joseph, Niels Roling, Joseph Kariuki, and **Fred Chege**. 1973b. *Extension and the Forgotten Farmer*. Nairobi, Kenya: Institute for Development Studies.

Bamberger, Michael. 1988. *The Role of Community Participation in Development Planning and Project Management*. Washington, D.C.: The World Bank, EDI Policy Seminar Report, No. 13.

Barkan, Joel et al. 1979. 'Small is Beautiful? The Organizational Conditions for Effective Small-Scale Self-Help Development Projects in Rural Kenya'. University of Iowa: Center for Comparative Legislative Research.

Barton, A. 1968. 'Bringing Society Back In: Survey Research and Macro-methodology'. *American Behavioral Scientist* 12: 1–9.

Belbase, Subhadra. 1987. 'Development Communication: A Nepali Experience'. *In* N. Jayaweera and S. Amunugama (eds.), *Rethinking Development Communication*, pp. 208–26. Singapore: Asian Mass Communication Research and Information Center.

Bellah, Robert N. (ed.). 1965. *Religion and Progress in Modern Asia*. New York: Free Press.

Beltran, Luis Ramiro, S. 1974. 'Rural Development and Social Communication: Relationships and Strategies'. Presentation to Cornell-CIAT International Symposium on *Communication Strategies for Rural Development*. Ithaca, New York: Cornell University.

———. 1976. 'Alien Premises, Objects, and Methods in Latin American Communication Research'. *In* E.M. Rogers (ed.), *Communication and Development: Critical Perspectives*, pp. 15–42. Beverly Hills: Sage Publications.

Berger, Peter L. 1976. *Pyramids of Sacrifice*. New York: Anchor Books.

Berlo, David K. 1960. *The Process of Communication: An Introduction to Theory and Practice*. San Francisco: Rinehart Press.

Bortei-Doku, E. 1978. 'A Fresh Look at the Traditional Small-Scale Farmer'. *The Ghana Farmer* XVIII (1): 4–6. Accra, Ghana: Ministry of Agriculture Review on Agricultural Development.

Brookfield, Harold. 1975. *Interdependent Development*. Pittsburgh: University of Pittsburgh Press.

Brundtland, Gro Harlem. 1989. 'Sustainable Development: An Overview'. *Development* 2/3: 13–14.

Casey, Randall. 1975. 'Folk Media in Development'. *Instructional Technology Report*, 12 (September): 1.

Ceres. 1977. FAO 'Review on Agriculture and Development'. 10 (4).

Chambers, Robert. 1983. *Rural Development: Putting the Last First*. New York: Longman.

Chander, Romesh. 1974. 'Television Treatment of Folk Forms in Family Planning Communication'. Paper presented to the Inter-Regional Seminar/Workshop on the Integrated Use of Folk Media and Mass Media in Family Planning Communication Programmes, New Delhi, 7–16 October.

Chayanov, A.V. 1966. 'Measure of Self-Exploitation of the Peasant Family Labor Force'. *In* Daniel Thorner et al. (eds.), *The Theory of Peasant Economy*, pp. 70–89. Illinois: American Economic Association.

Chenery, H., M.S. Ahluwalia, C.L.G. Bell, J.H. Duloy, and R. Jolly. 1974. *Redistribution with Growth*. Oxford University Press.

Chiao, Chen and **M.T.K. Wei.** 1984. 'The Chinese Revolutionary Opera: A Change of Theme'. *In* G. Wang and W. Dissanayake (eds.), *Continuity and Change in Communication Systems*, pp. 81–94. New Jersey: Ablex.

Childers, Erskine. 1976. 'Taking Humans into Account'. *Media Asia* 3(2): 87–90.

Chiranjit. 1974. 'Radio Treatment of Folk Forms'. Paper presented to the inter-regional seminar/workshop on the Integrated Use of Folk Media and Mass Media in Family Planning Communication Programmes, New Delhi, 7–16. October.

Chu, Godwin C. 1987. 'Development Communication in the year 2000'. *In* N. Jayaweera and S. Amunugama (eds.), *Rethinking Development Communication*, pp. 95–107. Singapore: Asian Mass Communication Research and Information Center.

Coleman, James S., Elihu Katz and **Herbert Menzel.** 1957. 'The Diffusion of an Innovation among Physicians'. *Sociometry* 20: 253–70.

Coleman, James S. 1958. 'Relational Analysis: A Study of Social Organization with Survey Methods'. *Human Organization* 17: 28–36.

Cooley, Charles H. 1962. *Social Organization*. Glencoe, Illinois: Free Press.

Daniels, Walter M. 1951. *The Point Four Program*. New York: H. W. Wilson.

Dasgupta, Sugata. 1979. 'Retooling of Social Work for the Eradication of Social Injustice'. Keynote Address to Asian Regional Social Work Seminar, Melbourne, Australia.

———. 1982. 'Towards a No Poverty Society'. *Social Development Issues* 6 (2): 4–14.

Davis, D and **Stanley J. Baran.** 1981. *Mass Communication and Everyday Life: A Perspective on Theory and Effects*. California: Wadsworth Publishing.

DeFleur, M. et al. 1975. *Theories of Mass Communication*. New York: David McKay.

Denison, E. 1962. *The Sources of Economic Growth in the United States and the Alternative Before Us*. New York: Committee for Economic Development.

Deutsch, Karl. 1961. 'Social Mobilization and Political Development'. *American Political Science Review* 55: 463–515.

Diaz-Bordenave, Juan. 1976. 'Communication of Agricultural Innovations in Latin America'. *In* E.M. Rogers (ed.), *Communication and Development: Critical Perspectives*, pp. 43–62. Beverly Hills: Sage Publications.

———. 1977. *Communication and Rural Development*. Paris: Unesco.

———. 1980. 'Participation in Communication Systems for Development'. Unpublished paper. Rio de Janeiro.

Diaz-Bordenave, Juan. 1989. 'Participative Communication as a Part of the Building of a Participative Society'. Paper prepared for the seminar on Participation: A Key Concept in Communication for Change and Development, Pune, India, February.

Dissanayake, W. 1984. 'A Buddhist Approach to Development: A Sri Lankan Endeavor'. *In* G. Wang and W. Dissanayake (eds.), *Continuity and Change in Communication Systems*, pp. 39–52. New Jersey: Ablex.

Douglass III, Edward Fenner. 1971. 'The Role of Mass Media in National Development: A Reformulation with Particular Reference to Sierra Leone'. Ph.D. dissertation, University of Illinois, Urbana-Champaign.

Dunn, P.D. 1978. *Appropriate Technology*. New York: Schocken Books.

Durkheim, Emile. 1933. *On the Division of Labor in Society*. New York: Macmillan.

Eapen, K.E. 1973. *The Media and Development: An Exploratory Survey in Indonesia and Zambia*. Leicester, England: Centre for Mass Communication Research, University of Leicester, England.

———. 1975. 'Appropriate Structures and Organisations for Communication Agencies'. *In* Mehra Masani (ed.), *Communication and Rural Progress*, pp. 35–40. Bombay: Leslie Sawhny Programme of Training in Democracy.

Eicher, C. and **L. Witt** (eds.). 1964. *Agriculture in Economic Development*. New York: McGraw Hill.

Eisenstadt, S.N. 1976. 'The Changing Vision of Modernization and Development'. *In* Schramm and Daniel Lerner (eds.), *Communication and Change: The Last Ten Years and the Next*, pp. 31–44. Honolulu: East-West Center, The University Press of Hawaii.

FAO. 1977. Review on Agriculture and Development. *Ceres* 10 (4).

Fair, Jo Ellen. 1989. '29 Years of Theory and Research on Media and Development: The Dominant Paradigm Impact'. *Gazette* 44: 129–50.

Firth, Raymond. 1964. 'Capital, Saving and Credit in Peasant Societies'. *In* Raymond Firth et al. (eds.), *Capital, Saving and Credit in Peasant Societies*, pp. 15–34. Chicago: Aldine Publishing Company.

———. 1965. *Primitive Polynesian Economy*. Second Edition. Hamden, Conn: Archon Books.

Fjes, Fred. 1976. 'Communications and Development'. Unpublished paper, College of Communications, University of Illinois, Urbana-Champaign.

Foster, George M. 1962. *Traditional Cultures and the Impact of Technological Change*. New York: Harper.

Frank, Andre G. 1969. *Latin America: Underdevelopment or Revolution*. New York: Monthly Review Press.

Freire, Paulo. 1971. *Education for Critical Consciousness*. New York: Continuum.

Frey, Frederick W. 1966. *The Mass Media and Rural Development in Turkey*. Cambridge: Massachusetts Institute of Technology, Center for International Studies, Rural Development Research Report 3.

———. 1973. 'Communications and Development'. *In* Ithiel De Sola Pool et al. (eds.), *Handbook of Communication*, pp. 337–461. Chicago: Rand McNally College Publishing Company.

Gans, H. 1962. *The Urban Villagers*. New York: The Free Press.

Gaur, R.A. 1981. 'Transfer of Technology: A Tool for Modernising Agriculture' *Management of Transfer of Farm Technology*, pp. 103–05. Hyderabad, India: National Institute of Rural Development.

Golding, Peter. 1974. 'Media Role in National Development: Critique of a Theoretical Orthodoxy'. *Journal of Communication* 24(3): 39–53.

Goldthorpe, J.E. 1975. *The Sociology of the Third World*. Cambridge: Cambridge University Press.

Goulet, D. 1971. *The Cruel Choice: A New Concept in Theory of Development*. New York: Atheneum.

————. 1973. 'Development—or Liberation'. *In* C. Wilber (ed.), *The Political Economy of Development and Underdevelopment*. New York: Random House.

Government of India. 1979. *India: A Reference Manual*. New Delhi: Ministry of Information and Broadcasting.

————. 1981. *Agricultural Extension: The Training and Visit System—Operational Notes*. New Delhi: Ministry of Agriculture and Cooperation.

————. 1982. *India: A Reference Manual*. New Delhi: Ministry of Information and Broadcasting.

Gran, Guy. 1983. *Development By People: Citizen Construction of a Just World*. New York: Praeger.

Grant, James P. 1978. *Disparity Reduction Rates in Social Indicators*. Overseas Development Council, Monograph No. 11.

Gusfield, J.R. 1971. 'Tradition and Modernity: Misplaced Polarities in the Study of Social Change'. *In* J. Finkle and R. Gable (eds.), *Political Development and Social Change*, pp. 15–26. New York: John Wiley.

Gyan-Apenteng, Kwasi. 1988. 'Refrigerators in China: Third World Reflects on "Civilization" vs. Nature'. *The Blade*, 25 December.

Hagen, Everett E. 1962. *On the Theory of Social change*. Homewood, Illinois: Dorsey.

Hamelink, Cees. 1983. *Cultural Autonomy in Global Communications*. New York: Longman.

Harrison, Paul. 1979. *Inside the Third World*. Penguin Books.

Havelock, R.G. 1971. *Planning for Innovation Through Dissemination and Utilization of Knowledge*. Cited in Juan Diaz-Bordenave, 1976, 'Communication for Agricultural Innovations in Latin America', *op. cit.*

Hedebro, Goran. 1982. *Communication and Social Change in Developing Nations: A Critical View*. Ames: Iowa State University Press.

Heine-Geldern, Robert. 1968. 'Diffusion: I. Cultural Diffusion'. *In* Sills (ed.), *International Encyclopedia of the Social Sciences*, vol. 4, pp. 169–73. New York: Macmillan.

Hellman, H. 1980. 'Idealism, Aggression, Apology, and Criticism: The Four Traditions of Research on International Communication'. Paper prepared for XII Congress of the IAMCR, Caracas.

Herskovits, Melville J. 1969. *Man and His Works*. New York: Knopf.

Hirschman, Albert O. 1958. *Strategy of Economic Development*. New Haven: Yale University Press.

Hobsbawm, E.J. 1968. *Industry and Empire: An Economic History of Britain Since 1750*. London: Weidenfeld and Nicolson.

Hornik, Robert. 1988. *Development Communication: Information, Agriculture, and Nutrition in the Third World*. New York: Longman.

Horowitz, Irving L. 1970. 'Personality and Structural Dimensions in Comparative International Development'. *Social Science Quarterly* 51 (December): 494–513.

Hoselitz, B.F. 1960. *Sociological Factors in Economic Development*. Glencoe: Free Press.

Hovland, C.I., A.A. Lumsdaine, and F.D. Sheffield. 1949. *Experiments in Mass Communication*. New York: Wiley.

Hovland, C.I., I.L. Janis, and H.H. Kelley. 1953. *Communication and Persuasion*. New Haven: Yale University Press.

Hudson, Heather. 1984. *When Telephones Reach the Village: The Role of Telecommunications in Rural Development*. Norwood: Ablex.

Hyden, G. 1980. *Beyond Ujamaa in Tanzania: Underdevelopment and an Uncaptured Peasantry*. Berkeley: University of California Press.

Illich, Ivan. 1969. *The Celebration of Awareness*. New York: Doubleday and Company.

Inkeles, Alex. 1966. 'The Modernization of Man'. *In* M. Weiner (ed.), *Modernization: The Dynamics of Growth*, pp. 138–50. New York: Basic Books.

———. 1969. 'Making Men Modern: On the Causes and Consequences of Individual Change in Six Countries'. *American Journal of Sociology* 75 (September): 208–25.

Inkeles, A. and D.H. Smith. 1974. *Becoming Modern: Individual Change in Six Developing Countries*. Cambridge: Harvard University Press.

Institute of Social Studies, The Hague. 1980. *Communication Research in Third World Realities*.

Jacobson, Thomas L. 1989. 'Old and New Approaches to Participatory Communication for Development'. Paper prepared for the seminar on Participation: A Key Concept in Communication for Change and Development, Pune, India, February.

Jayaweera, Neville. 1987a. 'Rethinking Development Communication: A Holistic View'. *In* N. Jayaweera and S. Amunugama (eds.), *Rethinking Development Communication*, pp. 76–94. Singapore: Asian Mass Communication Research and Information Center.

———. 1987b. 'Introduction'. *In* N. Jayaweera and S. Amunugama (eds.), *Rethinking Development Communication*, pp. xiii-xix. Singapore: Asian Mass Communication Research and Information Center.

Johnston, B and J. Mellor. 1961. 'The Role of Agriculture in Economic Development'. *American Economic Review* (September): 571–81.

Jones, E.E. and R. Kohler. 1958. 'The Effects of Plausibility on the Learning of Controversial Statements'. *Journal of Abnormal and Social Psychology* 57: 315–20.

Jussawala, Meheroo. 1985. 'International Telecommunication Policies'. *Development* 1: 64–66.

Kahl, Joseph A. 1968. *The Measurement of Modernism*. Austin: University of Texas Press.

Kantowski, D. 1980. *Sarvodaya: The Other Development*. New Delhi: Vikas Publishing House.

Katz, Elihu. 1957. 'The Two-Step Flow of Communication'. *Public Opinion Quarterly* 21: 61–78.

———. 1963. 'The Diffusion of New Ideas and Practices'. *In* Wilber Schramm (ed.), *The Science of Human Communication*, pp. 77–93. New York: Basic Books.

Katz, Elihu and P. Lazarsfeld. 1955. *Personal Influence*. New York: Free Press.

Kerblay, B. 1971. 'Chayanov and the Theory of Peasantry as a Specific Type of Economy'. *In* T.Shanin (ed.), *Peasants and Peasant Society*. London: Penguin Books.

Khan, A.W. 1987. 'Role of Radio in Development Communication: A Country Cousin Syndrome'. *In* K.E. Eapen (ed.), *The Role of Radio in Growth and Development*, pp. 29–36. Bangalore.

Kidd, Ross. 1984. 'The Performing Arts and Development in India: Three Case Studies and a Comparative Analysis'. *In* G. Wang and W. Dissanayake (eds.), *Continuity and Change in Communication Systems*, pp. 95–125. New Jersey: Ablex.

Kishore, D. 1968. 'A study of Effectiveness of Radio as a Mass Communication Medium in Dissemination of Agricultural Information'. Ph.D. dissertation, Indian Agricultural Research Institute, New Delhi, India.

Klapper, J.T. 1960. *The Effects of Mass Communication*. Glencoe, Illinois: Free Press.

Kothari, Rajni. 1984. 'Communications for Alternative Development: Towards a Paradigm'. *Development Dialogue*, pp. 1–2.

Krippendorff, Sultana. 1979. 'The Communication Approach to Development: A Critical Review'. *In* John Lent (guest ed.), *Third World Mass Media: Issues, Theory and Research*, pp. 71–82. Williamsburg, Virginia: Studies in Third World Societies, College of William and Mary.

Krishnaswamy, M.V. 1974. 'Film Treatment of Folk Forms'. Paper presented to the inter-regional seminar/workshop on the Integrated Use of Folk Media and Mass Media in Family Planning Communication Programmes, New Delhi, 7–16 October.

Kronenburg, J. 1986. *Empowerment of the Poor: A Comparative Analysis of Two Development Endeavours in Kenya*. Cited in Jan Servaes, 1989, *op. cit.*

Kroeber, A.L. 1944. *Configurations of Culture Growth*. Berkeley: University of California Press.

Lasswell, H.D. 1948. 'The Structure and Function of Communication in Society'. *In* Lyman Bryson (ed.), *The Communication of Ideas*. New York: Harper and Brothers. Also published in W. Schramm (1960), *Mass Communications*, pp. 117–30. Urbana: University of Illinois Press.

Lazarsfeld, P. 1941. 'Remarks on Administrative and Critical Communications Research'. *Studies in Philosophy and Social Science* 9: 2–16.

Lazarsfeld, P., B.Berelson, and **H.Gaudet.** 1948. *The People's Choice*. New York: Columbia University Press.

Lenglet, Frans. 1980. 'The Ivory Coast: Who Benefits from Education/Information in Rural Television?' *In* Emile G. McAnany (ed.), *Communications in the Rural Third World*, pp. 49–70. New York: Praegar.

Lent, John A. 1987. 'Devcom: A View from the United States'. *In* N. Jayaweera and S. Amunugama (eds.), *Rethinking Development Communication*, pp. 20–41. Singapore: Asian Mass Communication Research and Information Center.

Lerner, Daniel. 1958. *The Passing of Traditional Society: Modernizing the Middle East*. New York: Free Press.

———. 1963. 'Toward a Communication Theory of Modernization'. *In* Lucien Pye (ed.), *Communications and Political Development*, pp. 327–50. New Jersey: Princeton University Press.

Levine, J.M. and **G. Murphy.** 1958. 'The Learning and Forgetting of Controversial Material'. *In* E.E. Maccoby et al. (eds.), *Readings in Social Psychology*, pp. 94–101. Third Edition. New York: Holt, Rinehart and Winston.

Levy, Marion Jr. 1966. *Modernization and the Structure of Society.* Princeton University Press.

Lewis, Oscar. 1961. 'The Culture of Poverty'. *In* J.J. TePaska and S.N. Fisher (eds.), *Explosive Forces in Latin America,* pp. 149–73. Columbus, Ohio: Ohio State University Press.

Linton, Ralph. 1936. *The Study of Man.* New York: Appleton-Century-Crofts.

Lionberger, Herbert F. 1960. *Adoption of New Ideas and Practices.* Ames: Iowa State University Press.

Lowery, Shearon and **Melvin L. DeFleur.** 1988. *Milestones in Mass Communication Research.* Second Edition. New York: Longman.

Maine, Henry. 1907. *Ancient Law.* London: John Murray.

Maitland Commission. 1984. *The Missing Link: Report of the Independent Commission for Worldwide Telecommunications Development.* Geneva: International Telecommunication Union.

Mane, Vasant. 1974. 'Identification of Flexible Folk Drama in Family Planning Communication'. Paper presented to the inter-regional seminar/workshop on the Integrated Use of Folk Media and Mass Media in Family Planning Communication Programmes, New Delhi, 7–16 October.

Masani, Mehra. 1975. 'Introduction'. *In* M. Masani (ed.), *Communication and Rural Progress,* pp. 1–6. Bombay: Leslie Sawhny Programme of Training in Democracy.

McAnany, Emile G. 1980a. 'The Role of Information in Communicating with the Rural Poor: Some Reflections'. *In* E.G. McAnany (ed.), *Communications in the Rural Third World,* pp. 3–18. New York: Praeger.

———. 1980b. 'Overview'. *In* E.G. McAnany (ed.), *Communications in the Rural Third World,* pp. xi–xvi. New York: Praeger.

McClelland, David C. 1966. 'The Impulse to Modernisation'. *In* M. Weiner (ed.), *Modernization: The Dynamics of Growth,* pp. 28–39. New York: Basic Books.

———. 1967. *The Achieving Society.* New York: Free Press.

McQuail, D. 1983. *Mass Communication Theory.* Sage: London.

McQuail, Denis and **Sven Windahl.** 1981. *Communication Models.* New York: Longman.

Melkote, S. 1984. 'The Biases in Extension Communication: Revealing the Comprehension Gap'. Ph.D. dissertation, University of Iowa.

Migdal, J. 1974. *Peasants, Politics and Revolution.* New Jersey: Princeton University Press.

Morgan, James, K. Dickenson, J. Dickenson, J. Benus, and **G. Duncan.** 1974. *Five Thousand American Families: Patterns of Economic Progress.* Vol. 1. Ann Arbor: Survey Research Center, Institute for Social Research, University of Michigan.

Morris, Morris D. 1979. *Measuring the Condition of the World's Poor: The PQLI.* New York: Pergamon Press.

Mowlana, Hamid and **Laurie Wilson.** 1988. *Communication Technology and Development.* Paris: Unesco.

Myrdal, Gunnar. 1970. *The Challenge of World Poverty.* New York: Vintage Books.

Nair, K.S. and **Shirley White.** 1987. 'Participatory Message Development: A Conceptual Framework'. *Media Development* 34(3): 36–40.

Narula, Uma and **W.B. Pearce**. 1986. *Development as Communication*. Carbondale, Illinois: Southern Illinois University Press.

Neurath, Paul. 1962. 'Radio Farm Forum as a Tool of Change in Indian Villages'. *Economic Development and Cultural Change* 10: 275–83.

Nordenstreng, Kaarle. 1968. 'Communication Research in the United States: A Critical Perspective'. *Gazette* 14: 207–16.

Nurkse, Ragnar. 1953. *Problems of Capital Formation in Underdeveloped Countries*. Oxford University Press.

Nyerere, Julius. 1968. *Ujamaa: Essays in Socialism*. Dar es Salaam, Tanzania: Oxford Universtiy Press.

Oshima, Harry T. 1976a. 'Development and Mass Communication: A Re-Examination'. *In* W. Schramm and D. Lerner (eds.), *Communication and Change*, pp. 17–30. Honolulu: University Press of Hawaii.

———. 1976b. 'Old and New Strategies—An Economist's View'. *In* W. Schramm and D. Lerner (eds.), *Communication and Change*, pp. 53–56. Honolulu: University Press of Hawaii.

Parmar, Shyam. 1975. *Traditional Folk Media in India*. New Delhi: Geka Books.

Parsons, Talcott. 1964a. *The Social System*. New York: Free Press.

———. 1964b. 'Evolutionary Universals in Society'. *American Sociological Review* 29(3): 339–57.

Popkin, S. 1979. *The Rational Peasant*. Berkeley, California: University of California Press.

Portes, Alejandro. 1974. 'Modernity and Development: A Critique'. *Studies in Comparative International Development* 9 (Spring): 247–79.

———. 1976. 'On the Sociology of National Development: Theories and Issues'. *American Journal of Sociology* 82(1): 55–85.

Pye, L. 1963. *Communications and Political Development*. Princeton University Press.

Rahim, Syed A. 1976. 'Diffusion Research—Past, Present and Future'. *In* W. Schramm and D. Lerner (eds.), *Communication and Change*, pp. 223–25. Honolulu: University Press of Hawaii.

Rahman, M.A. 1981. 'Reflections'. *Development* 1: 43–51.

Ranganath, H.K. 1975. 'Traditional Media'. *Instructional Technology Report* 12 (September).

———. 1980. *Folk Media and Communication*. Bangalore: Chintana Prakashana Publishers.

Rao, Lakshmana. 1963. *Communication and Development: A Study of Two Indian Villages*. Ph.D. dissertation, University of Minnesota.

Ratnapala, N. (n.d.). *Study Service in Sarvodaya*. Colombo: Sarvodaya Research Center. Cited in W. Dissanayaka, 'A Buddhist Approach to Development', 1984, *op. cit.*

Reddi, Usha V. 1987. 'New Communication Technologies: What Sort of Development do they Bring in their Wake?' *In* N. Jayaweera and S. Amunugama (eds.), *Rethinking Development Communication*, pp. 42–60. Singapore: Asian Mass Communication Research and Information Center.

Redfield, Robert. 1965. *Peasant Society and Culture*. Chicago: University of Chicago Press.

Reich, Robert B. 1982. 'Ideologies of Survival'. *The New Republic* 3531 and 3532 (September): 32–37.

Riley, J.W. and **M.W. Riley.** 1959. 'Mass Communication and the Social System'. *In* R.K. Merton et al. (eds.), *Sociology Today* , pp. 537–78. New York: Basic Books.

Robertson, Ian. 1977. *Sociology.* New York: Worth Publishers.

Rogers, Everett M. 1962. *Diffusion of Innovations.* New York: The Free Press.

———. 1965. 'Mass Media Exposure and Modernisation Among Colombian Peasants'. *Public Opinion Quarterly* 29: 614–25.

———. 1969. *Modernisation Among Peasants.* New York: Holt, Rinehart and Winston.

———. 1975. 'Network Analysis of the Diffusion of Family Planning Innovations Over Time in Korean Villages: The Role of Mothers' Clubs'. Paper presented at the Population Association of America, Seattle.

———. 1976a. 'Where Are We In Understanding the Diffusion of Innovations?' *In* W. Schramm and D. Lerner (eds.), *Communication and Change,* pp. 204–22. Honolulu: Universtiy Press of Hawaii.

———. 1976b. 'Communication and Development—The Passing of the Dominant Paradigm'. *In* E.M. Rogers (ed.), *Communication and Development: Critical Perspectives,* Beverly Hills: Sage Publications.

———. 1976c. 'The Passing of the Dominant Paradigm—Reflections on Diffusion Research'. *In* W. Schramm and D. Lerner (eds.), *Communication and Change,* pp. 49–52. Honolulu: Universty Press of Hawaii.

———. 1983. *Diffusion of Innovations.* Third Edition. New York: The Free Press.

———. 1986. *Communication Technology: The New Media in Society.* New York: Free Press.

———. 1987. 'Communication and Development Today'. Paper presented at the seminar on Communication and Change: An Agenda for the New Age of Communication, Honolulu, 20 July–1 August.

Rogers, Everett M. and **Ronny Adhikarya.** 1979. 'Diffusion of Innovations: An Up-to-Date Review and Commentary'. *In* Dan Nimmo (ed.), *Communication Year Book* 3, pp. 67–81. New Jersey: International Communication Association.

Rogers, Everett M. and **D. Lawrence Kincaid.** 1981. *Communication Networks: Toward a New Paradigm for Research.* New York: The Free Press.

Rogers, Everett M., with **F.F. Shoemaker.** 1971. *Communication of Innovations: A Cross Cultural Approach.* New York: The Free Press.

Roling, Niels G. 1973. 'Problem Solving Research: A Strategy for Change'. Paper presented at the International Seminar on Extension Education, Helsinki.

Roling, Niels. 1982. 'Knowledge Utilisation: An Attempt to Relativate Some Reified Realities'. Paper presented to the conference on Knowledge Utilisation: Theory and Methods, East West Center, Honolulu.

Roling, Niels G., Joseph Ascroft, and **Fred Wa Chege.** 1976. 'The Diffusion of Innovations and the Issue of Equity in Rural Development'. *In* E.M. Rogers (ed.), *Communication and Development: Critical Perspectives,* pp. 63–78. Beverly Hills: Sage Publications.

Rose, Arnold M. 1970. 'Sociological Factors Affecting Economic Development in India'. *In* Monte Palmer (ed.), *The Human Factor in Political Development.* Waltham, Mass: Ginn and Company.

Rostow, W.W. 1960. *The Stages of Economic Growth: A Non-Communist Manifesto.* Cambridge: Cambridge University Press.

Ryan, William. 1976. *Blaming the Victim.* New York: Vintage Books.

Ryan, Bryce and **Neal Gross.** 1943. 'The Diffusion of Hybrid Seed Corn in Two Iowa Communities'. *Rural Sociology* 8: 15–24.

Samarajiwa, Rohan. 1987. 'The Murky Beginnings of the Communication and Development Field: Voice of America and the *Passing of Traditional Society'*. *In* N. Jayaweera and S. Amunugama (eds.), *Rethinking Development Communication*, pp. 3–19. Singapore: Asian Mass Communication Research and Information Center.

Sandhu, A.S. 1970. 'Characteristics, Listening Behaviour and Programme Preferences of Radio Owning Farmers in Punjab'. Ph.D. dissertation, Indian Agricultural Research Institute, New Delhi.

Schnaiberg, Allan. 1970. 'Measuring Modernism: Theoretical and Empirical Explorations'. *American Journal of Sociology* 76 (December): 399–425.

Schiller, Herbert. 1981. *Who Knows: Information in the Age of Fortune 500.* Norwood: Ablex.

———. 1986. 'The Erosion of National Sovereignty'. *In* Michael Traber (ed.), *The Myth of Information Revolution: Social and Ethical Implications of Communication Technology.* London: Sage.

Schramm, Wilbur. 1954. 'How Communication Works'. *In* W. Schramm (ed.), *The Process and Effects of Mass Communication.* Urbana: The University of Illinois Press.

———. 1964. *Mass Media and National Development.* California: Stanford University Press.

———. 1971, 'The Nature of Communication between Humans'. *In* W. Schramm et al. (eds.), *The Process and Effects of Mass Communication*, pp. 3–53. Urbana: University of Illinois Press.

———. 1976. 'End of an Old Paradigm'. *In* W. Schramm and D. Lerner (eds.), *Communication and Change*, pp. 45–48. Honolulu: East-West Center, The University Press of Hawaii.

———. 1977. 'Communication and Development—A Revaluation'. *Communicator* (April): 1–4.

Schramm, Wilbur and **W.L. Ruggels.** 1967. 'How Mass Media Systems Grow'. *In* W. Schramm and D. Lerner (eds.), *Communication and Change in Developing Countries*, pp. 57–75. Honolulu: East-West Center.

Schultz, T. 1963. *The Economic Value of Education.* New York: Columbia University Press.

Schultz, T.W. 1964. *Transforming Traditional Agriculture.* Connecticut: Yale University Press.

Schumacher, E.F. 1973. *Small is Beautiful.* New York: Harper and Row.

Schumpeter, J. 1934. *The Theory of Economic Development.* Harvard University Press.

Scott, J. 1976. *The Moral Economy of the Peasant.* Connecticut: Yale University Press.

Seers, Dudley. 1977a. 'The New Meaning of Development'. *International Development Review* XIX (3): 2–7.

———. 1977b. 'The Meaning of Development'. *International Development Review* XIX (2): 2–7.

Servaes, Jan. 1985. 'Toward an Alternative Concept of Communication and Development'. *Media Development* 32(4): 2–5.

————. 1989. 'Participatory Communication Research within Social Movements'. Paper prepared for the seminar on Participation: A Key Concept in Communication for Change and Development, Pune, India, February.

Severin, Werner and **James Tankard.** 1979. *Communication Theories*. New York: Hastings House. Second Edition 1987.

Shannon, C. and **W. Weaver.** 1949. *The Mathematical Theory of Communication*. Urbana, Illinois: University of Illinois Press.

Shaull, R. 1971. Cited in Paulo Freire, *Education for Critical Consciousness*, *op. cit.*

Shaw, Eugene. 1966. 'An Intra-India Analysis of Selected Communication-Development Variables'. Ph.D. dissertation, Stanford University.

Shingi, Prakash M. and **Bella Mody.** 1976. 'The Communication Effects Gap'. *In* E.M. Rogers (ed.), *Communication and Development: Critical Perspectives*, pp. 79–98. Beverly Hills: Sage Publications.

Shore, Larry. 1980. 'Mass Media for Development: A Re-Examination of Access, Exposure, and Impact'. In Emile G. McAnany (ed.), *Communications in the Rural Third World*, pp. 19–45. New York: Praeger Publishers.

Singer, Milton. 1966. 'Modernizing Religious Beliefs'. *In* Myron Weiner (ed.), *Modernization: The Dynamics of Growth*. New York: Basic Books.

————. 1972. *When a Great Tradition Modernizes: An Anthropological Approach to Indian Civilization*. New York: Praeger.

Singhal, Arvind and **Everett M. Rogers.** 1988. 'Television Soap Operas for Development in India'. *Gazette* 41 (2): 109–26.

————. 1989. *India's Information Revolution*. New Delhi: Sage.

Smelser, Neil J. 1973. 'Toward a General Theory of Modernization'. *In* Amitai Etzioni (ed.), *Social Change*, pp. 268–84. New York: Basic Books.

Smith, Adam. 1776. *An Inquiry into the Nature and Causes of the Wealth of Nations*.

Smith, Wilfred C. 1965. *Modernisation of a Traditional Society*. Bombay: Asia Publishing House.

Smythe, Dallas. 1985. 'Needs Before Tools—The Illusions of Technology'. *Media Development* 4: 8–17.

Social Studies (volume I). 1969. New Delhi: National Council of Educational Research and Training.

Srinivas, M.N. 1973. 'Comments on Milton Singer's Industrial Leadership, The Hindu Ethic and the Spirit of Socialism'. *In* Milton Singer (ed.), *Entrepreneurship and Modernization of Occupational Cultures in South Asia*, pp. 279–86. Duke University: Program in Comparative Studies on South Asia, Monograph No. 12.

Stover, William J. 1984. *Information Technology in the Third World*. Boulder, Colorado: Westview Press.

Streeten, Paul. 1979. 'Development Ideas in Historical Perspective'. *In* Kim Q. Hill (ed.), *Toward a New Strategy for Development*, pp. 21–52. New York: Pergamon Press.

Tarde, Gabriel. 1903. *The Laws of Imitation* (trans. Elsie Clews Parsons). New York: Holt, Rinehart and Winston.

Tehranian, Majid. 1985. 'Paradigms Lost: Development as Communication and Learning'. *Media Development*, xxxii (4): 5–8.

The Blade. 1990. 'Rescuing our Planet'. An Editorial, Section E, p. 4, 25 February.

Thorner, Daniel. 1966. 'Chayanov's Concept of Peasant Economy'. *In* Daniel Thorner et al. (eds.), *The Theory of Peasant Economy*, pp. xi–xxiii. Illinois: American Economic Association.

———. 1968. 'Peasantry'. *In* Sills (ed.), *International Encyclopedia of the Social Sciences*, Volume 2, pp. 503–11. New York: Macmillan and Free Press.

Tichenor, P.J. et al. 1970. 'Mass Media Flow and Differential Growth in Knowledge'. *Public Opinion Quarterly* 34: 159–70.

Toennies, Ferdinand. 1957. *Community and Society* . East Lansing: Michigan State University Press.

Tunstall, Jeremy. 1977. *The Media are American*. New York: Columbia University Press.

Uphoff, Norman and **M. Esman.** 1974. *Local Organisation for Rural Development: Analysis of Asian Experience*. Ithaca, New York: Center for International Studies, Cornell University.

Vallath, Chandrasekhar. 1989. 'Weakness of Agricultural Extension: A Study of Extension Message Comprehension'. Masters thesis, Bowling Green State University.

Van Hoosen, D. 1984. 'The Barefoot Actors: Folk Drama and Development Communication in Asia'. *In* G. Wang and W. Dissanayake (eds.), *Continuity and Change in Communication Systems*, pp. 127–37. New Jersey: Ablex.

Van Soet, Jaap. 1978. *The Start of International Development Cooperation in the United Nations 1945–1952*. Assen, The Netherlands: Van Gorcum Press.

Veblen, T. 1966. *Imperial Germany and the Industrial Revolution*. Ann Arbor: University of Michigan.

Vilanilam, John. 1979. 'The Meaning of Development'. *In* John Lent and John Vilanilam (eds.), *The Use of Development News*, pp. 2–19. Singapore: AMIC.

Vogeler, Ingolf and **A. De Souza.** 1980. *Dialectics of Third World Development*. New Jersey: Allanheld, Osmun and Co. Publishers.

Wall Street Journal. 1981. 'Sudan Farmers Find That New Methods Aren't Always Better'. Vol. LXII, No. 32. 27 November, p. 1, col. 4.

Wang, Georgette. 1984. 'Televised Puppetry in Taiwan—An Example of the Marriage Between a Modern Medium and a Folk Medium'. *In* G.Wang and W. Dissanayake (eds.), *Continuity and Change in Communication Systems*, pp. 169–80. New Jersey: Ablex.

Wang, Georgette and **Wimal Dissanayake.** 1984a. 'Culture, Development and Change: Some Explorative Observations'. *In* G. Wang and W. Dissanayake (eds.), *Continuity and Change in Communication Systems*, pp. 3–20. New Jersey: Ablex.

———. 1984b. 'Indigenous Communication Systems and Development: A Reappraisal'. *In* G. Wang and W. Dissanayake (eds.), *Continuity and Change in Communication Systems*, pp. 21–33. New Jersey: Ablex.

Weaver, James H. and **Kenneth Jameson.** 1978. *Economic Development: Competing Paradigms—Competing Parables*. Washington, D.C.: Development Studies Program, Agency for International Development.

Weber, Max. 1958. *The Protestant Ethic and the Spirit of Capitalism*. New York: Charles Scribner's Sons.
———. 1964. *The Sociology of Religion*. Boston: Beacon Press.
Weiner, Myron. 1966. 'Introduction'. *In* M. Weiner (ed.), *Modernization: The Dynamics of Growth*, pp. 1–14. New York: Basic Books.
Westley, B.H. and M. Maclean. 1957. 'A Conceptual Model for Communication Research'. *Journalism Quarterly* 34: 31–38.
White, Shirley and Pradeep Patel. 1988. 'Strategies for Message Development Using Participatory Video'. Paper presented to Inculdevcom Division, International Communication Association, New Orleans, June.
Williams, E. 1964. *Capitalism and Slavery*. London: Russell.
Williams, Maurice. 1989. 'Sustainable Development: An SID Perspective'. *Development* 2(3): 7–9.
Woods, John L. 1982. 'Making Rural Development Projects More Effective: A Systems Approach'. Paper prepared for the conference on Knowledge Utilization: Theory and Methodology, East West Center, Honolulu, Hawaii.
World Bank. 1973. Annual Address by Robert S. McNamara, President, World Bank, to the Annual Meeting of the Board of Governors, Nairobi, Kenya, 24–28 September.
Yount, Barbara. 1975. *IEC Newsletter*. No. 20. Honolulu: East West Communication Institute.
Zeitlin, Maurice. 1968. 'The Social Determinants of Political Democracy in Chile'. *In* J. Petras and M. Zeitlin (ed.), *Latin America: Reform or Revolution*, pp. 220–34. Greenwich, Connecticut: Fawcett.

Index